HUMAN RIGHTS
AND SOCIAL WORK

This book argues that incorporating the idea of three 'generations' of human rights allows us to move beyond the limitations of conventional legal frameworks. It examines current human rights issues and shows how a broader understanding of human rights can be used to ground a form of practice that is central to social work, community development and broader human services. The argument extends the idea of human rights beyond the realm of theoretical analysis and into the arena of professional practice and social action. This is set within the context of current debates about globalisation and the need to incorporate an internationalist viewpoint into all social work practice. This illuminating study adds a vital new perspective to the challenge of promoting international human rights.

Jim Ife is Professor of Social Work and Social Policy at Curtin University of Technology, Perth, Western Australia, and secretary of the Human Rights Commission of the International Federation of Social Workers. Previously he was Professor of Social Work and Social Policy at the University of Western Australia and is also a former president of Amnesty International Australia. His other publications include *Community Development* (2nd edition, 2001) and *Rethinking Social Work: Towards Critical Practice* (1997).

HUMAN RIGHTS AND SOCIAL WORK

Towards Rights-Based Practice

JIM IFE
Curtin University of Technology

CAMBRIDGE
UNIVERSITY PRESS

PUBLISHED BY THE PRESS SYNDICATE OF THE UNIVERSITY OF CAMBRIDGE
The Pitt Building, Trumpington Street, Cambridge, United Kingdom

CAMBRIDGE UNIVERSITY PRESS
The Edinburgh Building, Cambridge CB2 2RU, UK
40 West 20th Street, New York, NY 10011–4211, USA
477 Williamstown Rd, Port Melbourne, VIC 3207, Australia
Ruiz de Alarcón 13, 28014 Madrid, Spain
Dock House, The Waterfront, Cape Town 8001, South Africa

http://www.cambridge.org

First published 2001
Reprinted 2003

Printed in Singapore by Green Giant Press

Typeface New Baskerville (*Adobe*) 10/12 pt.   *System* QuarkXPress®   [PK]

A catalogue record for this book is available from the British Library

National Library of Australia Cataloguing in Publication data

Ife, Jim (James William), 1946– .
Human rights and social work: towards rights-based practice.
Bibliography.
Includes index.
ISBN 0 521 79291 6.
ISBN 0 521 79701 2 (pbk.).
1. Human rights. 2. Social service – Moral and ethical aspects.
3. Social workers – Professional ethics. I. Title.
323.01

ISBN 0 521 79291 6 hardback
ISBN 0 521 79701 2 paperback

Contents

Acknowledgements

For the author of a book to claim that the ideas it contains are all his/her own is both false and arrogant. Ideas are shared, developed and reconstructed through a process of continuous dialogue, reading and collaborative praxis, and any claim to individual 'ownership' of such ideas in the form of 'intellectual property' is a nonsense. Simply writing ideas in a book, with its corresponding claim to ownership and authority, is to privilege the author over others who have had a major influence in the creative endeavour, and is, for this author at least, a source of some discomfort. Many people have contributed, often unknowingly, to the ideas in this book, and it would be impossible to acknowledge, or even to remember, them all. I owe a great deal to many encounters with students, colleagues and friends, in several different universities and in the wider community.

There are, however, some people to whom I owe a particular debt of gratitude, who need to be specifically acknowledged. Louise Morley has made a substantial contribution in her invaluable assistance with library research, and also through her constructive input, her critical analysis, and her enthusiasm for dialogue. Barbara Black, Amanda Bolleter, Angela Fielding, Lucy Fiske, Nola Kunnen and Susan Young have all read part or all of the draft manuscript, and made many helpful comments and suggestions. I also need to acknowledge the support and friendship of many people associated with the Human Rights Commission of the International Federation of Social Workers, especially Terry Bamford, Imelda Dodds, Elis Envall, Tom Johannesen, and most particularly the inspirational Evelyn Balais Serrano. My long association with both Amnesty International and the Association for Services to Torture and Trauma Survivors, and my many friends from within both organisations, have also played a major role in stimulating my thinking about human rights. Students and colleagues at Curtin University and the University of

Western Australia have provided me with stimulating work environments, in which these ideas could be developed. Sharon Mullins, at Cambridge University Press, has been a most supportive and encouraging publisher, and Venetia Somerset has been a very thorough and helpful copy-editor.

Most of this book was written during a period of study leave at the University of British Columbia, and special thanks are due to Graham Riches and his colleagues at the School of Social Work and Family Studies for providing me with an excellent study leave environment, and for their collegial support. Particular thanks must also go to the residents of St John's College at UBC for their friendship and interest in my work, for creating a marvellous climate for sustained writing, and for some magnificent hikes in the mountains of coastal British Columbia. I cannot think of a better environment in which to write a book.

I owe an enormous debt of gratitude to Gwynneth for her continuing encouragement, love, understanding and support, and to Julia and Bronwyn for remaining an important part of my family life.

Finally, this book is dedicated to the people of Ermera and Gleno in East Timor, who in August 1999 taught me about human rights.

Introduction

Human rights represent one of the most powerful ideas in contemporary discourse. In a world of economic globalisation, where individualism, greed and becoming rich are seen as the most important things in life, and where at the same time the formerly secure moral positions for judging our actions seem to be declining into a morass of postmodern relativism, the idea of human rights provides an alternative moral reference point for those who would seek to reaffirm the values of humanity.

This book is written in the belief that human rights are important, and that they are particularly important for those in the human service professions in general, and for social workers in particular. By framing social work specifically as a human rights profession, many of the issues and dilemmas that face social work can be looked at in a new light. Further, human rights can provide social workers with a moral basis for their practice, both at the level of day-to-day work with 'clients', and also in community development and in policy advocacy and activism; indeed a human rights perspective can help to link these varying roles into a unified and holistic view of social work practice. This book seeks to articulate what it means to say that social work is a human rights profession, and to consider the implications of such a perspective for the practice of social work.

The opening chapter sets the background by defining human rights, and setting the context of an essentially discursive understanding of human rights that forms the basis for the remaining chapters. It also considers globalisation as the context within which we need to understand human rights practice; this is especially important because the recent upsurge of interest in human rights has been in part a reaction to globalisation, and because human rights have been the major theme around which the opposition to globalisation has crystallised.

Chapter 2 examines the three so-called 'generations' of human rights, and shows how this broader perspective can provide a framework for understanding social work as a human rights profession. Chapters 3 to 8 examine different theoretical or conceptual issues relating to human rights: the public/private divide, cultural difference, the link between rights and needs, the obligations that go with human rights, the relationship between rights and ethics, and participation in human rights discourse. In each case, the implications for social work of such a discussion are identified.

The remaining chapters then spell out what is involved in human rights-based social work. They examine how social workers might engage with the discursive construction of human rights as a basis for practice, how social work practice can work to realise and safeguard human rights, and the implications of a human rights perspective for the processes and structures of the social work profession itself.

Even though the theoretical issues around human rights are complex, and any exploration of human rights has to deal with them, social work requires that any theoretical exploration must be grounded in, and relevant to, the reality of the messy world of social work practice, with its contradictions, unpredictability and general chaos. This applied practical focus has been maintained throughout, and it is hoped that the book will therefore retain a relevance and utility for practitioners.

The book is written from an internationalist perspective. Although social work practice must always be contextualised within the culture and society in which it is located, human rights is a universalist discourse, based on ideas of a common humanity and global citizenship. It is therefore hoped that the book will have application in different national and cultural settings. It deals with issues that are the concern of social workers anywhere in the world, and a deliberate decision has been taken not to locate it exclusively within any particular national, political or cultural context. However, the fact that the writer is from a western cultural background, and represents the dominant voice of the white western male, means that many readers will no doubt wish to challenge or to reinterpret these ideas to suit their own practice needs. Indeed, the book has been written with that expectation, and the reader is invited to reconstruct these ideas to suit particular social work contexts.

Some points need to be made about the use of language. Rather than using the ungrammatical plural of the personal pronoun to avoid gendered language, I have used the more cumbersome terms 'his/her', 'she/he', and so on, randomly choosing the order in which the two words appear. For American readers in particular, the term 'liberal' may need some explanation: in this book it is not used in the sense popularised by the American media – namely someone with social democratic ideals – but rather in its more philosophical sense, of someone who values individualism and freedom, in the context of Enlightenment rationality and progress. Another word that has caused me considerable difficulty is the word 'client'. It is a word I do not like to use (for reasons that are explained in Chapter 11), but the alternatives 'consumer' or 'customer' are also highly unsatisfactory. Where possible I have used 'person' or 'individual', but sometimes, in order to avoid the clumsiness of 'person with whom a social worker is working' (or some similar wording) I have with reluctance resorted to the use of the traditional term 'client' for the sake of brevity and in the absence of a better alternative. Although social workers are the primary readership for whom this book is intended, the ideas explored in the book have application well beyond the field of social work, and in the hope that there are others who may find it of use, I have tried to keep social work jargon to a minimum.

One of the joys of writing my previous books has been the feedback I have received from many different people, leading to some important ongoing dialogues, and I would welcome comments from any reader – student, educator, practitioner or other – who would like to respond to anything in this book, in the spirit of dialogue.

CHAPTER 1

Human Rights in a Globalised World

The idea of human rights is one of the most powerful in contemporary social and political discourse. It is readily endorsed by people from many different cultural and ideological backgrounds and it is used rhetorically in support of a large number of different and sometimes conflicting causes. Because of its strong appeal and its rhetorical power, it is often used loosely and can have different meanings in different contexts, although those who use the idea so readily seldom stop to ponder its various meanings and its contradictions. This combination of its strong appeal and its contradictions makes the idea of human rights worth closer consideration, especially for social workers and those in other human service professions.

This book is concerned with what a human rights perspective means for social workers (Centre for Human Rights 1994). Framing social work as a human rights profession has certain consequences for the way in which social work is conceptualised and practised. In many instances such a perspective reinforces and validates the traditional understandings and practices of social work, while in other cases it challenges some of the assumptions of the social work profession. The position of this book is that a human rights perspective can strengthen social work and that it provides a strong basis for an assertive practice that seeks to realise the social justice goals of social workers, in whatever setting. Human rights, however, are also contested and problematic. To develop a human rights basis for social work requires that the idea of human rights, and the problems and criticisms associated with it, be carefully examined. In this and following chapters some of the issues and problems raised by human rights will be discussed, and the implications of these discussions for social work will be highlighted.

Many authors suggest that the idea of human rights is largely a product of Enlightenment thinking and is therefore inevitably contextualised

1

within an essentially western and modernist framework (Wronka 1992; Galtung 1994; Beetham 1995; Bobbio 1996; Pereira 1997; Bauer & Bell 1999). This has led to the criticism that human rights thinking and rhetoric are simply another manifestation of colonialist western domination, and to the suggestion that the concept of human rights should not be used (Aziz 1999). While it is true that much of the contemporary understanding of human rights has been shaped by western Enlightenment thinking, the same can be said of many other concepts that are frequently used in political debate, such as democracy, justice, freedom, equality and human dignity. To stop using such words simply because of their western Enlightenment associations would be to deny their power and importance across cultures and would lead to sterile and limited political debate. The task rather is to loosen them from the shackles of western modernism and to reconstruct them in more dynamic, inclusive and cross-cultural terms. That is the approach taken in this book, though of course cultural issues and the question of cultural relativism are critically important and will be discussed in some detail in Chapter 4.

There is a stronger reason, however, to resist the argument that the idea of human rights should be rejected because of its western connotations. This is because it is simply not true to say that human rights is an exclusively western concept. Notions of human rights are embedded in all the major religious traditions and can be found in many different cultural forms (Von Senger 1993; Ishay 1997), though the term 'human rights' may not always be used. Ideas of human dignity and worth, ideas that all people should be treated according to certain basic standards, ideas that people should be protected from what is frequently termed 'human rights abuse', and ideas of respect for the rights of others are not confined to the western intellectual tradition. To assume that they are is to devalue those other religious and cultural traditions that such critics often claim to be supporting. Nor is it true, as is commonly suggested, that human rights are a recent concept emerging only in the last two centuries, with their origins in Enlightenment thinking. Although the Enlightenment was crucial in the construction of the modern western framing of human rights, the idea of human rights has been reflected in writings from much earlier ages, even though the term itself may not always have been used (Blickle 1993; Coleman 1993; Dupont-Bouchat 1993; Von Senger 1993).

Human rights, indeed, represent a powerful discourse that seeks to overcome divisiveness and sectarianism and to unite people of different cultural and religious traditions in a single movement asserting human values and the universality of humanity, at a time when such values are seen to be under threat from the forces of economic globalisation (Rees & Wright 2000). The idea of human rights, by its very appeal to universally applicable ideas of the values of humanity, seems to resonate across cultures and traditions and represents an important rallying cry for those seeking to bring about a more just, peaceful and sustainable world.

As well as the criticism of cultural bias, two other criticisms are commonly made of a human rights perspective. One is that claims of human rights can be frivolous or selfish: people will claim something as a 'human right' when in fact they are simply expressing a simple selfish 'want'; for example people might claim the right to own a car, the right to take a luxury cruise, the right to smoke in a restaurant, the right to watch a video on an aircraft. Thus human rights become nothing more than a new language for consumerism and self-indulgence. The other criticism is that claims of human rights can conflict with each other and therefore one is left with the problem of reconciling competing claims, for example the right of freedom of expression as opposed to the right to protection from libel or slander (Holmes & Sunstein 1999). A human rights perspective needs to show how it will overcome those criticisms, and this will be undertaken in this and subsequent chapters.

Much of the academic debate about human rights remains at the theoretical level; less has been written about the *practice* of human rights. The important exception to this has been the legal profession, which has developed a significant specialisation in human rights law. While lawyers have played a very important role in the promotion and safeguarding of human rights, an exclusively legal framing of human rights practice has limited the applicability of human rights in other professions and occupations (Galtung 1994). The reasons for this, and its consequences, will be discussed in some detail in Chapter 2. Other professions, such as medicine, social work, teaching and nursing, are also concerned with human rights issues, and their practice can be seen as very much about the promotion of human rights in ways that extend beyond the more constrained practice of the law. The literature of these professions, however, while acknowledging that ideas of human rights are important for professional practice, does not for the most part define either theory or practice within a specific human rights framework. There is little articulation of what it means in practice for professionals to claim that their work is based on human rights, and so human rights remain a 'nice idea' rather than a solid foundation for the development of practice theories and methodologies. This book represents an attempt to fill this gap by examining what a human rights perspective means for the practice of human service professions such as social work. It identifies some of the important theoretical and conceptual issues about human rights and looks at how they might be applied to practice in a way that can identify a social worker more clearly as a human rights worker. In general use, the term 'human rights worker' applies either to lawyers with a human rights specialisation or to activists working for organisations such as Amnesty International. This book seeks to locate social workers also as human rights workers and to identify some key issues that emerge when social work is reframed as human rights work.

Social work

While much of the material in this book can be applied to a broad range of human service professions such as teaching, medicine and the other health-related professions, the primary focus of the book is social work. In this regard, 'social work' needs some clarification, as this term has different connotations in different national and cultural contexts (Tan & Envall 2000). In some societies, most notably Australia and North America, 'social worker' implies a fairly narrowly defined group of workers who have high professional qualifications, and excludes many others working in the human service field (Ife 1997a; Leighninger & Midgley 1997). In other societies the term has a much wider application, covering human service workers from a variety of backgrounds, with varying levels of educational qualifications. In some societies, such as the United Kingdom, social work has been seen as the implementation of the policies of the welfare state through the provision of statutory services, with relatively little role in community development or social change. In other societies, however, such as in Latin America (Aguilar 1997; Cornely & Bruno 1997; Queiro 1997), 'social work' has much more radical or activist connotations: it is concerned with bringing about social change, progressive movements for social justice and human rights, and opposition to prevalent forms of bureaucratic and political domination. In some contexts, such as the United States, individualised therapeutic roles for social workers are dominant (Leighninger & Midgley 1997), while in other contexts, particularly in 'the developing world' or 'the south', social work has a much stronger community development orientation. Even in societies that might superficially seem very similar, such as Australia and New Zealand, there can be significant differences in how social work is constructed and in what counts as good practice.

Given the importance of grounding social work in its cultural, social and political context, it is inevitable that social work will be constructed differently in different locations. This has considerable benefits for social work as it allows for a diversity of interests and practices. But it also poses problems, in that readers of the social work literature will be seeking to apply that literature in different contexts where the very idea of social work is contested. It is also a recipe for ambiguity and misunderstanding when social workers meet across cultural and national boundaries.

This book accepts a broad view of the nature of 'social work' and is not confined to specific professional, social control, conservative, radical, therapeutic or developmental formulations. The term is meant to be understood in its broadest sense and to include all those working in the social services or community development, including those seeking social change. The aim of this book is to show that a human rights perspective such as that developed in the following chapters provides a unifying framework within which the various activities identified as 'social work' can be incorporated, while still allowing for cultural, national and political difference (Centre for Human Rights 1994).

There is a strong tradition in social work of identifying a core value position for the profession (Tan & Envall 2000). Social work writers have consistently emphasised the importance of this value base; social work is not seen as a neutral, objective or 'value-free' activity, but rather as work which is grounded in values and which makes no apology for adopting partisan stances on a range of questions. In formulating this value base, the idea of human rights is often implicit, through phrases such as 'the inherent worth of the individual', the 'right to self-determination', and so on. Such statements serve to locate human rights, though perhaps in a fairly limited form, as having a central role in social work, though characteristically there is usually little explication of the nature of these 'rights', the contested nature of rights, what they mean in practice, and how adopting such rights as central actually affects what social workers do in their day-to-day work. Professional codes of ethics also tend to imply some commitment to an idea of human rights, since it is often from an implied human rights position that the ethics of social work are derived (Corey et al. 1998); this will be further discussed in Chapter 7. This again is a piecemeal approach to human rights and does not really confront the idea of human rights head on. Indeed it might be suggested that the construction of human rights contained in documents such as codes of ethics and introductory texts often treats human rights as if they are self-evident and non-problematic, a position which even the most cursory examination of the extensive literature on rights would show to be misguided and simplistic.

A discursive approach to human rights

Many of the issues and debates about human rights will be discussed in later chapters, and their applicability to social work practice will be identified. At the outset, however, it is important to make a clear statement about the approach to human rights adopted in this book. This is an approach that rejects a positivist notion of rights, implying that human rights somehow 'exist' in an objective form and can be identified, 'discovered', and empirically measured or verified. The idea of rights existing somehow independently of human agency is characteristic of the positivist world-view of the social sciences, which regards social phenomena as existing independently and objectively, and sees the task of the social scientist as objective empirical inquiry into the laws that govern how social phenomena interact. The positivist view has been the object of sustained critique in the social science literature (Fay 1975; Keat 1981; Lloyd & Thacker 1997; Crotty 1998), and the position of this book is one that rejects such a paradigm. Rather than regarding rights as 'existing' in some way, hence able to be uncovered through objective scientific inquiry, the arguments in later chapters see human rights as essentially discursive (Woodiwiss 1998), in other words rights are constructed through human interaction and through an ongoing dialogue about what should constitute a common humanity (Howard 1995). Hence human rights are not static but will vary over time and in different cultures and political contexts. The best-known statement of human rights, the Universal Declaration of Human Rights, though representing perhaps one of the more remarkable human achievements of the twentieth century, should not therefore be reified and seen as expressing a universal and unchanging truth. Rather, the Universal Declaration represents a statement of what was agreed by the leaders of the world's nations in 1948 as a statement of the basic rights of all people (see Appendix I for the full text of the Universal Declaration). It is an impressive and inspirational statement, with significant radical implications, and it has been used in many ways since to further many important causes in the name of humanity. But it is not holy writ, and it can and should be subject to challenge in different times, as different voices are heard and different issues are given priority. The same must apply to any other statement of human rights: what constitutes the basic rights of all human beings will be a matter for ongoing debate and redefinition and should always be open to challenge. The Universal Declaration has been criticised because of the dominance of western political leaders in the forum from which it was derived, leading to a perceived western bias (Wronka 1992; Chomsky 1998). This, however, is an argument not for the rejection of the idea of such a universal statement but rather for its continual reformulation in the light of different voices being validated and heard (Mahoney & Mahoney 1993).

The Enlightenment view of human rights, as argued by Locke, talks about 'natural' rights, namely the idea that the very nature of human beings implies that they have certain rights, as a consequence of their very humanity (Simmons 1992). By simply talking about 'human beings' we imply human rights arising from some notion of a common humanity which requires that people be treated in a certain way (Feinberg 1973). According to this view, at birth we are all equal and therefore we 'naturally' acquire equal rights. The idea of rights existing 'naturally' might at first sight sound like a positivist framing of human rights, but the idea of 'natural' rights in this sense is not necessarily inconsistent with the view of human rights as discursive. It is simply an affirmation of the view that our human rights are the consequence of our common humanity, but it is nevertheless quite consistent to talk about a discursive construction of how we understand those 'natural' rights.

The idea of human rights, by its very nature, implies the search for universal principles that apply to all humans, whatever their cultural background, belief system, age, sex, ability or circumstances. Such universality has been absent from many of the more traditional understandings of human rights, simply because not everybody has been thought of as 'human'. The discourse of the 'rights of man' and traditional views of patriarchal philosophers such as Locke have distanced women from the definition of 'human' and therefore from an understanding of what 'human rights' imply. Thomas Jefferson presumably saw no conflict between his advocacy of rights and freedoms and his ownership of slaves. The perpetrators of the Holocaust, while celebrating the high achievements of German civilisation, were able to justify their actions by effectively defining Jews as subhuman, and the same can be said of the Apartheid regime in South Africa, the Indonesian occupying army in East Timor, the Serb forces in Bosnia, and so on (Rorty 1998). Oppressors can justify their actions by effectively removing their victims from their understanding of 'human' and thereby avoiding the necessity of recognising their human rights. These examples may seem extreme and they bring instant condemnation, but it needs to be remembered that there are other classes of people who are regularly excluded from our construction of 'humanity', and hence from being ascribed human rights, about which we feel no such outrage. One obvious category is children, who are not seen as having the same rights as adults, even though many of those rights (such as the right to vote) are commonly labelled 'human rights'. People with intellectual disabilities represent another group who are readily denied 'human' rights, as are prisoners, refugees and many of the frail aged (Robinson & Sidoti 2000). By excluding them from categories of people to whom we ascribe human rights, we are thereby excluding them from our category of 'human', in the same way as Locke, Jefferson, the Nazis, and so on did in the above examples. In this sense, claiming that 'human rights are universal' is still a radical and challenging statement, even for those in the liberal democracies of the west.

The universality of human rights must not be confused with a static, unchangeable notion of human rights. Because human rights must be seen as constructed, rather than objectively existing, the important thing is the process of dialogue, discussion and exchange that seeks to articulate such universal values. Whose voices are privileged in the human rights discourse, and whose are not? How can other voices be heard, and are there other ways in which human rights might be conceptualised? Are some rights privileged over others, and does the way in which we have conceptualised human rights value some sorts of human action and marginalise others? These and other questions will be considered in later chapters, alongside a discussion of how social workers can be part of this ongoing discourse as human rights are constructed and reconstructed in a continuing discursive process.

Defining human rights

Understanding human rights as discursive means that human rights are not fixed or static, and therefore in that sense they cannot be fully defined. For this reason, this book will not attempt to outline or define a set of basic human rights; to do so would privilege the voice of the author over other voices, in what should ideally be a participatory and democratic process. It is important at this stage, however, to provide a definition, not of human rights per se, but of what we mean when we talk about a human rights discourse, or, in other words, what counts as a human right and what does not.

We hear many claims of rights, some contestable, some frivolous, and some applicable only to certain groups. Examples include the right to bear arms, women's rights, the right to manage, the rights of the child, Indigenous People's rights, the right to use corporal punishment on one's children, the right to advertise, the right to run for president, and so on. Not all rights claimed by people can be regarded as *human* rights. By human rights we generally mean those rights which we claim belong to all people, regardless of national origin, race, culture, age, sex, or anything else. Such rights are therefore universal and apply to everyone, everywhere, while more specific and circumscribed rights will only apply to certain people in certain circumstances. A human rights perspective, as outlined in this book, clearly implies that where there is a conflict, *human rights have priority over other claims of right*, in other words specific rights, claimed only for certain individuals or groups, cannot be allowed to contravene the fundamental human rights which belong to everyone. For example, I may claim a 'right' to a certain standard of office accommodation, a certain level of salary and an expense account, arising from my status in my university, but if this right can only be realised by the university reducing the quality of student education through diverting resources, then my 'exercising' my 'right' to these things is denying students the full realisation of their right to education. In this conflict of rights claims, education can be argued as a human right, whereas nice offices and expense accounts cannot, and so a case can be made that the right of students to education is the higher priority. This is fundamentally important in understanding a human rights approach. By defining something as a *human* right we are claiming that it has priority over other claims of right.

It is important to note that many claims for non-universal rights are made by the powerful, rather than the powerless. The powerless are largely concerned with claiming the universal rights that others take for granted, but in many instances the powerful claim specific and privileged additional 'rights', such as the right to manage, the right to bear arms, the right to maximise profits at whatever social and environmental cost, the right to exploit, and the right to unlimited ownership of private property. All these 'rights' cannot be universal, as it would be impossible for everybody to be able to exercise them, and hence they must be excluded from our category of 'human rights' as they are essentially the rights of the powerful and the privileged to continue their practices of domination.

Some claims of specific rights, however, are very different, and are not made by the privileged and the powerful. The claims of disadvantaged groups, for example the rights of women, the rights of children, the rights of refugees, and so on, cannot be dismissed so readily; to do so is to trivialise important issues of social justice and to reinforce discourses of oppression. Rather, such claims by disadvantaged groups must still be seen within the overall field of human rights. In many cases they are simply claims for human rights that are denied to particular groups; people with disabilities, for example, may find it especially difficult to obtain employment, and hence the right to meaningful work (recognised as a universal human right) takes on extra significance for people with disabilities and is included as part of a statement of their specific 'rights'. In this case the right itself is no different from the right of other members of the population, but the point is that oppressive structures and discourses mean that it is hard for this particular group to exercise that right, and hence special provision needs to be made. This is the position for many rights claimed as the rights of disadvantaged groups.

There is, however, another sense in which rights of disadvantaged groups can be regarded as human rights, even where they are rights that might not attach to the rest of the population. Claims of specific land rights for Indigenous People, for example, as a result of their aboriginality and their historical connection to the land, cannot be claimed as a right by everyone else. Yet these are still 'human' rights in the sense that they are necessary for the people concerned to realise their full humanity (Janke 2000). The right to realise one's full humanity is at the core of an idea of human rights, and hence the claim of indigenous land rights can be seen to fall within the category of human rights. The same argument can be made in relation to some aspects of women's rights, children's rights, rights of people with disabilities, older people's rights, and so on. Each group may have specific claims to rights which, while not necessarily generalisable to the entire population, are for them part of the fundamental human right to realise their own humanity. This fundamental right results in different claims of rights for specific groups, but can still be incorporated in a discourse of universal human rights.

This of course raises the question of how we define what is necessary for realising one's full humanity. Is the claim of a gun owner, for example, that the right to bear arms is necessary for him/her to realise full humanity, sufficient to qualify the 'right to bear arms' as a human right for that person? Rapists who claim that it is only in the act of committing rape that they can realise their own humanity may make a similar claim. Such claims, however, clearly conflict with the human rights of others, and a human rights perspective cannot allow as legitimate a claim for human rights that violates other people's human rights. It is also important to introduce the importance of an analysis of oppression and disadvantage. When we are talking about the rights of disadvantaged groups such as women or Indigenous People, we are acknowledging the existence and importance of structures and discourses of oppression which result in disadvantage and in the inability of people to realise their full humanity (Czerny 1993). Human rights have to be understood within this context, and it must be recognised that structures and discourses of oppression, by their very nature, run counter to human rights values. Hence a claim of rights that can be justified on the grounds that it helps to challenge and overcome structures and discourses of oppression can be included within the idea of 'human rights'.

From the above discussion, it is clear that claiming something as a 'human right' is stronger than just claiming a 'right' because I think I ought to have it, and many claims for rights cannot be justified on the grounds of *human* rights. To make a claim on the basis of human rights the following criteria must be met, and these will serve as a definition of human rights for the purposes of this book:

- Realisation of the claimed right is necessary for a person or group to be able to achieve their full humanity, in common with others.
- The claimed right is seen *either* as applying to all of humanity, and is something that the person or group claiming the right wishes to apply to all people anywhere, *or* as applying to people from specific disadvantaged or marginalised groups for whom realisation of that right is essential to their achieving their full human potential.
- There is substantial universal consensus on the legitimacy of the claimed right; it cannot be called a 'human right' unless there is widespread support for it across cultural and other divides.

- It is possible for the claimed right to be effectively realised for all legitimate claimants. This excludes rights to things that are in limited supply, for example the right to housing with a panoramic view, the right to own a TV channel, or the right to 'own' large tracts of land.
- The claimed right does not contradict other human rights. This would disallow as human rights the 'right' to bear arms, the 'right' to hold other people in slavery, a man's 'right' to beat his wife and children, the 'right' to excessive profits resulting in poverty for others, and so on.

This means that the class of 'human rights' does not include all the rights that people might claim, and that a claim to human rights has to pass certain stringent tests. The most frequent justification for claiming a human right is by reference to some agreed convention, the most common being of course the Universal Declaration of Human Rights. One reason why such human rights conventions are important is that they provide good grounds on which a claim for human rights can be made in any particular context.

Human rights are commonly seen as a package, 'universal and indivisible', which therefore cannot be separated from one another. This is the reason for the fifth criterion above: because human rights belong together, they must be consistent and cannot conflict with each other. This means that *within the field of human rights, giving priority to rights should not be necessary.* All are seen as important and it should not be necessary to affirm some as more significant than others. A human rights perspective says that once a claim of right has been established as a human right, it has top priority and takes precedence over any other claim of right. In practice, however, conflicting claims of human rights are not uncommon, and particular examples will be discussed in subsequent chapters. These need to be resolved, but this can often be achieved by applying the criteria above.

For social workers, this distinction between human and other rights, and the assertion that human rights must have priority, have particular relevance. There are many occasions when in social work practice there is a conflict between an apparent 'right' (though it may not be expressed in that way) and human rights. One example is where the demands of managers require that social workers deny services that can be justified on the grounds of human rights. The 'right to manage' certainly does not qualify as a human right on the basis of the above criteria (indeed it arguably fails on all five), and so if a social worker is in this position, human rights must have priority. A social worker would in this case be morally justified in challenging the management practices that lead to a denial of human rights, and if necessary she/he could make a good case for not obeying the instructions of management. Of course there are many situational factors that a social worker needs to take into account in determining whether such open confrontation would be a wise course of action, and it may be that some other option is chosen, such as careful research to document the human rights violations before moving to action, asking the social worker's union or professional association to take up the matter rather than pursuing it individually, talking informally to one's supervisor, and so on.

When human rights are discussed, they are commonly referred to as *universal, indivisible, inalienable,* and *inabrogable* (Cassese 1990; Centre for Human Rights 1994; Jones 1994). Universality and indivisibility have been covered in the above discussion; universality implies that human rights apply to all human beings, and indivisibility implies that human rights come as a package – one cannot pick and choose, accepting some and rejecting others. The statement that human rights are *inalienable* implies that they cannot be taken away from someone. This is somewhat controversial, as the application of the law sometimes sanctions the removal of some human rights, for example the rights of liberty, freedom of association and freedom to travel are denied to convicted prisoners. But as a general rule human rights cannot be taken away from us and remain with us as long as we live. The statement that human rights are *inabrogable* implies that one cannot voluntarily give up one's human rights or trade them for additional privileges – human rights are not to be idly dispensed with. We may choose not to exercise all our rights all the time, but we still have those rights, and even if we opt not to exercise them we are, at least in theory, always free to change our minds.

Further explication of the idea of human rights, and what it means for social workers, is the subject of the remainder of the book. The above definition and discussion, however, provide a basic understanding of what the term should be taken to mean in subsequent chapters.

Intergenerational rights

One of the most important changes to have taken place in the human rights discourse in the last decade or so has been the extension of our understanding of human rights obligations beyond the present. There have, of course, been major human rights violations in the past, but now there is a growing awareness that even if these events happened in the past there is some responsibility for people in the present to recognise them retrospectively, and to take appropriate action to provide some form of redress. The discussion about the Nazi fortunes apparently held in Swiss banks being appropriated for compensation to be awarded to Holocaust survivors is one such example. In other cases it is symbolic rather than monetary compensation that is at issue, for example the issue of apologies given by governments for the mistreatment of Indigenous People (HREOC 1997), though sometimes this issue also involves monetary compensation, as is the case in Canada. The way in which this responsibility for past human rights violations has been recognised has been haphazard and has been framed by differing contexts. Richard Falk (2000a), for example, points out how the retrospective recognition of the human rights violations committed in the Holocaust is very different from that given to the Nanking massacre of 1937. This is caused at least in part by the ideological imperatives of the cold war in western thinking, which would not have been served well by China being cast in the role of victim of human rights abuse at the hands of Japan. However, the whole issue of the extent to which we should act on the basis of human rights abuses in previous generations is of particular importance for social workers, who often find themselves dealing with issues of injustice, oppression and the violation of human rights that are of long standing and may have affected people over several generations.

The other way in which the temporal extension of human rights is changing the discourse is by extending the idea of human rights to include the rights of future generations. Everything we do affects the future of the world; the question is to what extent our actions should be guided by the need to protect the human rights of future generations as well as those living in the present. This of course has had particular importance within the environmental movement, where many have argued that it is immoral for us to take actions which deny rights to future generations: destroying wilderness, allowing global warming and ozone depletion to continue, destroying biodiversity, and so on. The argument is that future generations have human rights which we have a moral obligation to respect and protect (Attfield 1983; Goodin 1992). This perspective, too, can affect social workers, especially those working in community development or those working with environmental issues, but also social workers who may seek to break ongoing cycles of deprivation or violence which can span generations, and forms of oppression and structural disadvantage which (e.g. by destroying community structures or collective notions of mutual obligation) can affect future generations.

This temporal extension of human rights is a relatively new understanding of human rights and their corresponding obligations. We are used to thinking spatially about human rights – the obligations of communities or nations to each other – but not temporally, where there are human rights obligations that extend back into the past and forward into the future, but which affect our present behaviour. This dimension is important not only because of the human rights of those who have lived or will live in other generations but also because it forces us to think historically, to locate our actions in their historical context, and to understand that the definition and realisation of human rights are not static but have an important historical dimension.

Animal rights

While dealing with matters of definition it is important to touch on the issue of non-human rights in the sense that the term applies to other species. Animal rights have received increasing attention in recent decades, and the ecocentric perspective (Fox 1990; Eckersley 1992) as opposed to the anthropocentric perspective requires that rights should be considered as belonging not just to human beings but to all living creatures as part of the ecosystem.

This book does not consider the issues of animal rights. This is not because of a lack of sympathy with such a position on the part of the author, but rather because the book is concerned specifically with *human* rights, namely the rights that we assign to other members of the human species by virtue of their common humanity. The discursive approach to human rights adopted here means that there is a clear distinction between human and animal rights, in that humans are able to articulate and debate their rights together in a way that other species are not. Hence any attempt to articulate the rights of other species will be a case of humans defining those rights for themselves, as guides to how humans should act towards other species, but such definition does not imply any obligation on the part of members of other species to act towards each other in certain ways. Human rights, however, are different in that they are about humans defining their own rights and acting towards each other in ways that respect, protect and realise those rights. One of the recurring themes of this book will be the importance for social workers of facilitating processes whereby people can become engaged with the human rights discourse, and this simply would not apply in the case of non-human species. The treatment of other species in terms of rights must be dealt with in different terms, and while it is an important issue, related to how we define our own humanity, and essential for an ecological understanding of our place in the world, it is nonetheless outside the scope of this book.

It is important to note, however, that this position, and indeed the very idea of human rights, is, by definition, anthropocentric. It is a position that 'others' non-human species and requires that their rights be treated in a different way. A strong advocacy of animal rights is, however, fully consistent with a human rights perspective. While valuing human rights, an argument can be made that humans should not ride roughshod over the rights of other living species, and that human rights should not necessarily, or in all cases, have precedence over animal rights. It will be argued in Chapter 3 that one of the principles of human rights practice is that where there is a conflict of claims of rights, the rights of the weak and vulnerable should prevail over the rights of the more powerful, and this can readily be applied to our obligations to non-human species as well. It is therefore simplistic to set up anthropocentric human rights and an ecocentric view of animal rights as necessarily in opposition.

Globalisation

Human rights have been given an extra contemporary relevance by the pressures of globalisation. It is important to examine globalisation in some detail, because this provides the context within which social work will be practised in the early twenty-first century, and also because human rights represent a critically important element of the current debates about globalisation, and the opposition to it.

A global economy is not new. There has been world trade for many centuries, and indeed some form of global economy predates the emergence of the nation state, which is now perceived as under threat from the forces of globalisation. This, among other things, has led some writers (Hirst & Thompson 1996, 2000) to argue that globalisation is really not the new phenomenon it is usually claimed to be, and that we are seeing historical continuity rather than change. This is an important critique, and as will be suggested below, many of the historical continuities of globalisation are too readily ignored. But it can also be argued that there is an important discontinuity, which is caused by the sheer scale of the newly emerging global economy and the economic power of its major players. Until recently, global trade may have flourished but it was very much under the control of national governments, which could set the terms and limitations of such trade and in many cases could use world trade to further their own nations' interests. World trade, however, has now grown so large, and transnational corporations have become so powerful, that the capacity of governments to regulate, or deliberately profit from, world trade is severely limited. Most if not all national governments are subject to the dictates of global markets; they are unable to follow policies which might 'displease the markets' because the result would be an instant flight of capital, a currency crisis and economic collapse (Held et al. 1999; Meyer & Geschiere 1999; Mittelman 2000). National governments therefore have relatively little room to manoeuvre in the development of new or alternative policies; they have lost the ability to make independent decisions about the shape and direction of their nations' economic and social futures (Bauman 1998; Beck 2000). This has resulted in an effective loss of democratic control over important policy decisions. Key decisions affecting the futures of many millions of people are taken by individuals and groups who were not popularly elected and whose identities are unknown to most of the world's population. Conventional policy discourse has been framed largely within the confines of the nation state, but if it is not to become increasingly irrelevant it now needs to be reframed in order to take account of these changes. In later chapters it will be argued that a human rights approach to social work requires effective policy advocacy and development, and so this changing context of policy-making in a globalising world needs to be understood (Deacon 1997, 1999; Mishra 1999).

It is simplistic to suggest that globalisation will, by breaking down national boundaries, create a world of uniformity and, by implication, equality. Globalisation is, rather, creating new patterns of inequality. Castells (1996, 1997, 1998) has argued that in the 'network society' there are newly emerging networks of power, connected across national boundaries through new communications technology, and one's wealth, power and influence are determined by whether or not one is connected to these networks. Because these power networks take no account of national borders, in any society there will be some people who are included in the new global networks and others who are not. Hence inequality becomes less well defined by the boundaries of the nation state; in any nation, there will be people and communities who are advantaged by their access to the networks of power and others who are excluded and marginalised. We are used to thinking of national boundaries as determinants of relative advantage and disadvantage, for example we speak of rich and poor countries, developed and developing nations. While there is still obvious relevance to such a categorisation, given the persisting inequality between the rich and poor countries of the world, such a definition can serve to disguise the fact that there are wealthy elites in even the poorest societies, and that poverty (often at severe levels) can exist in affluent societies (Riches 1997). Indeed there is clear evidence that this inequality *within* nations is increasing, and Castells' analysis suggests that with the emergence of the network society this trend will continue.

It would also be simplistic to argue that globalisation simply increases inequality. Global inequality is nothing new and has been a tragic consequence of the combination of colonialism and global capitalism of the last two centuries. What has changed is not the obscene reality of an unequal world, but rather the boundaries of that inequality. Globalisation has meant that national borders are becoming less significant as boundaries of inequality; as capitalism 'goes global', the resulting social and economic inequality is similarly distributed in a pattern that makes national borders less relevant. For this reason, any attempt to understand the dimensions of inequality – something social workers are centrally concerned with by the very nature of their practice – requires an international analysis and an internationalist perspective. Human rights, because of their universalism, represent one attempt to develop such a perspective (see Chapter 4).

Although we can question Hirst and Thompson's claim that globalisation per se is not a new phenomenon, it is nevertheless true that much about globalisation has been with us for a long time; capitalism, colonialism, and their resulting exploitation and oppression are depressingly familiar and are hardly new creations of the globalised economy. Yet this is effectively denied by those who claim that globalisation, as a new phenomenon, needs a new analysis. The refrain of 'we need new solutions to new problems' effectively marginalises the very analytical frameworks needed to understand and address the issue. In many ways globalisation is simply the logical extension of capitalism, patriarchy, modernist rationality and colonialist exploitation, and the intellectual frameworks that critique these phenomena – Marxism, feminism, postmodernism and postcolonialism – are crucial to a critique of economic globalisation and the search for a viable and equitable alternative.

It is important, then, to recognise that there are both old and new elements in globalisation. In many ways what we are seeing is simply the reinvention in a new context of some old familiar stories of class, race and gender oppression, and the theoretical and activist wisdom of those who have been concerned with these oppressions in the past has much to teach the practitioner today. The people's struggle against globalisation is not therefore an entirely new struggle; it is a new form of some old struggles with which social workers have long been familiar. On the other hand, there are new aspects to globalisation, largely brought about by the revolution in information and communications technology and by the sheer scale of current global economic activity. This does open up new challenges, and also new opportunities. For social workers to come to terms with globalisation, it will be necessary therefore to be both familiar with the old and aware of the possibilities of the new. This has particular relevance to the human rights practice outlined in later chapters.

One of the characteristics of the current experience of globalisation is that it has been almost exclusively economic (Brecher & Costello 1994). There have been other international traditions, exemplified in the internationalist movements of the last century, that have been concerned with world peace, the environment, social justice, feminism and, of course, human rights. These saw the establishment of the League of Nations and then the United Nations, with its many agencies, and a host of international non-government organisations (NGOs), including the Red Cross, the Women's International League for Peace and Freedom, Save the Children, Amnesty International and Greenpeace. These were concerned with various visions for 'one world' based not so much on economic activity as on ideas of a universal humanity, global citizenship, international understanding and solidarity, and mutual responsibility. In recent times, however, the international agenda has been taken over by economic matters, and social justice, peace, environmental concerns and human rights have had to take second place. As an example, the current economic orthodoxy of world trade suggests that we should welcome those from elsewhere who want to invest in our local economy, and we should encourage our own nationals to intervene in other economies. Indeed the World Trade Organisation was established specifically to encourage such cross-national interference in other people's economies and to prevent governments or other groups from raising barriers to such investment and trade. As a consequence national governments (with the possible exception of the USA) now have little say in such matters.

National sovereignty may seem dead when it comes to trade, but it is very much alive in matters of human rights, where howls of protest will accompany any attempt to intervene in human rights matters across national borders. Human rights violations are seen as matters for careful persuasion and delicate negotiation, with an imperative not to offend national sensitivities; this is largely missing from trade negotiations, and if one government does not want to abide by international human rights standards little more can be done (unless, of course, there are other strategic interests in play, when human rights abuse can suddenly become an excuse for armed intervention). It is almost as if we live in one globalised world when it comes to the economy but in autonomous sovereign states when it comes to matters of human rights (Chomsky 1998).

The current experience of globalisation, therefore, is very one-sided. It is to do largely with economics, and in fact is little more than the imposition on a global scale of the kind of economic fundamentalism that has dominated western economic policies since the early 1980s, especially in English-speaking countries. This view sees the needs of the economy as paramount and suggests that it is necessary for all policy to be geared primarily towards economic development and prosperity. Other concerns, such as social justice and human rights, should not be allowed to supplant the economy as the priority for policy-makers; if they do, the resultant economic downturn will be in nobody's interests. The free market is to be relied on to represent the sum total of people's free choices and hence will realise the optimum in human well-being; any interference in the operation of the market will render it less effective, and hence all will suffer (Rees et al. 1993; Saunders 1994). This view results in policy that defines economic goals as paramount and all other goals as necessarily subservient to the needs of the economy. Such economic fundamentalism is familiar to social workers, especially in western English-speaking countries, where it has been used to justify the erosion of the welfare state and to define such erosion as economic necessity. It has affected the working conditions of social workers and, more importantly, has resulted in them having to limit both the quality and the quantity of service they are able to provide. We are now seeing the same phenomenon on a world scale, and again it becomes important to draw on the previous experience of social workers in dealing with such policies at national level.

The identification of this economic fundamentalism behind the current experience of globalisation is critically important. Much of the reaction against globalisation, including the activism of many consumer groups, human rights groups and other internationalist bodies, has been a reaction not so much against a globalisation that brings the world closer together, but against the economic fundamentalist form of globalisation that has so dominated the international agenda for the last two decades. It is not so much the idea of globalisation per se that has aroused such reaction, but rather the limited economic approach to globalisation that has eroded democratic accountability, has operated blatantly in the interests of the most powerful, appears to have exacerbated inequality, and has marginalised issues such as human rights and social justice in the interests of a narrowly conceived 'global economic interest'. From this point of view, the heated debates and popular demonstrations about globalisation are in reality not about globalisation at all but are about human rights, social justice and democracy (Rees & Wright 2000).

For this reason, the idea of human rights has been an important rallying cry for those who oppose the current processes of economic globalisation. Human rights, as we have seen, are commonly regarded as universal, and hence represent an alternative formulation of a universal ideal of humanity that rejects economic fundamentalism and asserts that human values, some idea of a common shared humanity, and a construction of global citizenship (implying both rights and responsibilities) should occupy the core of a 'new world order' brought about by new communications and information technologies. This resonates with the idea of 'globalisation from below' as advocated by writers such as Falk (1993, 2000b) and Brecher and Costello (1994) (see also Keck & Sikkink 1998). These writers argue that globalisation as currently experienced can be characterised as 'globalisation from above', in the interests of the rich and powerful, and with little or no democratic accountability. 'Globalisation from below' on the other hand would be globalisation that was in the interests of 'ordinary' people, would be essentially democratic, involving maximum participation in decision-making, and would be based on ideas of social justice and human rights rather than on narrow economic interests alone. From this perspective, the task is not to oppose globalisation per se, but rather to work towards an alternative globalisation that has primarily social rather than economic aims. In such a formulation, the idea of human rights plays a central role and has proved to be one of the most rhetorically powerful concepts used in popular demonstrations against globalisation.

Before leaving the discussion of globalisation, mention needs to be made of the opposing trend of localisation. Many communities have reacted against economic globalisation by seeking to invest new meaning in the local (Cox 1997; Hines 2000). The failure of the global economy to meet individual and community need has resulted in a large number of alternative currency and local economy schemes, such as LETS (Dauncey 1988). The failure of large banks to service local communities adequately, as they seek to compete in the global financial marketplace, has led to the establishment of community banks. Similarly, there are local community-based experiments in education, housing, policing and other community services, and a variety of cooperatives (Ekins 1992). These local initiatives clearly demonstrate that there are viable, sustainable, human-scale alternatives, and they represent possible future directions when (as seems sooner or later inevitable) the whole unstable and unsustainable global economic system collapses under its own weight. Some local reactions to globalisation are, however, more alarming, including the rise of militia and vigilante groups, and an apparent rise in parochialism, exclusion, racism and the scapegoating of minorities in many countries. Like globalisation, localisation is of itself neither beneficial nor harmful, and can promote or violate human rights. It is, however, a phenomenon of particular interest to social workers, who characteristically work with the local, and who occupy important community development roles seeking to turn the resurgence of interest in ideas of 'community' and localism into a progressive social movement rather than becoming immersed in the politics of exclusion and intolerance.

Rights-based practice

The remaining chapters in this book outline how human rights can be used as a basis for social work practice. It may seem axiomatic to say that social work is about human rights, but there are other formulations of social work which do not give such prominence to rights. One is needs-based social work, which emphasises the assessment of 'needs' and then the process of having those needs 'met'. The concept of need is of course central to social work, though this emphasis has been subject to criticism. Writers such as Illich (Illich et al. 1977) have criticised professionals, including social workers, for becoming society's professional need definers, thereby disempowering their clients, who are no longer permitted to define their own needs but who instead have their needs defined for them. There are other issues about needs-based practice, but it is also true that the idea of human needs is inextricably linked to ideas of human rights. The link between needs and rights will be explored in Chapter 5, as it represents an important aspect of the human rights approach to social work which is the main theme of this book. For the present, it is enough to note that 'human needs' have represented an alternative formulation for social workers rather than 'human rights', and that advocates of a rights-based approach have to demonstrate its advantages over a needs-based approach.

A second alternative formulation is a justice-based approach to social work. Most social workers, if asked to summarise the value base of their practice, would probably use the term 'social justice' rather than 'human rights'. As with needs, a clear link can be made between rights and justice. There are, however, two problems with a purely justice approach to social work which a human rights approach can overcome.

The first problem with justice is that it can imply simple revenge. 'We demand justice' is a commonly heard cry from advocates of the death penalty, punitive prison sentences and the like, causes which most social workers would be at least reluctant to support and more likely vigorously to oppose. Using a strong justice rhetoric for social work is in this sense hardly progressive and can simply help to legitimate a politics of revenge. The second problem is that justice is often defined procedurally: to be just, or to do justice, is to administer the laws in a just, fair and even-handed way. The laws themselves, however, may be highly discriminatory and oppressive, and the so-called 'justice system' can result in what is effectively the just administration of unjust laws; this indeed is the history of colonialism, when often brutal oppression was justified by the trappings of an apparently incorruptible system of 'justice' – magistrates, courts, laws, and so on. Similarly, an exclusive emphasis on procedure is problematic for social workers because it can lead to a practice which concentrates on the just administration of the existing system, ensuring that the client receives everything to which she/he is entitled, while not addressing the inequalities and structural oppression inherent in the system itself. In that sense it can result in conservative practice that passively accepts the existing order and merely seeks to make it work better; if the system itself is unjust, such practice is inadequate.

It is common to draw a distinction between retributive and restorative approaches to justice (Fatic 1995). The retributive approach seeks retribution: those who have broken the law, acted immorally or committed human rights abuses must be identified, hunted down, and made to 'pay' for their misdeeds. It is by exacting retribution in some form that justice can be both done and seen to be done; this results in punishment for the offender and is also seen to act as a deterrent for others. The restorative approach to justice, by contrast, seeks rather to recompense those whose rights have been violated, and it is less concerned with seeking retribution than with acknowledging that a wrong has been committed and allowing all concerned to move forward in a spirit of reconciliation. The contrast between the two is readily illustrated in the two conflicting approaches to human rights atrocities such as those that have occurred in Rwanda, East Timor and the former Yugoslavia: the retributive approach seeks to establish war crimes tribunals or other judicial bodies so that the guilty can be tried, convicted and 'brought to justice', while the restorative approach seeks rather to confront human rights abusers with their crimes, seek their public acknowledgement, and then move forward, as exemplified by the Truth and Reconciliation process in South Africa (Tutu 1999). The restorative approach, which seeks to 'restore' dignity, property, peace, safety, community, respect, or whatever else was violated, is based on Gandhian principles of non-violence (Little 1999), and it represents a more radical approach to the resolution of conflict, seeking to break rather than reinforce a cycle of violence. This distinction between retributive and restorative justice is also reflected at the more individual level, in contrasting ways of dealing with, for example, young offenders, domestic violence, family conflict or racist violence. It is a field where social workers have a good deal of expertise (Umbreit 1999), and as it has now become a major issue in the international human rights discourse, this represents an important area where social work expertise can make a contribution.

While 'justice' may be problematic and contested, it is not suggested here that the idea of 'social justice' is inappropriate for social work; indeed the term is used in a number of places in subsequent chapters. A human rights framework for social work, however, does get over some of the difficulties with justice as identified above. It moves social work well beyond the purely retributive approach of a politics of revenge, and indeed provides a critique of reactive calls for punitive 'justice' because these can be seen as violating human rights. And it does not divert attention from the structural causes of oppression and disadvantage; indeed, as will be argued in later chapters, a human rights approach demands that they be addressed.

A human rights approach should therefore not be seen as implying that the ideas of 'needs' and 'justice' have no value for social workers. On the contrary, they occupy important positions in any delineation of social work practice, and they are words which resonate strongly with practitioners. There are problems about each if it is understood in isolation, but, as the discussion in subsequent chapters will show, a social work practice based on a human rights framework can both enrich and contextualise ideas of needs and justice so that they become both more powerful and more useful.

Many of the issues discussed in this chapter will be revisited and explored further in later chapters. The chapter has been an introductory survey of some of the issues about human rights that are of particular relevance to social workers and that are relevant for constructing social work as a human rights profession. The field of human rights is fraught with conceptual ambiguity; it raises some of the most fundamental questions of social and political philosophy, which can only be touched on in a book of this nature. The reader who is seeking a detailed philosophical treatment of these questions will thus need to look elsewhere. The following chapters, while touching on some of these questions, are primarily grounded in the experience of social work theory and practice, and are therefore largely confined to a discussion of human rights within this context.

CHAPTER 2

The Three Generations of Human Rights

The academic literature on human rights has been dominated by three disciplines: law, philosophy and politics. Although social workers have for a long time liked to talk about rights (Centre for Human Rights 1994; Tan & Envall 2000), especially welfare rights, rights-based practice, and the rights of particular disadvantaged groups, a thorough analysis of human rights and their implications has not been prominent in the social work literature, and lawyers, political scientists and philosophers have dominated the discourse. In terms of human rights *practice* – the theme of this book – the field has been dominated by lawyers, who are widely regarded as the main human rights professionals. Most edited collections of articles on human rights, and journals dedicated to human rights, are written and edited by lawyers, and the law is commonly seen as the primary mechanism for the safeguarding of human rights and the prevention of human rights abuses (Beetham 1999). Emphasis has been on legislation and on human rights treaties and conventions, and much of the literature is concerned with their analysis and implementation (Mahoney & Mahoney 1993). Many countries have human rights commissions, whose membership is dominated by people with legal training, and which operate in a legal or quasi-legal way, for example by hearing complaints and making judgments which have legal force.

There is no doubt that legal processes and the practice of the legal profession have contributed a great deal towards the establishment and the safeguarding of human rights, and that lawyers have an important role to play in this regard. But the framing of human rights in largely legal terms limits both the scope of human rights and the possibilities for practice. It can leave social workers, community workers and non-legal activists marginalised and disempowered; more fundamentally, it can

24

leave many important areas of human rights concern undervalued and frequently ignored.

The discussion in this chapter is intended to broaden the construction of human rights beyond the narrow legal interpretations that dominate conventional discourse. This opens up the field of human rights in such a way that social work becomes a central focus of human rights practice and further demonstrates a human rights framework as central to all social work, rather than simply a field in which some advocacy-based social workers specialise.

Defining the three generations

It is common in the literature to consider human rights as having developed in three waves, or generations (Wronka 1992). This typology is central to the framing of social work as human rights practice that is developed in subsequent chapters.

Human rights of the *first generation* are also referred to as civil and political rights, and in their present form have their intellectual origins in the eighteenth century with the Enlightenment and the development of liberal political philosophy (Galtung 1994; Bobbio 1996). They are individually based and concern the fundamental freedoms seen as essential to the effective and fair organisation of democracy and civil society. They include the right to vote, the right to freedom of speech, the right to free assembly, the right to a fair trial and equality before the law, the right to citizenship, the right to privacy, the right to self-expression, the right to freedom of religion, the right to nominate for public office, and the right of free participation in the society and in the civic life of the nation. They also include the right to be treated with dignity, the right to public safety, freedom from discrimination (religious, racial, gender, etc.), protection in order to go about one's lawful business, and freedom from intimidation, harassment, torture, coercion, and so on. These rights are based on liberal notions of the value of the individual and constitute a strong assertion that these rights must be *protected*.

Because of this emphasis on protection, first-generation rights are sometimes also referred to as negative rights; they are rights which need to be protected rather than realised, rights which people are seen as somehow 'possessing', and the state is required to ensure that they are not threatened or violated. Campaigning for first-generation human rights tends to involve the *prevention* of human rights *abuses* and the *safeguarding* or *protection* of rights rather than the more positive assertion, provision and realisation of human rights.

Thus first-generation rights are often defined in the language of *natural rights*, that is, rights we somehow possess or inherit as part of the natural order (Bobbio 1996). Thus they cannot be granted, achieved or realised, but rather are to be protected and guaranteed. The traditional way in which first-generation rights have been guaranteed, or at least in which such guarantees have been sought, is through legal mechanisms. Bills of rights, constitutional safeguards and international human rights conventions have sought to define civil and political rights to provide mechanisms for people to appeal against the abuse or denial of these rights, and to establish sanctions against those who are responsible for violating them. The effectiveness of these legal instruments is, of course, variable, and many are regularly and knowingly breached. Indeed Amnesty International and Human Rights Watch reports contain many documented cases where governments that are signatories to UN conventions or that are supposedly subject to their own bills of rights engage in regular and systematic abuses of fundamental first-generation rights, or allow such abuse to be carried out with impunity.

The *second generation* of human rights is the constellation of rights known as economic, social and cultural rights. These are rights of the individual or group to receive various forms of social provision or services in order to realise their full potential as human beings: the right to employment, the right to an adequate wage, the right to housing, the right to adequate food and clothing, the right to education, the right to adequate health care, the right to social security, the right to be treated with dignity in old age, the right to reasonable recreation and leisure time, and so on. Rather than arising from eighteenth-century liberalism, second-generation rights, in their current form, have their intellectual origin more in nineteenth and twentieth-century social democracy or socialism, and other more collectivist movements. Because such collectivist ideologies are less accepted than liberalism in mainstream western political discourse, there is correspondingly less consensus around second-generation rights, and about the extent of implied state obligation, within the parties and interest groups of mainstream politics (Chomsky 1998; Beetham 1999); for example, should the state be required to guarantee the right to work, and does that mean it has to provide a job for everybody who wants one?

Second-generation rights are referred to as positive rights because they imply a much more active and positive role for the state. Rather than simply protecting rights, the state is required to take a stronger role in actually ensuring that these rights are realised, through various forms of social provision. Because they require a stronger and more resource-intensive role for the state, these rights are often more contentious than the first generation of civil and political rights, and the legal and constitutional guarantees around them are often weaker.

Second-generation rights are not as readily guaranteed by legal and constitutional mechanisms. While there are various conventions and human rights instruments that seek to cover second-generation rights, most notably the UN International Covenant on Economic, Social and Cultural Rights, they are not generally as effective, as it is more difficult to establish 'guilt' and apply 'sanctions'. Indeed the idea of human rights 'abuse' is less readily applied to second-generation rights, and so legal processes designed to prevent abuse are not as readily applicable. It is hard to imagine political leaders being taken to court for human rights abuse on the grounds of a country's inadequate education system, in the same way as they might be for torture or genocide, though this is the logical implication of second-generation human rights. For this reason legal processes and structures are less useful in helping people realise these rights, and hence lawyers have less of a central role in second-generation human rights practice.

The *third generation* of human rights involves rights which only make sense if defined at a collective level; they are rights that belong to a community, population, society or nation rather than being readily applicable to an individual, though individuals can clearly benefit from their realisation. These rights include the right to economic development, the right to benefit from world trade and economic growth, the right to live in a cohesive and harmonious society, and environmental rights such as the right to breathe unpolluted air, the right to clean water, the right to experience 'nature', and so on.

In their present form, these collective rights have only effectively been recognised as human rights in the twentieth century (though of course they have been of concern to some writers for much longer), and arise from twentieth-century struggles against colonialism and unsustainable economic and social development, as well as the struggles promoting self-determination for colonised peoples and the struggles of environmental activists. Their codification in treaties and conventions is only at a very preliminary stage, and legal and constitutional mechanisms for their protection or realisation do not exist in anything other than embryonic form. For many people, especially in western political systems, they would not at first sight be identified as 'human rights' because of the dominance of individual liberal views of what constitute human rights and of what it means to be human. Third-generation rights, however, represent an important arena for human rights struggle and a significant arena for debate. Much of the critique of dominant western views of human rights, and the advocacy of human rights based on so-called 'Asian values' (Pereira 1997; Woodiwiss 1998; Bauer & Bell 1999), is in effect an advocacy for third-generation rights in the face of the dominance given in traditional liberal western political discourse to first-generation human rights.

The dominance of first-generation views of human rights

When people talk about human rights, they often mean first-generation civil and political rights. When the media and politicians discuss the 'human rights record' of a particular country they are usually not referring to the adequacy of that country's health, education and social security systems, or its environmental standards, as they would be if they included second and third-generation human rights in the term. Rather, they are referring to a government's adequacy at protecting the abuse of civil and political rights. Hence the term 'human rights worker', when used by social workers and others, conjures up images of people working for the protection of first-generation human rights abuses: political prisoners, detention without fair trial, torture, extra-judicial executions, deportation of refugees, suppression of political dissent, death squads, suppression of trade unions, violence by police and security forces, and so on. In social work, this leads to a view of human rights work as the domain of only a minority of social workers, whereas the inclusion of second and third-generation rights would effectively define all social workers as doing human rights work.

Several reasons can be suggested for this popular concentration on civil and political rights and the tendency to equate 'human rights' only with first-generation rights. As the first to be recognised historically within the dominant western political discourse, civil and political rights have occupied a significant place in western political thought since the eighteenth century, and hence there has been a longer time in which some form of consensus could develop about their importance. The clear association of first-generation rights with liberalism has meant that they have developed a legitimacy as part of the project of liberal democracy. This liberal foundation makes civil and political rights more acceptable and less threatening to western governments and western-owned media, which owe much of their legitimacy to eighteenth-century liberal views of the role of the state, and western governments and media have played a powerful role in defining global political discourse and determining the international human rights agenda (Chomsky 1998).

A concentration on first-generation rights has also been politically convenient for governments. It enables a government to claim a 'good human rights record' even though it may be reducing public services in health, education and welfare. First-generation rights are a necessary prerequisite for a just society, but they do not of themselves produce social equality or social justice, as these are understood by most social workers. For such goals to be achieved, at least second-generation rights also need to be taken into account, and a strong case can be made for the inclusion of third-generation rights as well, as preconditions for social justice. But second and third-generation rights are expensive. While there is some public expenditure required for first-generation rights to be safeguarded (Holmes & Sunstein 1999), the level of expenditure required for the adequate meeting of second and third-generation rights is significantly greater, and represents a commitment few governments are prepared to make in the era of economic globalisation and the perceived wisdom of reductions in public social spending. Defining such programs as human rights increases a government's obligation to provide adequately to have those rights met, and hence it is not surprising that governments are happy to retain a more limited first-generation construction of human rights.

Another reason for the dominance of first-generation human rights is to be found in the way in which 'human rights campaigns', the 'human rights movement' and 'human rights activism' are portrayed by those most centrally involved. Undoubtedly the best-known international 'human rights organisation' is Amnesty International, an organisation whose focus, at least until recently, has been almost exclusively on a narrowly defined range of civil and political rights. Amnesty International has not campaigned publicly on rights to health care, to education or to a clean environment, though it does advocate and promote broader human rights education and awareness, which cover such areas. It has, understandably, preferred to concentrate on its particular area of expertise, but the identification of Amnesty International as 'a leading human rights organisation', and Amnesty International's self-promotion in these terms, result in a ready definition of 'human rights' as equivalent to Amnesty International's self-defined mandate of civil and political rights (the full mandate of Amnesty International can be found in its annual reports and other documents readily available from its national offices, from the International Secretariat in London, or from the Internet).

A further reason for the dominance of first-generation human rights in popular discourse is the role that lawyers and the law have played in human rights. As noted above, first-generation rights can be protected and guaranteed by laws, conventions, regulations and legal sanctions, and this has become the implicitly accepted way in which activists seek to guarantee first-generation rights. This makes it a natural arena for the practice of law, and it is hardly surprising that activist or socially committed lawyers have been at the forefront of first-generation human rights activism. Second-generation rights, however, are more complex and require more than legal guarantees; they involve policy development, political change, the design and delivery of effective human services, and so on. These are less the natural territory of the lawyer and more the natural territory of the social worker. Third-generation rights, similarly, might be seen more as the natural realm of the politician, the economist, the environmentalist or the community development worker.

The legal profession has immense power in contemporary western societies, and legal action is increasingly defined as the most appropriate way to seek solutions to problems, through litigation, class actions, and so on (Carty 1990). Lawyers are disproportionally represented in parliaments, in political parties, and in the power elites of most societies, and indeed the Westminster system of politics is founded on a legal model of adversarial debate. In such a climate it is hardly surprising that the construction of human rights which is most closely compatible with legal definitions and legal practice, and which is most readily enforceable through legal structures and processes, is the one that is dominant.

Yet another reason for the dominance of first-generation human rights can be found by subjecting human rights to a gender analysis. First-generation rights protect many traditional male roles; they seek to protect those who take public stands on issues, those who are active in civil and political life, and those who publicly dissent. Characteristically, these have been largely (though of course not exclusively) men. The very term 'civil and political' applied to human rights conjures up a male-dominated arena of essentially patriarchal structures, and hence a concentration on civil and political rights is a concentration on the traditional rights of men. For many women, human rights abuse occurs not in the 'civil and political' domain but in the domestic arena, through domestic violence, rape, exploitation, economic dependence, and the denial of opportunities for meaningful self-expression and for participation in the society. These are largely (though not entirely) ignored by traditional understandings of first-generation rights. From this perspective, the concentration on civil and political rights represents, and is a consequence of, the dominance of patriarchal structures and discourses, in much the same way that it also represents the dominance of western liberal structures and discourses.

Most of these issues will be taken up in later chapters in which an approach to human rights will be developed that is consistent with social work principles. For present purposes, the important point is to acknowledge that human rights extend beyond the traditional western, patriarchal assumptions of traditional first-generation human rights (though these, it must be stressed, remain crucial) and incorporate the more contentious but also more inclusive categories of second and third-generation rights.

Implications of a broader perspective

Beyond the legal

Moving to a broader construction of human rights incorporating the three generations allows a conceptualisation that moves beyond some of the limitations of the conventional view. First, as already suggested, it allows us to move beyond the legal framework of human rights. The legal domination of the human rights discourse has limited the range of both thinking and practice. This is not to suggest that the legal approach – concerned with treaties, conventions, sanctions and enforcement – is unimportant. Clearly a good deal has been achieved towards the realisation of civil and political rights within this framework (Mahoney & Mahoney 1993). The legal hegemony over the idea of human rights practice, however, has limited the potential contribution of other intellectual and professional traditions and has emphasised those rights that can be most readily codified and protected through the law.

Moving beyond the legal perspective enables second and third-generation rights to be taken more seriously, and emphasises the connection between them. It requires an intellectual framework which incorporates all three and seeks the positive *realisation* of human rights as well as the negative *protection* of human rights. It assumes a more active role for the state (or for whatever historically might take its place) in the provision of services, resources and facilities to enable people's human rights to be realised. Hence it broadens the idea of human rights *practice* well beyond the practice of law. This has major implications for other professions, especially social work.

Beyond the western

First-generation human rights, with their association with eighteenth-century western liberalism, have understandably been of particular concern in western societies. It is in these societies that first-generation rights generally have the strongest level of *de facto* protection. While the human rights discourse is tacitly limited to these rights, the accusation that human rights are essentially a western preoccupation, providing another excuse for western cultures to dominate other cultural traditions, remains strong. The other generations of human rights, however, resonate differently across cultural traditions. Concern for second-generation rights has been at the centre of the critique of conventional 'development' (Beetham 1999), and of the parallel critique of the way orthodox economic wisdom seems to require the dismantling of public services and low standards of health care, education, housing and employment conditions. Thus second-generation rights are central to the concerns of many nations outside the economically developed western world, and they extend the struggle for human rights to a critique of western models of development. Third-generation rights, through their concern for the right to development and to a clean, healthy environment, are even more strongly felt in cultures of the 'developing' nations. From this perspective the 'Asian critique' of human rights is not a stance against human rights per se but rather is a critique of the western dominance of the human rights discourse, which is seen as having marginalised claims for third-generation rights in nations of the south (Woodiwiss 1998).

One of the important aspects of human rights, as we have seen, is their indivisibility and interconnectedness. A framework of human rights which is to be both conceptually strong and also relevant for practice, in a world of diversity, must therefore encapsulate the three generations and not seek to emphasise one at the expense of others. This moves beyond the limitations of conventional western constructions of human rights and enables the development of a re-evaluation of the critique of human rights as simply another form of western intellectual hegemony (see Chapter 4).

Beyond the patriarchal

Taking a more holistic view of the three generations also moves the construction of human rights beyond the patriarchal assumptions that lie behind some of the concentration on first-generation rights in the public discourse. It enables the human rights issues which are of particular concern to women to be incorporated, and works against the privileging of the male participant in civil and political society as being the principal beneficiary of the protection and guaranteeing of human rights.

The incorporation of a feminist analysis is therefore an essential component of a more inclusive human rights framework, and this applies not only at the theoretical level. As long as the practice of human rights is confined to first-generation rights, protected through legal mechanisms, human rights practice remains essentially conflictual, competitive and male. Some forms of feminist practice can add a new dimension to the understanding of human rights work, involving consensus-seeking, collective decision-making and conflict resolution (Pettman 1996).

A further important contribution of a feminist perspective is the linking of the personal and the political (Coote & Campbell 1982). This requires that human rights be understood not only in terms of the role of public figures in civil society but also in terms of private or domestic experience, and, moreover, that these two arenas be linked. Human rights, from this perspective, must be about the personal and the political, and human rights practice will only be effective if it is able to link them successfully (see Chapter 3).

Towards the postmodern

The above discussion emphasises the importance of the critiques of post-colonialism, feminism and post-structuralism in the deconstruction and reconstruction of human rights within a more postmodern context. The privileging of other voices than that of the western male with a law degree is imperative if human rights are to remain an authentic discourse within which human needs, aspirations and visions can be articulated. This points clearly towards a more postmodern perspective, where a diversity of voices is valued and where any claim to universal truth is suspect (Harvey 1989; Seidman 1994; Kumar 1995). However, the discussion of human rights poses a particular logical problem for such a view. Human rights, after all, are a discourse about universality. The very idea of human rights assumes that there are some 'rights' which can be claimed by all people as a consequence of their common humanity, and the struggle to articulate human rights is essentially a struggle to articulate a universal discourse of 'the human spirit'. A postmodernism which denies the possibility of such a discourse is thus incompatible with notions of human rights, and for this reason a negative or sceptical postmodernism (Rosenau 1992) must be rejected by those concerned with human rights.

This does not mean, however, that the postmodern critique must be rejected in its entirety, and it can be argued that 'affirmative' or 'critical' forms of postmodernism (Rosenau 1992; Pease & Fook 1999) are more compatible with some constructions of 'universal' human rights. But there remains an inevitable tension between the two, and people concerned with the ideas of human rights must live and work with this tension. Working with tension and contradiction is nothing new for social workers and others in the human service field, and it is the exploration of this tension, within the context of praxis, that is the theme of later chapters. The paradigm of critical theory – which attempts to value and legitimise alternative voices and aspirations while at the same time acknowledging the importance of universal themes of human suffering and oppression (Geuss 1981; Fay 1987; Ray 1993; Touraine 1995) – will be used as a framework for this analysis. The struggle to articulate and realise human rights can be seen in terms of different constructions of what are defined as universal themes, and hence a critical paradigm based on discursive rationality (Habermas 1984) becomes a particularly useful perspective.

Practice

Many of the issues raised here will be explored in more detail in later chapters. The remainder of this chapter examines the implications of such a broad conceptualisation of human rights for social work practice. Understanding social work practice as extending across the three generations is central to framing social work as a human rights profession.

First-generation practice: advocacy

First-generation human rights are an important area of social work practice, especially in relation to advocacy models. Such social work is readily characterised as 'human rights work' in the more narrow conventional sense of the term. Civil and political rights, although they may be the least contested in public discourse, remain flagrantly violated in many parts of the world, as is indicated in regular reports by Amnesty International and Human Rights Watch. A number of social workers play an important role in working for the protection of civil and political rights, through work with advocacy groups, refugees, prison reform, attempting to secure adequate legal representation for people, work on behalf of the relatives of the 'disappeared', work in community legal centres, and so on. As a direct result of the work they do, social workers themselves can sometimes be the victims of first-generation human rights abuse. Social workers have been arrested, imprisoned without trial, tortured and 'disappeared' because the social work profession, by its commitment to social justice, will sometimes come directly into conflict with oppressive regimes, will ask questions that the powerful prefer not to have asked, or will advocate on behalf of the disadvantaged when it is dangerous to do so. In 1988 the International Federation of Social Workers established a Human Rights Commission whose role is to support social workers who take such risks and to work for the release of those who have been detained as a result of practising social work in such hostile environments.

Such first-generation human rights practice is critically important, as long as civil and political rights are violated, as happens daily. One of the important problems that needs to be addressed is that first-generation human rights abuse is not distributed evenly around the world. It tends to be concentrated, at least in its more extreme forms, in the nations of 'the south' or 'the developing world', as the stronger democratic and legal structures in many countries of 'the north' make such abuses less likely, at least in their extreme form. This readily leads to a framing of first-generation rights which makes the nations of the north appear superior and more 'advanced', and hence has racist and colonialist connotations. A litany of violations of first-generation human rights can sound very like the north preaching to the south and showing up the latter's apparent inadequacies while basking in a form of moral superiority. It is important for social workers and others concerned with first-generation human rights abuse to help deconstruct such racist and colonialist framings of human rights. This can be achieved by pointing out the historical and political context of human rights abuse in the nations of the south, showing how the tensions, conflicts, corruption and weaker legal structures are the consequence of a colonialist history of domination and oppression, national boundaries that reflected the needs of colonisers and the whims of map-makers rather than cultural loyalties, economic globalisation that is exacerbating global inequalities, and racist attitudes by the colonisers which left newly independent nations ill equipped to join a 'global community' in terms defined by the nations of the north. It is also important to emphasise that first-generation human rights abuse is not the sole prerogative of the south. So-called 'developed' nations also commit first-generation human rights abuse, as is clearly evident in the treatment of Indigenous People in Australia, imprisonment rates and the use of the death penalty in the USA, and so on. The human rights abuses in the former Yugoslavia show that European nations are not immune from gross violations of first-generation rights, and the Holocaust stands as a stark reminder that even in one of the most supposedly 'civilised' European nations – the land of Beethoven, Schubert, Goethe, Schiller and Kant, among many other standard-bearers of western culture – governments can be guilty of the most horrendous crimes against humanity.

Such contextualising, political analysis and historical perspective are therefore central to an understanding of human rights abuse, even in the more restricted first-generation sense. It shows that the abuse is linked to international forces and must not be seen as a simple condemnation of particular people or groups, in a specific country, acting in isolation. Such systemic analysis is central to social work and is one of its greatest strengths. The familiar phenomenon of blaming the victim (Jamrozik & Nocella 1998), seen so often in day-to-day social work practice, applies equally to claims of first-generation human rights abuse, and in this sense the social work contribution to the furthering of human rights can be very significant. This emphasises the importance of all social work being consciously located within its historical and political context. The study of history, politics and culture is necessary for good social work, and social workers need to understand the historical and political environment within which they and their clients are working, rather then merely addressing the 'presenting problem'.

In thinking about social work practice in the arena of first-generation human rights, advocacy models of social work are clearly important (Bateman 1995). Social workers have frequently taken advocacy roles, on behalf of either individual people or disadvantaged groups. There are, however, some problems with the advocacy model of social work. Briefly, advocacy is a form of legal practice which does not necessarily transfer readily to social work. Lawyers have been able to separate the advocacy and judicial arms of the profession, so that advocates do not need to consider balancing arguments or other interests; this is left to judges and magistrates. Social workers, on the other hand, do not usually have such a luxury and are often expected to undertake some form of 'assessment', which involves judgement, rather than simply representing only one side of the story.

A further problem with advocacy is that it is potentially disempowering. Advocacy involves representing, or speaking on behalf of, a person, group, family or community. For the powerless and the disadvantaged, it may well be argued that the last thing they need is to have yet another person, however well intentioned, speaking on their behalf, and that the emphasis has to be much more on empowering them to speak for themselves. Simply entering into a social work relationship and assuming an advocacy role can represent profoundly conservative practice, reinforcing the powerlessness of the people concerned, and this is made more insidious by the apparently radical nature of the word 'advocacy' as used by many social workers.

The above criticisms of advocacy models should not be taken as implying that advocacy should be abandoned by social workers; there are many instances when advocacy is important, and where it can serve the goals of human rights and social justice. The argument is simply that advocacy should be used with caution, rather than embraced uncritically as a form of necessarily progressive practice. If advocacy is not to be conservatising, it needs to be practised within an empowerment framework which seeks to show how an advocacy approach, far from reinforcing the dependence of the client on the social worker, is actually geared towards the skilling of the client. The active involvement of the client in this process is therefore crucial, and this approach indeed has been followed by many social workers who have sought to reframe advocacy in a more empowering way. This will be elaborated further when a dialogical praxis model of social work is discussed in Chapter 10.

Second-generation practice: direct practice, organisational practice, policy development, research and action

Consideration of the second generation of economic, social and cultural rights moves a human rights discourse to the core of mainstream social work. While only a minority of social workers would be seen as concerned primarily with first-generation rights, most if not all social workers are concerned with helping people realise second-generation rights. Social workers in the public welfare system, and indeed many others, are concerned daily with poverty and with people who have to make do on very low incomes. The right to an adequate income and standard of living, and the right to income security, are central to the work of such social workers. Similarly, the right to adequate shelter and housing is a fundamental principle for many social workers concerned with homelessness or with residential care, and with finding appropriate accommodation for vulnerable groups such as the aged, people with disabilities, children in care, single parents and refugees. The right to an adequate standard of health care is of major importance for social workers in hospitals, health centres and clinics. Social workers in the education field, and those working with children, have a primary concern for the right to education, and almost all social workers find themselves involved with the right to meaningful work, through helping to find employment for those whose access to the employment market is restricted because of age, disability, sexuality, gender, race, ethnicity, inadequate education or training, geographical location, global corporations, or simple bad luck. The conventional approach to social work suggests that these second-generation rights can best be met by *the provision of social services*, to provide the guaranteed basic minimum standards of health, housing, education, and so on. This is fully consistent with the social democratic ideology of many social workers (Bryson 1992; George & Wilding 1994), which suggests that the provision of adequate services is the way to overcome social problems. It also suggests that social work practice, which in many contexts is about delivering the social services, is essentially concerned with ensuring that people's second-generation human rights are met. Thus in their regular day-to-day practice social workers involved in direct service with individuals and families can be seen as human rights workers.

Social workers working in organisational practice, for example in management roles and in organisational development, can also be seen as playing a role in securing second-generation human rights. Such rights are commonly met through the workings of social agencies, whether within the welfare state, in the so-called 'third sector' (the community sector, or non-profit, non-government sector), or in the private sector. Social workers who are working to make those organisations more effective (through, for example, providing better and more appropriate health care, or providing better standards of housing more suited to people's varying needs) are therefore working towards the more effective meeting of second-generation human rights, simply by helping the agencies to work more effectively and appropriately.

There is another level, however, at which second-generation human rights become significant for social work. As was noted above, these human rights require a more committed response from governments. They are positive rights, which need to be *met* rather than merely *protected*, and this involves a level of public expenditure in areas such as health, education, housing, employment and income security which governments find it difficult to maintain given the power of neo-liberal economic orthodoxy, and the corresponding power of global markets. The adequate realisation of second-generation human rights, then, cannot be achieved only by social workers working in the social services, with the declining resources of decaying welfare state structures. If social work is a human rights profession, concerned with second-generation rights, this requires social workers to be active politically in seeking to effect policy change so that adequate levels of social provision can be made available to people who need it. This naturally incorporates many of the traditional macro approaches to social work as essential components of human rights practice. Social policy analysis and advocacy are clearly of fundamental importance if second-generation human rights are to be met, whether this practice takes place from within policy-making structures (e.g. government policy officers) or outside them (e.g. activist groups). Part of such policy work is, of course, research, which again can be valuable whether it is undertaken from within the policy bureaucracy or from external agencies. Social action towards change is also obviously important, and a significant aspect of work for human rights. All these 'macro' skills have an important place in social work, and hence the idea of human rights practice concerning second-generation human rights sits very comfortably alongside social work and suggests that social workers have a major contribution to make to human rights work.

Third-generation practice: community development

The third generation of human rights is concerned with collective rights, or those rights which make little sense if applied only to individuals, but which belong to a collective (whether a community or a nation) and which need to be understood in a collective context. The dominant liberal individualism of western political thought since the eighteenth century has led these rights to be undervalued and has resulted in their status as 'third-generation' relative newcomers, somehow seen as more of a 'luxury' compared with first and second-generation rights, and therefore not as 'fundamental'. Critics from other cultures, and especially from Asian countries influenced by the Confucian tradition, however, have argued that in these cultures collective rights are of fundamental importance, and at least in some circumstances should precede individual first or second-generation rights (Gangjian & Gang 1995; De Bary & Weiming 1998). The Confucian tradition values social harmony, solidarity, and the individual belonging to a larger social unit – indeed that is seen as the way in which full individual potential can be realised – and hence collective rights are regarded as of particular importance. In this way it can be seen that the very terms 'first generation', 'second generation' and 'third generation' represent a western bias, simply reflecting their historical emergence and perceived priority in western liberal thought.

Third-generation rights include the right to economic development, the right to belong to a stable, cohesive society, and environmental rights, namely rights to clean and uncontaminated air, water and food, and a physical environment which allows humans to reach their full human potential. This understanding of human rights extends the conventional western first-generation view still further. It sees environmental activism as part of the struggle for human rights, and regards communities that are suffering the effects of pollution as experiencing a human rights violation. It also clearly links human rights with economic development, which complicates the often simplistic view that economic development violates human rights, as is argued by many opponents of globalisation.

The western undervaluing of third-generation rights is paralleled in western social work, which has largely concentrated on social work practice provided to individuals or families, or 'casework'. Social work dealing with communities – 'community work', 'community organisation' or 'community development' – has been marginalised by comparison (Mullaly 1997); in many western countries it is either a minor aspect of contemporary social work (e.g. the USA) or is defined as outside the concerns of social work (e.g. the UK). While social work cannot claim a monopoly on community work (any more than it can on casework or group work), there has been a tradition of social workers undertaking and pioneering community work, and yet this has largely, in the west, had the status of a poor relation of the more individually oriented therapeutic and public welfare approaches (McDonald 1999). Western social work in this way has reflected the dominant liberal individualism of first and second-generation rights, and devalued third-generation collective rights. But if people are truly to live up to their full human potential, which social work commonly claims as its goal, the communal as well as the individual must be taken into account, and it can be argued that the dominant individualism of the west, with its devaluing of the collective, has led to alienation, loneliness, depression, suicide, crime, loss of community, and to a peculiarly limited and individualistic understanding of citizenship and the human spirit.

If third-generation rights are to be taken into account in framing social work as a human rights profession, community work (or 'community development', the term used in this book from now on) becomes of critical importance. In this way the collective expression and realisation of human rights can be included alongside the more individually oriented constructions of human rights which have so dominated western discourse. This is not a case of arguing whether collective rights are more important than individual rights, but is rather a more inclusive position that sees both as important and as necessary if full human potential is to be realised. Similarly, it is not a case of arguing whether community development is more or less important than casework as a priority for social workers; rather it is saying that both are necessary and that they need to complement each other. Indeed there are a number of models of social work practice that refuse to make such a macro/micro distinction but seek instead to incorporate both into social work theory and practice (Fook 1993; Fisher & Karger 1997; Mullaly 1997; Healy 2000).

In understanding the role of social work in community development, and in the realisation of third-generation human rights, a model of community development that I have developed elsewhere can be useful (Ife 1995). This takes a holistic view of community development, identifying six dimensions on which community development can be understood: social, economic, political, cultural, environmental and personal/spiritual. It is important that community development be understood as occurring along all six dimensions, each of which is necessary if any community is to reach its optimum level of development. This rejects the fundamentalism of any single approach, for example the view that economic development is of itself sufficient to ensure the development of a community, or the view that all it takes is personal development and the rest will somehow magically follow. For social work practice to be effective in community development, it is therefore necessary for it to operate along all six dimensions, thereby incorporating third-generation human rights.

Social development involves working with a community to help strengthen its social structures, cohesion and interaction. It may include working towards the provision of services which will typically meet second-generation human rights, but understood on the basis of collective need (the needs of a community) rather than only the needs of isolated individuals. Community *economic development* recognises the importance of community-based economics and the need for sustainable economic activity that benefits, strengthens and supports a community rather than simply serving the needs of the global economy. *Political development* requires the community worker to focus on decision-making and power structures within the community with a view to helping them develop strength, inclusivity and effectiveness. *Cultural development* emphasises the importance of a community's cultural history, norms, values and traditions, and seeks to strengthen community-level cultural activity in the face of the commodification and the globalisation of culture. *Environmental development* asserts that a sense of place and a connectedness to our physical environment are essential to human well-being, and seeks to integrate environmental protection and development within a broader community development structure. The environmental movement has some important lessons for social work, about the need for sustainability in all structures and processes and about the need to link the human condition with a sense of place and with the health of both local and global environments. Finally, *personal/spiritual development* maintains that personal fulfilment and community are necessarily linked, that it is only through a strong experience of human community that we can feel our complete humanity, and that the personal and spiritual sides of community must not be neglected but need to be incorporated in our understandings of community structures and processes. For some, this will be framed in terms of personal growth and fulfilment, while for others it will be framed in terms of the importance of spirituality, both individually and collectively experienced, and hence the terms 'personal' and 'spiritual' have been linked (for a fuller discussion see Ife 1995).

These six dimensions of community development encapsulate the essence of third-generation human rights, which might be reframed as the rights to social, economic, political, cultural, environmental and personal/spiritual development, within a collective or community context. By extending our understanding of human rights to include the third generation, we extend our understanding of social work as a human rights profession to include community development theory, roles and skills. Such a broader view of human rights also does much to address the critique of western first-generation understandings of human rights as too individualistic and as ignoring the collective aspects of human rights. Hence a more inclusive understanding of human rights, and a more inclusive social work practice, become achievable.

Conclusion

The theme of this chapter has been the extension of our understanding of human rights from the more traditional first-generation approach to include second and third-generation understandings. This goes some way to addressing the criticism of human rights as being too western and individualistic, and also moves human rights beyond the narrow legalistic framing characteristic of first-generation human rights to one where social workers can be seen to play a central role as human rights practitioners. It serves as a framework to bring together the various aspects of social work that have often been fragmented and seen as in conflict: casework, advocacy, organisational practice, policy development/advocacy, research, and community development. Many of the themes raised in this chapter will be returned to in later chapters, where their implications for human rights practice will be further elaborated. The approach taken in this chapter can be summarised in the following table.

The three generations of human rights

	First generation	Second generation	Third generation
Name	Civil and political rights	Economic, social and cultural rights	Collective rights
Origin	Liberalism	Socialism; social democracy	Economics; development studies; green ideology
Examples	Rights to vote, free speech, fair trial; freedom from torture, abuse; protection of the law; freedom from discrimination	Rights to education housing, health, employment, adequate income, social security, etc.	Rights to economic development and prosperity; benefit from economic growth; social harmony; healthy environment, clean air, etc.
Agency	Legal clinic; Amnesty International; Human Rights Watch; refugee work	Welfare state; third sector; private market welfare	Economic development agencies; community projects; Greenpeace, etc.
Dominant professional	Law	Social work	Community development
Social work	Advocacy; refugee work; asylum seekers; prison reform, etc.	Direct service; management of the welfare state; policy development and advocacy; research	Community development: social economic, political, cultural, environmental, personal/spiritual

This three-generation framework for understanding human rights and social work practice will be used throughout the remaining chapters in developing human rights-based social work practice. However, the concentration on first-generation human rights is not the only way in which the idea of human rights has been restricted, and in subsequent chapters it will be necessary to extend our conceptualisation of human rights in other directions.

CHAPTER 3

Public and Private Human Rights

As was indicated in Chapter 2, one of the major criticisms of conventional human rights discourse, largely confined to civil and political rights, has been that it has concentrated on the protection of human rights and the prevention of human rights abuse only in the public sphere (Clapham 1993; Bröhmer 1997; Ratner & Abrams 1997). The very idea of 'civil and political' rights implies that rights are about the capacity to engage freely in the structures and processes of civil society and the body politic. The fact remains, however, that for many people it is not in the public or 'civil and political' domain where human rights are threatened or denied and where it is necessary for human rights to be promoted and protected. It is in the private or domestic sphere that, arguably, the greater human rights violations occur and where there is most need for social work practice to seek to redress abuses. A number of groups can be identified to whom such human rights practice most particularly applies. In discussing these particular groups in this chapter, several important issues about human rights, and human rights practice, will emerge and will be considered. The chapter will therefore not only consider the human rights of vulnerable groups but will use these considerations to identify a number of important theoretical and practical issues that apply to any examination of human rights and social work practice.

The conventional identification of human rights as being located in the public sphere has been one of the factors that has led to social work not being closely identified as a human rights profession. This is because social work has been commonly located in the private domain, dealing with private troubles rather than public issues (Van Den Bergh & Cooper 1986; Dominelli & McLeod 1989; Fook 1993). Hence with human rights seen as concerned with the public, and social work as concerned with the private, there has not been a ready identification of

43

mainstream social work with human rights work. The position taken in this book is that both social work and human rights have to extend across the public/private divide and must be concerned with both private troubles and public issues. The common identification of social work as private and human rights as public leads to a weakening of both, whereas making clear connections between the private and the public brings the two much closer and makes a framing of social work as human rights practice seem quite natural.

The oppression of women and the contribution of feminism

There is no doubt that for many women the most significant struggle for human rights lies in the domestic sphere, as that is where they are the victims of human rights abuse on a massive scale. Domestic violence, rape and sexual assault are now well documented, and it is clear that there has been a gross (and many would add deliberate) underreporting of such abuse for many years (Walby 1990; French 1992). Indeed there is undoubtedly still a significant degree of underreporting of human rights abuse against women in the home, given the persisting dominance of patriarchal structures in the police and judicial systems that are required to deal with such complaints. This is reinforced by feelings of shame, inadequacy and personal guilt, which are still widespread despite the best efforts of feminist groups to raise women's consciousness in this regard.

Women can also be regarded as victims of human rights abuse in ways that do not involve direct personal violence. They still receive significantly less of the world's wealth and resources than do men, whether in terms of wages and salaries in the workplace or in terms of distribution of household income (French 1992). In terms of education, earning power, representation at the top levels of government and business, participation in political leadership and financial influence, women are significantly disadvantaged when compared with men (Jacobsen 1994). While it must be acknowledged that these differences have been narrowing somewhat in the countries of the north, in many other nations the gap remains as wide as ever. There can be no doubt that women are greatly discriminated against, and this is clearly a matter of human rights. It makes no sense to talk about the achievement of human rights unless the struggle for gender equity is included – to quote the slogan used by feminist human rights activists, 'human rights are women's right, and women's rights are human rights'.

The struggle for women's rights has frequently been victim of the same liberal thinking that has confined human rights discourse to civil and political rights. Liberal feminism has concerned itself simply with achieving 'equal rights' for women in the existing structures of society, without incorporating a critique of those structures and seeking their transformation. It has therefore concentrated on such things as the right to equal work and equal pay, and the removal of the 'glass ceiling' preventing women from reaching the most senior positions in their chosen fields. While such goals are undoubtedly important, this approach to feminism does not address the underlying causes of the oppression of women, nor does it seek to transform the society, as is advocated by more structural, post-structural and radical forms of feminism (Tong 1989). This has the same limitations as the human rights discourse that privileges civil and political rights over other rights, and it confines the struggle for 'equal rights' for women to the public sphere, rather than asking what equal rights in the private or domestic sphere might imply.

This discussion of the limitations of liberal feminism suggests another critique of the liberal approach to human rights. In the same way that liberal feminism can be regarded as inadequate because it seeks liberation while not challenging oppressive structures, it can be argued that human rights for all will never be achieved by merely advocating for those whose rights are denied and seeking to use existing societal mechanisms and structures to bring about social justice. Feminists have argued that it is the very structures of a patriarchal society that disadvantage women, and that a just outcome will not be achieved until those structures are changed through some form of transformative practice (Plumwood 1993). Similarly, a more structural approach to human rights will maintain that human rights for all will never be achieved while there are structures of domination and oppression, and that it is these that need to be addressed. The implications of such a position for social work are profound. It means not only that social work must seek to advocate human rights within the existing system, but that social workers also need to regard human rights violations or denials as systemic in origin and to address fundamental structural issues through their practice.

Can such an argument for the need for structural change be sustained in relation to human rights? A conservative position, valuing the existing system as it has evolved, would be cautious about accepting such a radical notion. It would argue that we are unlikely to be able to improve significantly on the existing system for the protection and promotion of human rights, and that we should therefore concentrate on making the system work better and should use it to promote human rights in every possible way. This is, in fact, the assumption behind much human rights advocacy, and particularly the use of legal structures, processes and precedents. The practice of law, with its acceptance of the body of law and its concentration on interpreting the law, in particular through its use of precedents, is inherently conservative, and advocacy models of social work practice are similar, in that they imply a basic acceptance of the existing system and the need for advocacy to ensure that people and groups receive their entitlements. A structural perspective, however, links human rights practice with attempts not only to make the system work better but to change the system to one more consistent with human rights principles. It sees human rights abuse and denial as having basic structural causes, to do with the distribution of wealth, power, gender, language, capitalism, and so on.

It is certainly possible to mount an essentially liberal case for first-generation human rights, divorced from a structural analysis. This would argue that legal and constitutional structures are now in place in many countries of the world guaranteeing civil and political rights, and that the main task is therefore to make the system work (while not denying that there is room for some incremental improvement) and to establish it in all countries. Such an argument can be criticised, however, as even in the case of first-generation rights there are structural causes of human rights abuse and denial. The detention and torture of political prisoners, the erosion of labour standards, denial of the right to form trade unions, and curbs on freedom of speech, can all be seen as linked to the need to maintain the system of global capitalism, and hence as having significant structural causes; in this light a purely liberal approach to human rights is clearly insufficient. If second and third-generation human rights are taken into account, however, it is clear that a simple liberal account is not merely insufficient but grossly inadequate. Poverty, unemployment, inadequate health care, homelessness, environmental degradation and unequal economic development are all clearly linked to the needs of global capitalism and the so-called economic 'imperatives' that are the determinants of social policy in all countries of the world. To deny these structural causes and to think that second and third-generation rights can be achieved simply by making the existing system work better is to fly in the face of overwhelming evidence to the contrary, and simply cannot be sustained.

Human rights practice, therefore, requires that existing structures of inequality be addressed, and hence it implies some form of radical practice. This has been raised at this point because it emerges as a direct consequence of a discussion of feminism and the oppression of women in relation to human rights. A similar argument could also be made on the basis of Marxism or postcolonialism, involving the use of a class or race analysis of human rights. In each case the need for a more radical analysis that takes account of structural causes is easily demonstrated.

There is another important contribution of feminism to human rights practice, which needs to be acknowledged at this point. Through their rejection of patriarchal structures, many feminist writers have emphasised more holistic, liberating and non-violent processes, and the need to replace existing patriarchal structures of violence and domination with more inclusive alternatives (Braidotti et al. 1994; Harcourt 1994). This inclusiveness is obviously fully consistent with human rights practice, and indeed the dominance of patriarchal structures is so significant that a feminist analysis (of the more radical or structural variety, rather than liberal feminism) is a necessary component of human rights practice.

Children, dependency and competing claims for rights

Children represent another group where human rights abuse occurs largely outside the public domain, in the private or domestic sphere. The place of children in society and in the family has changed with time (Mitterauer & Seider 1982) and also varies in different cultural contexts (Alston 1994). Because of this, the idea of the rights of the child, as part of an overall understanding of human rights, is controversial. In earlier times the child was regarded as the 'property' of his/her parent(s), and there was no legitimacy for others to intervene to protect the child against physical, sexual or emotional abuse. This view has changed, but there remains a strongly held belief that treatment of children is the responsibility of the parent(s), and that other actors such as the state (and social workers acting on the state's behalf) have little role in determining how a child shall or shall not be treated in the home.

This is clearly illustrated in attitudes to corporal punishment. In many western countries corporal punishment of children in the public location of the school is now strictly prohibited, and if a teacher administers even the mildest slap to a child that teacher will be prosecuted and is likely to be dismissed and effectively banned from ever teaching again, however extreme the provocation may have been. By comparison, the sanctions against a parent assaulting a child in the privacy of the home are much less severe. Corporal punishment in the home is now also illegal in many countries, though this was much harder to bring into law than a ban on corporal punishment in schools. But the state will normally not interfere and take any form of legal action unless the abuse was of a much more serious nature. Certainly a single light slap would not be regarded as sufficient grounds for taking legal action against the parent, and would not be sufficient to justify that parent from being 'dismissed' and prevented from ever being a parent again, as is the case with the teacher. A teacher hitting a child at school is clearly regarded very differently from a parent hitting a child at home, even though the latter may in reality be more emotionally damaging for the child, given the psychological importance of the parent–child relationship in comparison with the teacher–pupil relationship.

This example illustrates the complexity of the issue of children's rights and the conflict with the idea of parents' rights. It is one of many cases where there are competing and conflicting claims for rights, and such conflicts occur whenever human rights are discussed and debated. The clash of the rights of children and the rights of parents has particular significance for social workers because child welfare is a major area of social work practice in any country or culture, and social workers often find themselves mediating between these competing claims for rights and involved in decisions about whether a child should be removed from its parents 'in the child's best interests'. Social workers practise in an arena where society has conflicting values (protection of children versus the integrity of 'the family'), and they are expected to make difficult and controversial moral and professional judgements on behalf of society, where a poor decision can have serious, even tragic, consequences (Clark 2000).

In this case of a conflict of rights, it is necessary to analyse the situation in more detail. The two actors on whose behalf rights are claimed, parent and child, are in an unequal power relationship because the child is powerless in most situations when compared with the parent. This alone suggests that there is a strong case for the rights of the child to be favoured rather than the rights of the parent, since social work has a clear value base which locates it as working in the interests of the less powerful. Similarly, the child is likely to be less able to express her/his wishes effectively and is more in need of representation and advocacy than is likely to be the case with the parent. There is also a more fundamental reason for favouring the rights of the child over the rights of the parent. This is because so-called 'parental rights' are in reality the right of one person (or two people) to control, and exercise power over, another person, whereas the rights of the child are rights to self-determination and control over his/her own life. A strong case can be made, in line with various human rights agreements and conventions, that the right of self-determination should take precedence over a right to control another person, unless there are very exceptional circumstances to suggest otherwise. Indeed this would be consistent with the position outlined in Chapter 1, since the right to self-determination meets the criteria for a 'human right', whereas the right to control another person does not. Hence a human rights perspective must give priority to the right of the child. A similar argument can also be applied in other circumstances where a right to self-determination conflicts with a right to control, such as the rights of women and men in cases of domestic violence, the rights of managers and workers, and the right to bear arms as against the public right to safety.

Deciding between competing claims of rights is therefore a matter for moral reasoning and for the application of values, which can be helped by the principle of human rights having priority over other rights, as outlined in Chapter 1. This moral reasoning cannot be undertaken by attempting simplistically to determine 'the greatest good for the greatest number' using Bentham's 'calculus of happiness' (Benn & Peters 1959; Bentham 1983) in an apparently objective way; value debate is inevitable. Given the discursive nature of human rights, as outlined in Chapter 1, there will often be such competing claims, and their resolution requires moral debate. Social workers are in a very important position to contribute to that debate because of the strong integration of values and morality into their practice and because the value base of social work requires that it take stands on particular issues. In the case of the competing claims of the rights of parents and children, it locates social work clearly on the side of the rights of the child, as the more vulnerable and less powerful and articulate claimant. This is further strengthened by the principle of the priority of human rights over other claims of rights, and is also consistent with most child welfare practice, which insists that the interests of the child come first in any decision about a child's future (Goddard & Carew 1993).

There is, however, another side to the idea of practising 'in the best interests of the child'. There may be a strong moral case to justify such a stance, but how do we know that we are really acting in the best interests of another person? Using an analysis of the rights of the child may be necessary in many cases where intervention is required, but it can also be dangerous. Whenever we take on the role of speaking on behalf of somebody else we are denying that person's ability to speak for him/herself, and we run the risk of colonising and oppressive practice. Many of social work's most regrettable practices have been justified on the grounds of 'acting in the best interests' of someone. The removal of Aboriginal children from their parents in Australia, over an extended period, resulted in major trauma for both parents and children, and many shattered lives; many Indigenous People in Australia are today living with the tragic consequences of this policy, and indeed the impact of the 'stolen generations' on the wider Australian society has been significant (HREOC 1997). Yet this policy – now regarded as inhumane, misguided, oppressive, discriminatory and a gross violation of human rights – was confidently justified at the time as being 'in the best interests' of Aboriginal children. Many of the welfare officers of the time firmly believed they were doing the right thing, and that the interests of the children were their primary concern. This is a cautionary tale for all social workers who confidently claim to be acting 'in the best interests' of somebody else. Who can say with certainty that today's practice, accepted as meeting all the highest standards of professional conduct, will not in the future be similarly seen as oppressive?

It is not only in the case of indigenous Australians that adoption practice has resulted in what was later seen as human rights abuse. There are similar stories from other countries with indigenous populations (e.g. in North America: Berger 1991), and in the case of the British 'child migrants' it was not even a question of racism driving what is now seen as utterly inappropriate and inhumane adoption practice (Humphreys 1994). In the light of such experiences, any social worker should be very wary of the phrase 'in the best interests of the child' as a justification for action.

How can social workers reassure themselves that their apparently justifiable interventions are not making the same mistakes, causing similar tragedies, and that they will not earn the condemnation of future generations? We can never, of course, be fully confident in such matters, as we can never judge our current actions with the benefit of hindsight. But there are things that can be done to reduce the possibility of oppressive, if well-meaning, practice. One element that the above examples have in common is that the children themselves were not consulted and had no part in the decision about what was to happen to them. Acting 'in the best interests of the child' does not mean that a worker is justified in ignoring the child's wishes or has no responsibility to seek the views of the child in whatever way is possible. This of course is not possible with infants, but older children can communicate, and social workers in more recent times have taken much more notice of the child's expressed wishes (Goddard & Carew 1993); indeed not to take such wishes into account can be seen as a violation of the child's right to self-determination. A human rights approach to social work requires that the client, especially a vulnerable and powerless client such as a child, must have maximum input into any decisions regarding her/his future, and social workers are therefore required to make maximum effort to facilitate such input, through whatever form of communication is available to the person concerned. This includes providing interpreters for people who speak a different language, allowing people to communicate orally, or in writing, through art or drama, by computer, or any other relevant medium.

Another safeguard against oppressive practice is for the social worker to be fully informed not only about the case with which he/she is dealing but also about the broader political, historical, social and cultural contexts within which social work practice is taking place. Welfare workers who were more aware of Aboriginal culture and of cultural oppression would have been less likely to collude with removing Aboriginal children from their families. Welfare workers in Britain who understood the pressure for labour in the former colonies and the processes by which such policy decisions were taken would have been less likely to be willing participants in the child migration scheme, and so on. We may never know the full consequences of any action we may take, but the more we are informed about the context of our decision, and the more we take the trouble to find out about the likely outcomes of our actions, the less likely we are to make decisions which, however well intentioned, result in oppression. There is therefore a responsibility for every social worker, when making decisions 'in the interests of' powerless and vulnerable people, to be thoroughly informed about the political, historical, cultural and social contexts of his/her practice. This suggests that the social work profession and educational bodies have a responsibility to ensure that social workers are not only well trained in specific practice methodologies but are also well educated about the contexts within which their practice is located. It further suggests that any move to reduce the scope of social work education, or to concentrate on the acquiring of specific 'practice competencies' at the expense of a broader contextual analysis, should be strongly resisted.

These are just some of the theoretical and practice issues raised by social work practice with children, as understood from a human rights perspective. Child welfare has always been a major part of social work and it raises particularly difficult and sensitive questions around cultural issues, competing claims of rights, and the potential for oppressive practice. These issues, however, extend well beyond the specific field of working with children and have implications for work with all vulnerable groups.

Older people

Older people are another group that is at risk of human rights abuse in the domestic or private sphere. The phenomenon of elder abuse has only been documented in recent years, and it is a problem that has remained largely unrecognised until the last twenty years or so (Biggs et al. 1995). Like child abuse, elder abuse can be physical, emotional or sexual. However, there is an additional category with elder abuse, namely financial abuse, and this requires a different human rights formulation. It is not only a case of the right to protection from physical or emotional harm but also a case of the right to self-determination regarding one's property and financial affairs. While financial abuse of the elderly can be perpetrated by unscrupulous sales representatives, financial advisors and brokers, most abuse comes from members of the person's immediate family seeking access to the person's savings, wealth or property, either immediately through fraud and deceit or in the longer term through pressuring the elderly person to change her/his will. Social workers have a specific responsibility to ensure that these human rights of older persons are respected and safeguarded, both formally through legal mechanisms that exist to protect older people's rights, and in a non-legal way in their work with families.

There is another important difference between the rights of children and those of older people. While children may not have the full capacity to manage their own affairs and make decisions for themselves, as they grow up and mature this capacity increases. A social worker can therefore work in an educative and empowering role as the young person increases her/his ability to be self-directing and a responsible decision-maker. With many older people, however, the capacity to make such independent decisions decreases over time, especially if there is some form of dementia. Capacity, autonomy and independence therefore decrease, rather than increasing as is the case with children. This means that the person is with time becoming more vulnerable to abuse and less able to control his/her own life. For this reason, empowerment-based practice, though still certainly possible, must take on a rather different set of assumptions about what the older person can realistically be expected to achieve, and it is a case of moving towards greater rather than less dependency. The human rights issues are therefore different, with an expectation of increasing vulnerability to abuse in whatever form. And the right to a healthy, happy and fulfilling lifestyle, while still clearly important, needs to be framed in a rather different way than is the case in work with young people. The decreasing capacity of many older people to define, demand and realise their human rights means that empowerment of older people by social workers takes on a particular significance (Neysmith 1999). One way in which this can be achieved is by working with older people to plan their future realistically, including planning for a time when they may not be able to exercise the same level of self-determination and may have increased levels of dependency on others.

It is also true that a concentration on such an approach to social work with older people can serve to pathologise old age, focusing attention only on its negative or debilitating aspects. This feeds into age discrimination against older people, many of whom are denied opportunities to contribute to the community and find their wisdom and experience devalued. This criticism has been levelled at policy on ageing, which has put far more resources into developing programs for the sick or frail aged (hostels, nursing homes, community care) and has ignored the fact that most older people do not need such intensive services and are able to lead healthy and fulfilling lives (Office of Seniors' Interests 1999). Obviously issues of elder abuse, the rights of older people with diminished capacity to make decisions, and adequate care for the frail aged are important and need to be adequately addressed. But a more positive view of older people would value them as citizens still able to make an important contribution to society.

Age discrimination can take place in any setting, at a number of levels, and is itself a human rights issue that social workers need to address. This is a clear example of how a social work concern for the most vulnerable can unintentionally reinforce the pathologising and marginalising of a particular group. It is essential that social workers should not fall into this trap but should frame the human rights issues surrounding older people in a more positive and systemic way. Social work that concentrates only on the negative, and that as a result pathologises entire groups, can do more harm than good. This principle applies also to the other vulnerable groups discussed in this chapter. It emphasises the need for a strong *developmental* approach to social work practice that is based on human rights.

People with disabilities

People with disabilities are a group that has long been subject to human rights abuses of one kind or another (Dreidger 1989). In the context of this chapter, dealing specifically with human rights in the private or domestic sphere, we are less concerned with the important issues of the rights of people with disabilities in the public arena, such as rights of access and mobility, the right to work, the right to freedom from discrimination, and so on. Rather, we are concerned with the denial of human rights to people with disabilities within families and households, and the significant problems of abuse of people who because of their vulnerability can be easily taken advantage of by others. Here it is important to distinguish two different groups of people with disabilities: those whose disability reduces their capacity to make decisions and represent their interests in public (e.g. people with an intellectual disability, or those suffering from serious mental health problems); and those whose disability does not reduce their capacity for decision-making and self-advocacy (e.g. people with a physical disability).

The reason for making this distinction is that social work practice with the two groups is different. With the latter group, human rights-based practice centres on breaking down the barriers to participation and a meaningful life, countering discrimination, building confidence in people with disabilities so that they are able to advocate for themselves. For a social worker to speak on their behalf, or to claim to understand their needs better than they do themselves, amounts to colonialist and oppressive practice. It is necessary in such cases to maintain a strong dialogical and empowerment perspective (see Chapter 10). With the group whose decision-making or communication capacity is impaired, however, there are additional issues involving the protection of their interests and the prevention of abuse. Here it may be necessary for a social worker to act 'in the best interests' of the person with a disability, and this raises the same issues as those identified in the discussion on children. Again, social work practice in the past has at times been responsible for reinforcing the oppression of people with disabilities (Barnes 1990), for example by encouraging institutionalisation, or by colluding with programs of 'community care' which do not have adequate supports or opportunities and which have left the person actually worse off than she/he would have been in institutional care. The same issues apply as noted earlier: the need to seek maximum feasible participation by the person in the decision-making process, and the need to be aware of the broader systemic context of practice.

In discussing work with people with disabilities, it is important to mention the move towards 'normalisation' which so affected this area of work from the 1980s (Barnes 1990). This perspective aims to maximise the extent to which a person with a disability can lead a 'normal' life and concentrates on defining such people as 'normal' rather than in some way deviant. The problem with this, of course, is that it assumes a construction of what is 'normal' and can in that way lead to very conservative and conformist practice, where the person is pressured to fit some idea of 'normality' (Wendell 1996). This approach has declined in importance in more recent years as a result of the increasing emphasis on the value of diversity in many areas of practice. The valuing of difference rather than conformity and 'normality' represents a major change not only in social work thinking but throughout much of social policy. It has come about because of the influence of the women's movement, the movement for gay and lesbian rights, the valuing of multiculturalism, and a postmodernist rejection of a single reality or 'right' way to do things.

While there is no doubt that valuing diversity has resulted in a more liberating and empowering approach to practice, which opens up many more possibilities for all social work clients, it also poses potential problems, in that it can lead to an attitude that says 'it's OK to be different, so we don't have to do anything about people with disabilities', and hence it can become an excuse for lack of action. This is why it is necessary for the valuing of difference to be informed by a strong human rights perspective which would maintain that it is necessary to incorporate an analysis of why people with disabilities are disadvantaged in a multitude of ways and would argue for the realisation of some form of universal human rights. It is very important that the valuing of difference should not be used as an excuse for accepting the status quo; this would be tantamount to acknowledging that the system as it is represents the best that can be achieved, and is in that sense profoundly conservative. This is why some form of structural analysis of disadvantage is necessary to be set alongside the valuing of difference and the acceptance and celebration of diversity.

Other issues

It is important at this stage to identify two areas that have not been covered so far. This chapter has focused on human rights issues in the domestic or private sphere, but this must not be taken as implying that these are the only human rights issues around work with women, children, older people and people with disabilities. There are also significant issues in the public arena for each of these groups: issues of discrimination, of access, of opportunity, of stigma, and so on. It is of course essential that these be addressed by social workers working for human rights. Their omission from discussion in this chapter does not imply that they are less important than human rights issues in the private or domestic domain. Rather, the aim of this chapter was to emphasise the importance of understanding social work in the personal, private or domestic sphere as being about human rights, in contrast to the dominant first-generation public-sphere framing of human rights issues. From this perspective a social worker undertaking nursing home placements for the frail elderly is a human rights worker, as is a child protection social worker, a social worker at a women's refuge, a social worker in an assessment team for people with physical disabilities, and a social worker implementing community care programs for those with chronic mental health problems. It is not common for such workers to think of themselves specifically as human rights workers, yet a human rights perspective on their work can provide a more robust and clear framework for practice.

The other point that needs to be made is that the groups discussed in this chapter are not meant to be an exhaustive list of vulnerable or disadvantaged groups with which social workers practise. This is clearly not the case. They are, however, the four groups which are perhaps most vulnerable to human rights abuse in the home and in the private domestic arena.

Non-state abusers of human rights

One of the important things to be emphasised as a result of this discussion is that the state is not the only perpetrator of human rights abuse, nor should the state bear sole responsibility for the protection and the realisation of human rights. The human rights abuses discussed in this chapter are commonly carried out by private individuals or groups, most often family members. Yet the more conventional understanding of human rights (in its first-generation sense) tends to hold the state responsible, and talks about the 'human rights record' of particular governments. But the state per se does not, for the most part, commit rape, domestic violence, elder abuse, child abuse and so on. We may argue that the state has a responsibility to prevent such abuse from occurring, but this abuse is not state-initiated or state-sanctioned, except in certain particular circumstances (e.g. rape in war, corporal punishment in schools). We are concerned for the most part with human rights abuses committed by individuals or, in some cases, groups, acting in their own private capacity.

The idea that other bodies than the state are responsible for human rights violations is important if we are to extend our human rights perspective beyond the limitations of the conventional view outlined in Chapter 2. It is not only individuals who are non-state violators of human rights, however. In an era of globalisation and privatisation, corporations, especially transnational corporations, wield considerable power and have been often accused of abusing human rights (Rees & Wright 2000). Criticisms of oil companies for ignoring the needs of local communities and supporting authoritarian regimes, of mining companies' disregard for the rights of Indigenous People, of the marketing strategies of tobacco companies, of the marketing of baby formula in the developing world and many other instances have been based on arguments that the activities of the corporations concerned amount to abuse of human rights. And extending the view of human rights into the third generation, any company that knowingly causes pollution of the environment can also be said to be engaging in the abuse of human rights. Not only corporations but international NGOs and agencies of the UN may be criticised for human rights abuse, for example in their treatment of local workers who are employed on aid programs, or their collusion with local military authorities who are engaging in oppressive practices.

Human rights matters are therefore not only matters for states, though this is not to say that states should abrogate their responsibilities in the human rights field. For our purposes, it suggests that social workers, in their policy, advocacy, social action and research work, should not only be concerned with the action (or non-action) and the responsibilities of states. They also, obviously, need to be concerned with the actions of private individuals, and of course this has long been the case with social work practice. But they further need to consider carefully the role of other non-state actors in human rights abuses, specifically corporations, transnational bodies, private security firms, religious organisations, and NGOs of all kinds. Such a broad view of course complicates the idea of human rights abuse, but it also legitimates social work action, in the name of human rights, in a number of fields where social workers have not been traditionally active.

Conclusion

Because social workers often deal with vulnerable and marginalised populations, and those whose human rights are violated in the private or domestic sphere, it is important for human rights-based social work to frame both social work and human rights as spanning the public/private divide. In discussing the private/public divide of human rights and social work, a number of important practice issues have been raised in this chapter. These include the importance of social work linking the public and the private, the need to understand problems in their historical, political and cultural contexts, the importance of a structural analysis, the importance of appropriate advocacy on behalf of the vulnerable, the corresponding dangers of working 'in the best interests' of another, the importance of moral reasoning for social workers, and the need for diversity to be framed within a universal human rights analysis if it is not to become oppressive and exploitative. These principles will be returned to in later chapters, when the characteristics of human rights-based social work are elaborated.

CHAPTER 4

Culture and Human Rights

The issue of cultural relativism has been a major one for theorists of human rights; arguments about cultural difference represent perhaps the strongest criticisms of the idea of human rights, and for many they are the most difficult to deal with (Brown 1998, 1999). This is especially true for social workers from western traditions, who are generally aware of the role of the west in colonising other world-views and who wish to value cultural diversity. This results in western social workers (among many others) feeling somewhat guilty about supporting something called 'human rights' and being particularly susceptible to the criticisms of human rights as a western concept and therefore somehow not to be trusted. The aim of this chapter is to explore this difficult area, with a view to developing an approach to human rights that overcomes these dilemmas.

While it is true that the western cultural tradition has been the origin of many oppressive and colonising practices, including some aspects of conventional social work practice, the feelings of guilt about all things western, so commonly expressed by people like social workers, represents an inappropriate and unhelpful reaction. While there are many things that can be criticised about mainstream western culture, there are other aspects of western culture which, from a human rights perspective, one would want to defend. And exactly the same can be said of other cultural traditions; glorifying another culture and assuming that it should be beyond criticism is as naïve and misleading as it is to criticise everything about western culture as oppressive. Herein lies the key to dealing with cultural difference: the capacity to look critically at all cultural traditions, to see human rights as important in all cultures, to see how human rights are contextualised differently in different cultures, and to see that human rights violations and the struggle for human rights occur in all cultural contexts. The challenge for western social workers is to move beyond the two extremes of western triumphalism and western self-flagellation to a more sensitive and realistic appraisal of cultural difference.

Culture is a centrally important aspect of human existence; indeed we are nothing without our cultural context. It is culture that gives meaning to life, and it is culture that determines a good deal of human behaviour (Jenks 1993). An understanding of cultural issues is therefore essential for social workers, and this applies to more than cross-cultural issues or issues of cultural difference: in understanding any individual, family or community, the culture in which that person or group is located is of primary significance. To take account only of psychological or social structural factors in understanding human behaviour is therefore to omit many of the most important determinants of behaviour. To understand, for example, why an elderly person may resist the idea of moving into a nursing home, one needs to understand the cultural values around home, old age, family and institutional care in the particular experience of the elderly person her/himself. It is cultural factors that play a large role in determining why a child may be missing school, why a woman is isolated and depressed in the family home, why a young person becomes dependent on drugs. Of course psychological factors and social structural factors also play a part, and social work writers will disagree on the relative importance to be given to each, but there is no doubt that culture must be seen as a critical determinant of human behaviour, human emotion and human well-being. For this reason alone, the cultural aspects of human rights must be taken seriously.

The western domination of human rights discourse

There can be no doubt that the western intellectual tradition has been dominant in shaping mainstream human rights discourse since the eighteenth century. But this does not mean that human rights are purely a western invention. Although the term 'human rights' may not be used as such, the idea of human rights can be found in many philosophical and religious traditions, including Judaism, Islam, Buddhism, Hinduism and Christianity, and in Greek, Arabic and Indian philosophies (Von Senger 1993; Ishay 1997). All these traditions contain some notion of people being entitled to be treated in a certain way, and the valuing of the experience of humanity. To claim that human rights are purely a western construct is not only misleading but it devalues other religious and philosophical traditions and ironically reflects quite racist assumptions to the effect that only western thinkers have come up with the idea. Having said this, however, the western domination of the human rights discourse needs to be acknowledged. The very idea of first, second and third-generation rights, as outlined in Chapter 2, betrays a western bias, as it reflects the order in which these concerns entered modern western thought. The western intellectual tradition has dominated social and political discourse across a wide variety of fields, not just human rights, and one could make the same statement about ethics, justice, music, science, psychology, law, medicine, and many other fields, including, of course, social work. Human rights are not alone in having had their construction affected by the dominance and triumphalism of the modern western tradition. The mistake is to assume that human rights per se are a western concept and to dismiss them as such. We do not do this in other fields; just because western thought has dominated ethics we do not dismiss ethics as unimportant, and the western domination of music surely does not imply that we should give up music as a form of human expression, any more than the western domination of food production means that we should stop eating. Rather, the task is to reconstruct our ideas of ethics, music, food, and the rest, so that they are freed from the constraints of western domination and can be enriched by a variety of cultural traditions and understandings. The same applies to human rights. Western domination of human rights is no reason to reject the idea altogether; rather it represents an imperative to undertake a task of reconstruction of human rights in such a way that does not privilege the apparently dominant western world-view.

What does it mean to say that the western tradition has dominated human rights discourse? There are several characteristics of the western world-view that have affected the construction of human rights, and it is important that these be identified and discussed.

Individualism

First, there is the characteristic individualism of western liberal thought. Liberalism, the principal ideology of the western intellectual tradition, has been an ideology of the individual (Machan 1989). It is individual experience that is important, and individual achievement that is celebrated. The phrases 'the nature of man' and 'the spirit of man' emphasise this individualism (quite apart from the gender implications, which will be considered in due course). We talk about history as the history of individual achievements, even when these were manifestly collective. Columbus 'discovered' America (was nobody else there with him to sail the ship?); Wellington defeated Napoleon at Waterloo (without mention of the armies that actually did the fighting); Christopher Wren built St Paul's Cathedral (by himself); Herbert von Karajan made wonderful music (apparently without the help of the players of the Berlin Philharmonic), and so on. Human achievement is largely cast in individual terms, and similarly when there is evil we need to find an individual to take the blame; Hitler is individually blamed for the tragedies of World War II and the Holocaust, often without acknowledgement of the influence of any others, or the importance of other political, economic and historical factors. And at a more local level, whenever there is some sort of accident or disaster we seem intent on finding out 'who is responsible' so that the blame can be sheeted home to an individual rather than understood systemically (a phenomenon with which social workers in child protection are all too familiar).

This individualism is so entrenched in western thought that it is often impossible for people living in western cultures to recognise its dominance; hence alternative views, such as the Confucian position emphasising harmony and the value of the whole, are almost incomprehensible to many westerners. In Australian universities for example, many 'mainstream' academics find it difficult to understand Aboriginal academics' reluctance to take individual credit for intellectual work in the traditional western academic way, because of the Aboriginal recognition of the collective shared nature of wisdom and understanding, and a reluctance to promote individual interests ahead of those of the collective. Yet examples such as this remind us that western individualism is not the natural order of things, that it is only one tradition among others.

The dominance of individualism in traditional understandings of human rights has already been mentioned, and this has been the cause of much of the mistrust of the human rights movement by individuals and governments from non-western countries. It is a strong argument for the validation of third-generation understandings of human rights, which emphasise that human rights can also be understood collectively and are more than simply the sum total of individual rights. A further exploration of third-generation collective rights is therefore of particular importance in the reconstruction of our understandings of universal human rights. This does not mean that individual rights should be abandoned – to do so would be to fall into the trap of western self-recrimination discussed above – but rather that individual and collective rights should be both recognised and validated, and discussed and debated.

For social workers, the dominant individualism of the western tradition has led to the dominance in the west of individual understandings of social problems, and of individualised forms of practice. Despite the rhetoric of a number of social work writers, in most western countries collective analyses and collective practices (such as community development) take second place to more individualised forms of practice, ranging from 'therapy' to public welfare casework. If social workers are to see themselves as a human rights profession, and if they are serious about accepting the critique of human rights as having been framed from a dominant western perspective, it will be necessary for them to question more strongly the individualist biases in their own theory and practice – not to reject the individual perspective entirely but rather to validate the collective and to include both, on equal terms. This has been a long-standing argument from those social work writers who have been concerned with structural analysis and community development practice (Fisher & Karger 1997; Mullaly 1997; Gil 1998; Pease & Fook 1999; Healy 2000), so it is hardly a new argument for social workers, but it is one that, from an inclusive human rights perspective, demands to be taken more seriously in western social work than it has in recent decades. For the social worker, this means a reaffirmation of the links between the individual and the collective, or the personal and the political, across all social work, and an integration of the 'macro' and 'micro' approaches to social work practice.

Patriarchy

The western world-view is characteristically patriarchal, and this has influenced the construction of human rights in ways that have already been indicated. Phrases like 'the spirit of man' and 'the nature of man', mentioned above in relation to individualism, reflect the patriarchal assumptions behind the traditional western view of the human spirit. Women's history has largely been excluded from the historical record and is only now being rehabilitated through the efforts of feminist historians (Du Bois 1998). Of course western culture is not the only culture to be influenced by patriarchal structures and ways of thinking. Patriarchy is experienced across many cultural traditions; indeed in many non-western cultures, where the feminist movement has not been as strong, it could be argued that the oppression of women and the dominance of patriarchy are now greater than in western countries. Groups such as the Taliban in Afghanistan, seeking to react against western domination, can impose regimes that are far more oppressive of women than anything that is practised in the patriarchal west. The struggle for the liberation of women, and the need to dismantle structures of patriarchal domination, transcend cultural boundaries, and this is in fact a good example of the need for a human rights framework. For the phrases 'the oppression of women' or 'the liberation of women' to have any meaning that can be used to criticise the practices of the Taliban (to take an extreme example), they need to encompass some idea of the rights of women, and the way women are denied human rights, that transcends grounding in a particular culture and that is described with reference to some sort of universal human rights framework.

Despite the less than perfect record of non-western nations in relation to the rights of women, the important point for present purposes is to identify that the western world-view has been largely defined by men, in the interests of men, recognising the achievements of men and valuing the work of men. This has led to the unquestioned acceptance of structures of domination and violence, and has marginalised women while privileging men. If we are to engage in a reconstruction of human rights and a vision of the human spirit that move beyond the limitations of the traditional western world-view, it is essential that this be addressed, and hence a feminist analysis is a necessary component of such a reframing. There cannot therefore be an inclusive understanding of universal human rights without a feminist perspective being centrally incorporated.

For social workers, this means that progressive social work practice has to be informed by feminism. Of course there is no single feminism, and there is insufficient space here to explore the rich variety of thought that has contributed to the various strands of feminist scholarship (Tong 1989). It is important to restate, however, that a simple liberal feminism (helping women to compete with men and behave like men) is inadequate. Some form of radical, structural or post-structural feminism is necessary if structures and discourses of patriarchy are to be addressed and a more inclusive view of human rights established. Such a feminist perspective can inform social work at all levels. It is not only about working with women as clients or victims of human rights abuse. It is also about a feminist analysis informing social work practice with men, with children, with families, or with any population group, because we are all affected (and dehumanised) by patriarchal structures and the continued oppression of women. A further important area is social work's organisational context. It is in the structures and processes of the organisations within which social workers work, and which impinge on their clients, that patriarchy is practised and reproduced. An important part of progressive social work practice is to address these organisational issues and to find ways to work transformatively within organisations in order to help set up more inclusive, accepting, organic and consensus-based structures and processes.

Colonialism, racism and progress

The western world-view has a strong tradition of colonialism, and its associated racism. The importance of the Enlightenment in this process needs to be emphasised. The period known as the Enlightenment towards the end of the eighteenth century, associated with thinkers such as Voltaire, Locke, Adam Smith and others, provided the intellectual rationale for the modern western world-view that is associated with individual freedom, reason, progress, science, and freedom from the 'bonds' of superstition and religion. One of the important aspects of the Enlightenment was the belief in progress: that we are engaged in an unfolding adventure of human discovery and development, where we are constantly improving on what has gone before, where the present is an improvement on the past and the future will be an improvement on the present. This idea of inevitable progress is so ingrained in modern western thinking that it is very difficult to step outside it and to realise that this has not always been the dominant world-view or construction of human activity. In other cultures (such as traditional Hindu or Buddhist cultures: Hershock 2000) and at other times (such as the medieval period in Europe: Cook & Herzman 1983), the idea of necessary progress has not been as strongly embraced.

The belief in progress is enshrined in the very name 'the Enlightenment'. It was assumed that because of the revolution in ways of thinking in the west at that time, people there were now more 'enlightened' than they had been before (Foucault 1972; Touraine 1995; Rorty 1998; Jenkins 1999). This naturally led to an arrogance and a feeling of superiority over those who were not so 'enlightened' or who were at an earlier stage on the great journey of progress, namely the rest of the world. It was thus a natural step for the west to assume the role of bringing this 'enlightenment' to the 'less enlightened' elsewhere, and this became the intellectual justification for the colonial domination of 'less civilised' nations. It thus paved the way for traders, missionaries, soldiers, governors and 'pioneers' to impose the more 'enlightened' western ways on the remainder of the world, in the assured knowledge of their self-evident superiority. This of course served the ends of economic exploitation and provided a strong justification for the nineteenth-century economic oppression of colonised peoples.

Racism is a natural consequence of such a world-view. If people really believe they have achieved a degree of enlightenment and progress that others have not, they can define themselves as superior and others as less than fully 'human'. Then they are fully justified in exploiting them (e.g. by extracting the resources that founded modern industrial capitalism) or 'rescuing' them (as in much Christian missionary work). There remains to this day an unspoken racism on the part of the people of the west, a view that somehow they have achieved a superior quality of life and that the rest of the world has much to learn from their wisdom. It is western expertise that is seen as providing the solutions for the problems of the rest of the world, despite the fact that it was the inappropriate application of that same western 'expertise' that caused many of the problems in the first place.

Within such a world-view, it is hardly surprising that the formulation of human rights has been criticised as colonialist by those in non-western countries (Davis 1995; Pereira 1997; De Bary & Weiming 1998; Bauer & Bell 1999). The challenge is to address this by genuinely validating and including voices from other cultural traditions in the debates about human rights and the articulation of what it means to be human. This will be taken up in more detail in Chapter 8.

For social workers, this means that just as feminism must have a place at the core of social work theory and practice, the same must be said of anti-racist and anti-colonialist analyses. Again, as with feminism, this not only applies to working with people of different racial or cultural backgrounds but has to inform all social work, because colonialist practice can be subtle and insidious. Examples of colonialist practice include:

- only reading social work texts and journals from 'developed' countries
- organising training programs for social workers from the south so that they can learn the lessons of the north, in a one-way flow of communication
- imposing one's world-view on another person
- playing the role of 'visiting expert', or validating another in playing that role
- specifying the objectives and outcomes of practice before engaging in dialogue with the client
- privileging one's own wisdom over that of another.

The issue of anti-colonialist practice will be taken up in more detail in Chapter 10. It is a fundamental aspect of human rights-based social work, since colonialism in all its forms is the antithesis of human rights.

Rationality

The western world-view, so strongly grounded in the Enlightenment, emphasises rationality and rational logical thinking, or to be more specific, it emphasises a certain type of rationality, grounded in logical positivism. This strongly influences what is to count as 'real' knowledge and as legitimate inquiry, research, theory and practice. Again, as with the assumption of progress, the acceptance of a certain form of rational logic is so ingrained in the western consciousness that it is very difficult for people from within that tradition to value other ways of knowing or arriving at the truth. While there may be an acceptance that there are other ways of knowing, it still remains the case that, in much western scholarship, rational, scientific, logical (and, many would argue, patriarchal) forms of thinking are privileged over any other (Touraine 1995).

The western tradition values positive knowledge, namely knowledge that is understood as 'factual', that exists in an objective sense, that can be acquired through objective, value-free scientific inquiry, and that can be precisely defined, described and measured (Fay 1975; Lloyd & Thacker 1997). It also values knowledge that is derived as a result of careful and rigorous 'logical' argument, based on empirical observation.

Feelings, emotion, subjectivity or the unmeasurable have no place in this rationality; they are to be banished if at all possible, and their presence gets in the way of 'real' intellectual work. This is, however, only one sort of knowledge, and only one way of 'knowing' the world (and a very sterile one indeed). There has been a series of significant challenges to the privileging of this sort of knowledge and rational scientific reasoning. Indigenous People have emphasised the importance of magic, religion, spirituality, dreaming, and so on – a very different sort of understanding and a different dimension of knowledge that simply cannot be contained by the formal tenets of western logic (Knudtson & Suzuki 1992). Feminists have also questioned the patriarchal assumptions behind much traditional western reasoning and inquiry (Plumwood 1993) and have argued that there are other ways of knowing the world and each other arising from women's traditions that have been undervalued in the dominant male discourse.

Another aspect of western rationality has been its reliance on dualistic thinking. Such thinking constantly makes divisions into two dichotomous and opposing categories: mind/body, male/female, right/wrong, radical/conservative, winner/loser, pass/fail, guilty/innocent, adequate/inadequate, individual/collective, private/public, good/evil, healthy/unhealthy. It is the way that people in the west have come to make sense of the world, the way they organise it and find a place for everything and everyone. But dualistic thinking has its limitations: it is constantly dividing instead of uniting, and it excludes rather than includes. It is a world based on 'either X or Y' instead of 'both X and Y', a world of black and white which can sometimes, with difficulty, tolerate shades of grey but has no concept of the richness of multiple colours. Some feminist thinkers, such as Plumwood (1993), have identified the importance and limitations of dualistic thinking and have sought to move towards forms of logic and rationality that transcend such dualisms. Feminism is of course not the only source of a critique of dualism, as such a critique has been widespread in many non-dualistic philosophical and religious traditions (e.g. Hinduism).

A further aspect of western rationality is its tendency to linear thinking. Reasoning proceeds along a single line, with a beginning and an end, one step at a time, with no going back or jumping ahead, and no excursions into 'left field'. Other forms of more holistic or systemic thinking therefore are undervalued, and those who try to follow them have difficulty in fitting their ideas into 'acceptable standards'. The limitations of linear thinking have been identified by a number of critics, and while there is significant interest in more holistic approaches, there are still serious obstacles faced by holistic thinkers, caused by the structures and practices of western forms of communication. A book, thesis or article, for example, represents a linear process. It has a beginning, a middle and an end, and proceeds along a linear path. The author may not have actually written it in that order, and the reader may well choose not to read it in that order either, but the end-product presented for the consumption by the reader is necessarily linear, and its very form reinforces linear thinking and the linear transmission of knowledge. One of the more interesting aspects of postmodernism has been the attempt to move beyond such linearity in the writing of novels, and particularly in the use of computers to create a work that can be 'read' in many different orders, none of which is necessarily the 'right' one. Linearity, however, remains dominant in western thought and is seen in the persistent appeal of all varieties of fundamentalism, of which economic rationalism is only one example.

All this has obvious implications for social work. Western social work has based itself, inevitably, on western forms of rationality. The scientific, positivist tradition in social work has valued rigorous empirical research with the aim of establishing an apparently context-free 'body of knowledge'. Dualisms, linear thinking and the privileging of positive knowledge are all strong traditions in social work (Ife 1997b). In the computer age such forms of knowledge are even more highly valued: 'knowledge' is becoming something which can be stored and transmitted digitally and made available via the Internet, and this inevitably means the further valuing of positive knowledge and linear processes and the marginalising of other forms of knowledge that cannot be so readily communicated via digital impulses.

The experience of social workers, however, is often at odds with this narrow western rationality. Intuition, magic, love, laughter, games, drama, music, and so on are all important ways in which we can 'know' ourselves and others, and they have always been part of social work practice, however much they may have been disapproved by the scientific traditions of academic social work. Indeed social workers know well that often the way they can best help people is not through carefully planned and evaluated scientific 'interventions' but by an experience of their common humanity, by sharing something special and significant that comes from their human experiences (Ragg 1977; Wilkes 1981), and which can never be measured empirically, entered into a database, or made available on the World Wide Web. And social workers have been particularly concerned with holistic systemic understandings that deny simple linear thinking and seek a very different way of understanding, communicating and sharing. The influence of other theoretical traditions, such as the critique of positivism, interpretive social science, narrative, feminist methodology, postmodernism, critical theory and so on, has also helped social workers to move beyond the sterility of positivism and the western tradition.

This is not to say that all empirical investigation is worthless, that hypothetico-deductive science has nothing to offer, or that careful, methodical linear investigation has no value. This is clearly not the case, as there can be no doubt that there have been many very important achievements of conventional western rationality. It is simply to recognise that there are other forms of knowledge that also need to be validated, and that add rich layers of understanding that the conventional western rational approach by itself can never hope to achieve. Social work practice, and indeed all other aspects of human life and action, will be incomparably richer if multiple and inclusive forms of knowing and communicating are acknowledged.

This also has significant implications for our understanding of human rights. It suggests that human rights should not only be subject to traditional empirical investigation and logical western reasoning. Indeed some of the most powerful affirmations of human rights are not made within this tradition, but are expressed through poetry, drama, or the power of human action. The rhetoric of Martin Luther King's famous 'I have a dream' speech did more to express the importance of human rights than a whole library of carefully argued philosophical treatises. Vaclav Havel, who inspired not only the Czech people but many others throughout the world, was a playwright and used his creative talents to great effect. The courage of Nelson Mandela, Aung San Suu Kyi and others has inspired millions to the cause of human rights without their lives and actions necessarily being subjected to critical intellectual analysis. And to cite a personal example, those of us who were privileged to attend the independence ballot in East Timor as observers will never forget the strength and courage of the East Timorese people, in the face of real and significant intimidation. The sight of thousands of people lining up at polling stations at 6 a.m. on the day of the vote, in the face of severe intimidation and in full knowledge of the likely consequences of their actions, was a moving statement of the power of human rights, which taught us all something that could never be learned from a lifetime of reading, research or seminars. There are different ways of arriving at, and communicating, the deep truths about human rights, and the western intellectual tradition, for all its undoubted strengths, is merely one of these.

Culturalism, diversity and change

One of the biggest mistakes in thinking about culture is the temptation of 'culturalism' (Booth 1999). This is the assumption that if something is a cultural tradition this makes it above criticism and somehow sacrosanct. Culturalism reifies culture, and in effect allows the continuation of the most abusive and oppressive practices, all in the name of cultural integrity.

It is a temptation to which many social workers are prone, in their understandable desire to value and embrace diversity and to engage in culturally sensitive practice. But the valuing of diversity and the desire for culturally sensitive practice do not imply an acceptance of culturalism that means 'if it's cultural, it's good'.

The culturalist position makes two false assumptions about culture. The first is that cultures are static, whereas in fact they are continuously changing and evolving; no culture will be the same as it was even ten years ago, and it will be different again in another ten years' time. Norms, values and practices are changing, and any categorical statement about a characteristic of a particular culture may soon be out of date. The other false assumption is that cultures are monolithic. In fact cultural traditions tend to be pluralistic; many cultural values and practices are not held universally in a particular culture or group but are contested and debated. For example, many western commentators are reluctant to criticise the practice of female circumcision because it is seen as valued within the cultures in which it is practised, and to criticise it is seen as being culturally insensitive, not respecting the integrity of the culture, and reinforcing colonialist domination. While it is true that criticisms of the practice of female circumcision can often be couched in culturally insensitive terms, it also must be remembered that the practice of female circumcision is not universally valued within those cultures, and there are many from *within* those cultures who are campaigning for its abolition on the grounds that it is an abuse of human rights, and who would welcome appropriate external support in their campaign. This is a case where cultural values and practice are under challenge, where there is a variety of views within the culture, and where the culture itself is undergoing change. To take a narrow culturalist perspective, and thereby to remain silent and inactive, is to misunderstand that in this instance, as in many others, the norm is plurality and change rather than a static and universally held set of beliefs and practices. This is not to deny that the issue of female circumcision is a difficult and sensitive one which requires a high level of understanding and cultural sensitivity on the part of people from other traditions. Rather, it is to identify it as an arena of struggle, contest and change, with diverse views within the cultures in which it is practised, and to move beyond thinking of other cultures as if they are permanent museum exhibits.

The same holds with other issues of women's liberation. The struggle for the liberation of women from patriarchal structures and practices is one which crosses cultural boundaries and which is being acted out in many contexts around the world. This struggle may have achieved more in some places than in others, and it will take very different forms in some places than it will in others, as women find their own culturally appropriate ways to work towards the realisation of their human rights. But it is nonetheless the same struggle, taking different forms in different contexts. This is the pivotal point when it comes to issues of cultural relativism and human rights (Brown 1998, 1999). The struggle for human rights (for women or any other group) takes place across cultural boundaries; by saying that human rights are universal we imply that they are issues for people in all cultural contexts, and that it is a common, global struggle of which we can all be a part. But this does not mean that the struggle will be played out in the same way in different places. Human rights may be universal but they may be defined differently, realised differently, guaranteed differently, and protected differently, in different contexts; the right may be the same, but it can be met in different ways. This then is the challenge for the human rights worker: to maintain a strong human rights perspective which says that universal human rights are important, but also to work towards culturally appropriate ways in which they can be realised in different cultural contexts, remembering that those cultural contexts themselves are subject to change and that cultural values tend to be pluralistic rather than monolithic.

This is of central concern for social work, as social workers are typically in positions where they can assist the struggle for human rights and the contextualising of those rights within different cultural traditions. The way in which this can be achieved will be discussed in Chapter 5, in terms of the relationship between rights and needs. For present purposes, the important point is that it is possible to find a way to move beyond the paralysing constraints of culturalism and seek culturally sensitive and respectful forms of human rights work across cultural boundaries; indeed if human rights are truly universal and involve struggles such as that for the liberation of women discussed in this section, such practice becomes essential. And of course what applies to the feminist struggle applies equally to other struggles for human rights, involving children, people with disabilities, race, sexual preference, poverty, or whatever. By framing these as human rights struggles one is framing them also as universal struggles, which therefore are the concern of all people and which must of necessity take place across national and cultural borders.

Global citizenship

The concept of human rights, understood as universal, is strongly linked to the understanding of citizenship; our citizenship entitles us to certain rights which must be met by the state of which we are citizens, and this has been the basis for social policy formulation. In the era of globalisation, however, we have not seen the globalisation of citizenship keeping pace with the globalisation of the economy. As the state is 'hollowed out'

(Jessop 1994), it is proving less able to meet all the citizenship rights that people may wish to claim This is especially so in terms of second-generation rights, dependent as they are on substantial levels of public spending, which governments are finding impossible to maintain given the power of the global economy and the ideology of the free market. It is therefore necessary, in a globalised world, to examine the idea of global citizenship, though this has to date been inadequately defined or realised.

The weaknesses in the realisation of global citizenship can be illustrated by the case of personal mobility. In the globalised world, the wealthy and powerful are able to move around the globe with ease and are welcomed wherever they go. They are highly sought after, and in some cases will readily change their nominal citizenship for convenience, financial gain, and to avoid being held too accountable for their actions. For such people national identity and citizenship have little meaning, and they proudly call themselves 'citizens of the world'. By contrast, refugees, asylum seekers and migrant workers, who are either fleeing persecution or simply seeking a better life for themselves and their families, are discriminated against, coerced, moved on, denied basic human rights, punished and incarcerated (Loescher 1999). It is evidently quite acceptable for the rich to change countries in pursuit of wealth, but it is not so fine for the poor to do so. Strident calls from sections of the media to 'send them back to their own country' are reminiscent of the British poor laws, when to be poor meant to have one's freedom of movement severely curtailed, at the risk of draconian punishment, and when the generosity of the parish was strictly limited to its own people and denied to strangers, who, if they were poor, would be whipped and sent home (De Schweinitz 1943). It is a sobering thought that it took centuries for the British poor laws to be reformed, and new universal provisions established, as a right of citizenship, for all people in Britain, wherever they lived. Clearly it is now necessary to take more seriously some notion of global citizenship which will protect the rights of such people, and which will see the poor, as well as the rich, able to call themselves 'citizens of the world'.

The same argument can be applied to other human rights issues, as well as personal mobility and the rights of refugees, asylum seekers and migrant workers. One need only consider the issue of world poverty to see how unevenly any notion of global citizenship, and its corresponding rights, is applied. Indeed the very idea of universal human rights implies some notion of global citizenship; they are rights which we claim not because we are citizens of a particular country but simply because we are human, and hence they are part of the global citizenship entitlements of every person. The Universal Declaration of Human Rights and other human rights treaties and protocols represent the initial steps to establish a charter of global citizenship rights, and in the era of globalisation the task to establish such citizenship rights becomes all the more urgent as national rights regimes become less effective in a globalised world.

The idea of global citizenship therefore carries with it the idea of universal human rights. Hence as the process of globalisation continues, and with it the corresponding search for a conception of global citizenship (even if only for the more advantaged), the idea of human rights inevitably achieves a greater significance. We should not be surprised, therefore, that at this particular time in history there seems to be a renewed interest in the idea of human rights, and the term is frequently used by the opponents of the current form of globalisation (see Chapter 1). It is interesting that globalisation is commonly seen as in opposition to human rights, whereas if it were more inclusive and less concentrated solely on the economic, one would expect globalisation and human rights to go hand in hand. This only serves to emphasise the narrow nature of the current experience of globalisation and the urgent need to establish a form of globalisation that embraces rather than opposes universal human rights.

Global practice

The implications for social work of ideas of global citizenship have barely been acknowledged in the social work literature. But it is a major area of development for the social work of the future, if social work is to continue to be relevant in the era of globalisation and if a human rights base to social work practice is to be realised.

One way of understanding social work practice is to see it as the process of helping people to articulate their rights and to have those rights realised and protected. This means that social work must have a universal, international perspective, and that it is not enough to be concerned only with the local and the immediate context in which social work is located. On the other hand, it is essential that social work not ignore the local, as this remains the important location for human activity, and is if anything becoming more so. As was mentioned in Chapter 1, one of the most significant reactions to globalisation has been a counter-trend towards localisation, as people in local communities, who feel that the global economic system is failing them, seek to establish their own locally based alternatives. These may be promising community-based programs, or they may be parochial, exclusive and racist. Social workers, particularly those working in community development roles, have a clear task in helping to support the former and challenge the latter.

As the role of the nation state declines in importance, the policy intervention of social workers needs to change. Social workers, in drawing the natural link between private troubles and public issues (Mills 1970), have traditionally seen the importance of policy development and advocacy with national governments in order to bring about improvements in services and policies more designed to promote social justice. With the decline of effective state power and the increase in globalisation, however, such intervention at the national level recedes in importance. National governments, after all, are severely limited in their policy options because of the demands of global markets. There is much more room to move at the local level; global markets may be able to intimidate a government into not following certain policies, but there is much less they can do to stop a local community from setting up its own local currency scheme or economic development cooperative. The other important arena for practice is the global, since this is where the key decisions are made and it is global forces that control the lives of social workers and their clients. Thus the location for social action and policy advocacy needs to shift from the national to both the local and the global, and it is the capacity to link these two that will determine the future success of social work. The forces that affect social workers' clients are now strongly global, whereas the experience of private troubles, and indeed the major experience of life for the overwhelming majority of the earth's population, remain stubbornly local. If social work is to be effective, it must be able to operate at both levels, and to link the two in a local–global frame of reference that has been termed 'glocal' (Lawson 2000).

It is therefore essential for social workers to understand the global dimensions of apparently local problems. As an example, a case which received a good deal of media coverage internationally, and which caused a degree of self-examination by Americans, was the incident in Michigan in 2000 when a six-year-old boy shot and killed another child in his school. At the same time, in Sierra Leone, there were alarming reports of child soldiers, sometimes as young as six, trained to shoot, to terrorise, and to kill. While at first sight these may seem unconnected, the two are linked by common global phenomena: a powerful and cynical global arms trade, a culture of violence that promotes violent solutions to problems and values macho aggression, and a weak human rights regime which is powerless to prevent such abuses, and which has yet to convince the world that the rights of children should be taken seriously. Yet such events are commonly understood as national or local problems, and the two were treated as quite separate by the world's media, even though they happened at the same time and both involved armed six-year-olds killing people. Social workers in Michigan were working with the young boy and his relatives at the same time as social workers in Sierra Leone were working to rehabilitate child soldiers, yet the connections between the six-year-old killers of America and of Africa were not made by the social workers concerned.

Truly global practice would seek to bring together, perhaps through the Internet, people from both continents who have suffered from these tragedies, and the social workers in both places who were working with victims and perpetrators, trying to prevent it happening again. If social work is to be effective, it is necessary to be able to make those links and to work across borders to seek common solutions. Social workers in child welfare, whether in Michigan, Sierra Leone or anywhere else, need to conceptualise their practice, and their ideas of children's rights, to include these global issues. The important point is that these two situations must not be thought of as individual events, understood only from within national boundaries and taking a national perspective, such as 'how has American society become so violent', and this requires a major change in the way social workers think and act.

Another example is public expenditure on health care. In many western nations health expenditure is effectively in decline and the health system is defined by critics and by the media as being 'in crisis'. Yet these crises in health care are for the most part framed as isolated national problems, with lots of criticism and advice to national governments about how to solve them but with little acknowledgement that it is a shared global problem, with global causes and inevitably requiring global solutions. Even with refugees and asylum seekers, an issue so obviously global and internationally linked, which cries out for a strong global analysis, the response by activists is depressingly confined within national perspectives, seen as 'Canada's refugee problem' or 'Australia's treatment of illegal immigrants', or 'the need for Kosovo to be made safe again'. As long as this is the only way, or even the predominant way, in which social workers think about such problems, social work will become increasingly ineffective and irrelevant in a globalised world.

The forces of globalisation are such that they affect all social workers, and all the people with whom they interact: clients, managers, community members, colleagues and students. If we wish to understand why a person is unable to find work, why a manager is required to make yet more cuts to services, why a patient has to wait years for elective surgery, why a community is suffering economic decline, why there are beggars on the streets, why a colleague is too busy to stop for a coffee, why a young person feels that life has so little to offer that he/she tries to take his/her own life, why a student falls asleep in class after working late on a part-time job, or why there are millions of people dying of preventable diseases, we need to understand global forces and the global factors that contribute to these problems. Thus all social work must be concerned with the global, and all social work is in this sense international social work. International social work has a long tradition within the profession, but it has largely been seen as a specialist field occupied by relatively few social workers: those who work for international agencies, who are involved in intercountry adoptions, who work with refugees, and so on. For most social workers international social work might be seen as an interesting specialisation but one with little relevance to 'mainstream' practice. In the era of globalisation, however, an international perspective has everything to do with all social work practice, mainstream or otherwise.

Conclusion

The discussion of cultural issues, the main theme of this chapter, has led to the identification of some further issues of human rights-based practice. These relate to the need for social workers to be not only culturally sensitive but also to locate cultural difference within a broader human rights perspective. The struggle for human rights transcends cultural and national boundaries, and although human rights will be contextualised in different ways, they are also part of a discourse of global citizenship that naturally leads social workers to develop a more internationalist approach both to the analysis of social problems and to practice. In the era of globalisation this is appropriate and necessary if social work is to remain relevant to the needs of those who seek its services, and if it is to be able to address issues of social justice.

CHAPTER 5

Human Rights and Human Needs

This chapter is about the relationship between needs and rights, and what that means for social work practice. Social workers can be regarded as professional need definers. They are constantly in the process of identifying, and then trying to meet, human needs, as described back in 1945 by Charlotte Towle (Towle 1965). Scarcely a day would pass in any social worker's life when the word 'need' is not used on dozens of occasions. Social workers do 'needs assessments', talk about the needs of individuals, of families, of client groups (e.g. the aged), of communities, of agencies, of service delivery systems (e.g. the health care system) and of the whole society (e.g. the need for a better income security system). Social workers talk about 'unmet need', 'needing more resources', 'doing a needs survey', 'needing more social workers', 'needing supervision', and so on. 'Need' is one of the most commonly used words in the social work vocabulary, and it is significant that more often than not it is used, in the words of Noel and Rita Timms, 'in the absence of any deep sense of puzzlement about the concept' (Timms & Timms 1977: 141). Need, however, is a complex issue and requires a good deal more examination than is common in the social work literature. This book seeks to frame social work as a human rights profession rather than a human needs profession. Instead of seeing social work practice as about the assessment and meeting of human needs, we can see it as about the defining, realising and guaranteeing of human rights. To understand the difference, it is necessary to look in more detail at the relationship between needs and rights in the context of social work practice, so that the implications of an idea of rights-based practice can become clearer.

The problem of needs

Although the concept of need is treated unproblematically by most social workers, it is in fact both complex and controversial (Doyal & Gough 1991). It is an instance where the paradigm of positivism has had a major impact, and this remains the case for many social workers. The positivist view of need sees 'needs' as existing in their own right, as phenomena to be objectively identified and measured (Ife 1995). The very phrase 'needs assessment' suggests such a view; clients, communities, agencies, organisations and so on all have 'needs' which somehow we are able to describe and measure as if they were independent phenomena. It is assumed that different social workers, if given the same 'case' (whether an individual, a family or a community) and asked to do a needs assessment, would come up with the same answer. If they do not, it would be grounds for questioning the competence of one of the workers, who presumably did not do the needs assessment 'properly'. Such a view is characteristically positivist, with its emphasis on the apparently neutral and objective assessment of social phenomena, and if there are differences in assessment, attention is given to methodological deficiencies. It is like asking two people to measure the width of a desk; if they come up with different answers, then the problem lies in the methods of measurement, and one of them either had an inaccurate ruler or did not know how to use the ruler properly. The objective 'fact' of the width of the desk is not in question; it is the same for the two measurers, and so they should come up with the same answer.

If we accept that human needs exist objectively in the same way as a desk, then the positivist paradigm is quite an appropriate way of understanding need. But it is clear that human needs are not the same as desks. Needs are, by their very nature, value-laden. Different value positions will have very different views on what, if anything, is 'needed' in a particular situation. A social worker with a strong feminist perspective, who sees traditional family structures as highly oppressive, will define different 'needs' in a case of domestic violence from the definition of a social worker with conservative patriarchal 'family values'. These two social workers will probably never agree on the 'needs' of the victim, the perpetrator and the family in a domestic violence case. The needs as defined by these two social workers are not just objective measurements; they are affected by theoretical understandings, and in particular by ideologies. Needs must therefore be understood as statements of values, of ideologies, rather than statements of 'fact'. This does not mean that they are not also matters for professional expertise; when a social worker defines what is 'needed' in any particular circumstance, the need definition is based on a professional understanding of what is likely to 'work' in that situation and hence what form of practice or service provision is likely to lead to a desired result. Such a judgement is based on professional expertise, on relevant research, on practice wisdom, on theory, and so on. Judgements of need are both value/ideology judgements and also judgements reflecting expertise (Ife 1980).

The important point emerging from this is that with questions of need, the act of definition and the perspective of the need definer are of paramount importance. Not only will two social workers define the 'needs' of a particular individual, family or community in different ways, but other actors in the case will also have different definitions of what is 'needed', including the client her/himself, other family members, community leaders, other professionals, and so on. Social workers in the reality of day-to-day practice spend a good deal of time negotiating these various perspectives on 'need'.

One of the criticisms of all human service professionals, and perhaps particularly of social workers, is that they use their professional position to privilege their definitions of need over the definitions made by others. Illich's well-known critique of the various professions as 'disabling' specifically includes social workers (Illich et al. 1977). He claims that by increasingly taking on the role of defining people's needs for them, professions have disempowered people by preventing them from defining their needs for themselves. In the era of professionalism, we have professionals exercising control over increasing aspects of our lives. It seems as if there are professionals telling us the right way to do everything: to eat, to relax, to make love, to give birth, to raise children, to learn about the world, to deal with personal problems, to keep fit and healthy, to grieve, to grow old, even to die. There are right and wrong ways to do everything and there is an apparent army of professionals ready to teach us how to do it properly and to imply that somehow if we do not do these things in the approved way we are less than fully human. When we have any sort of problem, we are expected to seek the advice of a professional, who implicitly knows better than we do what we need. This has the effect of disempowering people and giving them less control over their own lives. It devalues human choice and renders people passive 'consumers' of professionalised services. It does not acknowledge the efforts of people to provide for themselves in their own ways: self-education is devalued in comparison to formal qualifications; representing oneself in court without legal assistance is discouraged; self-care in the health field is devalued (unless of course it means buying a book by an expert about how to 'do' self-care properly). Professionals – medical practitioners, lawyers, planners, accountants, architects, psychologists, teachers, social workers, counsellors, health and fitness experts, and so on – seem to be in control of every aspect of our lives. When such criticism is voiced in the popular media it is commonly social workers that are singled out for criticism (Franklin & Parton 1991); they are labelled as 'do-gooders' trying to interfere in people's lives and tell people what is good for them, as 'social engineers' and as people whose prescriptions have led to a worsening rather than a resolving of many social problems. While such popular criticisms are usually based on a limited understanding of social work practice and grossly oversimplify complex social problems, many social workers nevertheless feel a twinge of discomfort that there might be more than a grain of truth in what is being said. It is, basically, the same criticism as that of Illich, though from Illich's position it applies to all professions, and social work, though as guilty as the rest, does not deserve to be singled out for special criticism.

The key to this criticism is that it is based on the definition of need and on the tendency of professionals to appropriate the right of individuals, families or communities to define their own needs. For the purposes of the present discussion, it emphasises that need definition is far from unproblematic and is certainly not neutral or objective; indeed the very act of professional need definition is itself ideological, and privileges the professional while disempowering the person, group or community whose 'needs' are being determined. It also suggests that a significant human right is the right to define one's own needs, and that professional practice is therefore a form of human rights abuse.

Such an argument suggests the desirability of reformulating social work practice so that it seeks to return to people the power to define their own needs and seek to have them met. This is either implicit or explicit in a number of formulations of social work, particularly those regarded as in the more critical or radical tradition, or those that seek a goal of genuine empowerment (Benn 1981, 1991; Rees 1991; Fook 1993; Fisher & Karger 1997; Ife 1997b; Mullaly 1997; Gil 1998; Pease & Fook 1999; Healy 2000). It is the intention here to demonstrate that by replacing 'needs-based' practice with 'rights-based' practice, such a goal can be more readily realised and some of the problems of need definition can be avoided.

Needs and rights

When we make a statement of need, we are saying that something is *necessary* in order for something else to occur. We are talking, essentially, about a means to a particular end. I need a pen in order to write, I need food in order to stay alive, I need medication in order to cure an illness, I need a car in order to drive around the city, I need new clothes in order to look smart, I need to listen to music in order to feel relaxed, and so on. All my 'needs' are actually not ends in themselves but are means to achieve other desired ends. There are two things to notice about these statements of needs. One is that some of the desired ends might be regarded as more important than others (e.g. staying alive as opposed to looking smart), and the other is that some of these statements might be questioned as to whether the 'needed' thing is the best or only way to achieve the desired end (e.g. I could use public transport to get around the city, and there are other ways to help me feel relaxed as well as listening to music). These two points will be taken up in later discussion and are important in developing a rights-based approach to social work.

When social workers make statements of need, the desired end state can be described in terms of the meeting of a claimed right, and this is the essence of the link between needs and rights in social work practice. When we say that a community needs a child care centre, we are basing that statement on an assumption about the rights of parents to be able to participate in the workplace or have other time away from the duties of caring, and the rights of children to receive adequate care. When we say that a child needs special educational programs, we are doing so on the basis of an understanding of the right of children to an appropriate education, and the right to achieve one's maximum educational potential. When we say that an elderly person needs a nursing home placement, we are making assumptions about the right of that person to an adequate standard of care, and the rights of family members to be able to do other things with their lives than look after the needs of their dependent relative twenty-four hours a day.

Statements of need within social work are therefore also statements about rights. The problem has been that the associated rights nearly always remain implicit and unstated. There is a confident assertion of need – for nursing home-placement, for a child care centre, or whatever – but the corresponding rights are seldom spelled out. Indeed the social worker her/himself may not have thought through the rights issues involved but may have taken them as given, or may even be largely unaware of them, having been so affected by policy manuals, agency procedures, office culture and the pressing requirements of the day-to-day job that questions of rights hardly seem significant. These rights are, however, at the basis of practice. One important practice principle for human rights social work, therefore, is that social workers should seek to identify the rights issues behind the statements of need that they make every day. Rights-based practice is a form of social work where the word 'right' is used more than the word 'need' in the day-to-day discourse of social workers, and where whenever a 'need' is talked about, the rights that lie behind that need are identified and explored.

It was noted above that in talking about needs and relating them to desired consequences, not all the desired consequences would be seen as having a similar priority. Hence my need for food in order to survive would be seen as having a higher priority than my need for new clothes in order to look smart; most people would presumably agree that survival has a higher claim than looking smart. By saying I 'need' these things, I am effectively claiming a right to have those needs met, and presumably my claim to survival has a stronger claim to be met than my need to look smart. To evaluate the strength of my claim to a 'right' to new clothes, we have to examine how important it is for me to look smart. A case might be made, for example, that because of my position, and the importance of appearance in encouraging people to trust me, it is very important that I look smart, as I will not be able to do my job properly unless I do. Such a claim obviously is more readily justified with some occupations than with others. Another case might be made that it is important for my own mental health that I look smart; for some people, looks are unimportant at a personal level, but I may be someone for whom looking smart is very important to my sense of personal well-being, for good cultural or psychological reasons.

This leads to the issue of how do we prioritise rights as the basis for claims of need. Clearly, some rights are more important than others, and it is necessary to make decisions about which rights should have priority because sometimes the rights will conflict (e.g. the right to bear arms and the right to personal safety) and also because we are often faced with limited resources, which means that not all needs can be met. Equally clearly, we cannot make firm decisions about the priority of rights in the abstract; some rights, such as the right to look smart, need to be properly contextualised, and in these cases the end becomes a means: it is not just the right to look smart that is at issue but the right to be able to do one's job well, or the right to mental health and a sense of personal well-being. Hence ends can become means to another end, and the distinction between means and ends is not always easy; indeed it can be argued that it is really a false distinction. This question of the validity of separating means and ends, and hence rights and needs, and the implications for social work, will be taken up later in the chapter. The important point for present purposes is that it is not easy to assign relative priorities to claims of rights and that this cannot be done without an examination of the context within which a right is claimed.

Giving priority to different needs and rights

To assign priority to some rights (and therefore needs) over others requires some kind of universal framework or hierarchy of rights, but this is fraught with difficulty. We have already seen how the western tendency to give priority to first-generation rights over third-generation rights has led to a significant critique from Asian commentators of a cultural bias in human rights discourse. We have also seen that different claims for rights cannot be treated in the abstract but must be contextualised; we cannot say, for example, that the 'right' to look smart should take precedence over the 'right' to be able to drive around a city. Each has to be looked at in its context if we are to assign relative importance to these two (perhaps trivial) claims for rights (Doyal & Gough 1991).

In Chapter 1, when the definition of human rights was discussed, it was noted that one of the characteristics of human rights is that they are indivisible. Human rights belong together, and hence one should never be in a position of having to make a choice between two competing 'human' rights. One of the criteria for a claimed right to count as a human right was that it should not be in conflict with other human rights. Hence human rights should not conflict with each other, and when there is a conflict between a *human* right and another right, the human rights perspective requires that the *human* right should have priority. That is one important principle which can apply when competing claims for rights need to be evaluated.

How can we tell if a claimed right, or need (with its implicit right) is a claim for a *human* right, and then whether it can be justified as such? One way is to keep asking means and ends questions. For example:

- Why do I need (or have a right to) new clothes? *In order to look smart.*
- Why do I need (or have a right) to look smart? *In order to improve my mental health and sense of well-being.*
- Why do I need to improve my sense of well-being? *Because it is part of my being human.*

Once the inquiry reaches an assertion that it is 'part of being human', 'what I have a right to expect as a human being', or some such statement, we have entered the domain of human rights. We can then evaluate the claim in two ways. First, we can see whether the claim satisfies the five criteria for a human right as outlined in Chapter 1. If it does, we also need to evaluate the strength of the various claims at each step of the chain. For example we may want to object that I can look smart without new clothes (a trip to the dry-cleaners may be all that is required), or that my appearance is so shabby that even a suit of new clothes will do nothing to make me look smart. We might also argue that I can improve my mental health and sense of well-being in less expensive ways than by buying new clothes (e.g. buying a new CD may serve the purpose just as well), and so on. Only if we can be satisfied of the validity of each claim in the chain can we accept the claim as a claim *of human rights*, and therefore assign it the top priority that such a claim deserves. Many of the claims of social work clients, however, will satisfy such criteria, as for the most part it is precisely because these rights have not been met that the person concerned has ended up seeking the assistance of a social worker.

Hierarchies of needs and rights

One of the best-known formulations of human need is Maslow's hierarchy of needs. Maslow (1970) outlined five 'levels' of human needs, the most fundamental being physiological needs, followed by safety needs, needs for belongingness and love, needs for esteem, and finally needs for self-actualisation. The important point about Maslow's hierarchy is that he maintained that if needs at one level are not satisfied, needs at higher levels become less significant, as the individual concerned concentrates on meeting the more fundamental needs. As the more basic needs are realised, however, the higher-order needs emerge as more important. One's need for self-actualisation is of little importance or concern if one is starving, cold and homeless, but the need for self-actualisation can become all-encompassing for an individual fortunate enough to have the needs at the four lower levels effectively met.

As we have already seen, needs are strongly linked to rights. Maslow himself, in the foreword to the second edition of his book *Motivation and Personality*, suggests that the needs he has described can in fact also be regarded as rights:

> It is legitimate and fruitful to regard instinctoid basic needs and metaneeds as *rights* as well as needs. This follows immediately upon granting that human beings have a right to be human in the same sense that cats have a right to be cats. In order to be fully human, these need and metaneed gratifications are necessary, and may therefore be considered to be natural rights. (Maslow 1970: xiii; italics in original)

If we accept a hierarchy of human needs, and that needs are inevitably linked to rights, is there also, then, a hierarchy of human rights? If there were, it would mean that some rights are more fundamental and that they need to be met before we can turn our attention to 'higher-order' rights. The western construction of first-generation rights as somehow more fundamental than second or third-generation rights has something of this hierarchical flavour, and might be seen as a Maslow-like approach to attaching priority to human rights. As we have seen in earlier chapters, this privileging of first-generation rights has caused difficulties. It is necessary to reject such a framing of human rights, and instead to accept the idea of human rights as 'universal and indivisible', namely that human rights come together as a package that includes all three generations, and to privilege none of them over the others. In this sense, the 'essential' components of our common humanity, which is what human rights attempt to encapsulate, should not be ranked in a hierarchy but belong together; each is necessary and none is sufficient without the others.

Maslow's hierarchy of needs does nonetheless represent a useful way of thinking about human rights. Because needs imply rights, all five levels of Maslow's hierarchy have rights implicit in them. From a human rights perspective – this is also implicit in Maslow's work – we can see the goal of self-actualisation as a right of all human beings. This means that there is a powerful case for the rights implied in all four of the lower levels of Maslow's hierarchy to be seen as human rights, since from Maslow's position it is necessary to achieve them all if one is to achieve self-actualisation. This does not imply that the human rights inherent in Maslow's work are hierarchical in the sense that one is more important than the others (though it does suggest that some rights may precede others in that if some rights are not realised others seem to be of less immediate priority). Interestingly, this implied 'hierarchy' of rights does not correspond with the priority implicit in the 'three generations' framework. From the perspective of Maslow's hierarchy, civil and political rights would not be the first to be met (a reading of Maslow's definitions suggests that these rights belong with the second 'highest' level of need, namely the need for esteem), and rights to food, clothing, shelter, health and some degree of economic security, namely second-generation rights, are more fundamental for the meeting of human need than are first-generation rights. Indeed one could even make a case that third-generation environmental rights come first, since without an environment in which we can breathe the air and drink the water, other rights become irrelevant. But one should be cautious about applying a hierarchical view of human rights too strongly because such a view militates against the notion of human rights as indivisible, which is one of the strengths of a human rights perspective. It may be that at some times and in some circumstances particular human rights are seen as of more immediate concern than others, for example when people are without food and shelter, other rights that are also being denied may receive less immediate attention. But the danger in this is that those other rights will be ignored; for example aid agencies will provide adequate food and shelter but will not bother with education, even though education is also a human right and is certainly necessary if people are to achieve the self-actualisation discussed by Maslow, which is surely the goal of human rights-based practice.

Needs as contextualised rights

Another way of thinking about the relationship between needs and rights is to relate it to the issues of universalism and cultural relativism, as discussed in Chapter 4. Human rights, by their very nature, are universal, but this does not mean they have to be applied or realised in the same way in different cultural contexts. If we take a view that sees human *rights* as universal, but *needs* as being the way in which those universals are applied in different contexts, we have come a long way towards resolving the problems of universal rights and cultural relativities. As we have already seen, need statements contain implicit rights, and hence it is by making need statements that we often try to operationalise rights and show how those rights can be met. For example, we can accept that the *right* to education is a universal human right, but this does not mean that educational *needs* are, or should be, the same in all cultural contexts. The right to education can be met in different ways, using different structures and processes. It may mean school buildings in one context but something else in another. For example in remote areas with sparse populations, communication using computers, telephones and video may be a much more appropriate way of realising the right of each child to an education. In other contexts it may mean something different again, such as itinerant teachers without a formal classroom, or it may mean education provided largely through a tribal or extended family structure. Thus there will be a large range of 'needs' associated with meeting a single human right of education. In one context it will mean a need for buildings, in another it will mean a need for computers, in another it will mean the need to train local people in basic educational methods, in another it will mean the need for books and videos, and so on. Similarly, the right to shelter means very different 'housing needs' in different parts of the world, depending on such factors as climate, culture or family structure.

In this way, statements of need become the way in which cultural and other variations can be incorporated into a universal human rights framework. The *rights* are universal, and constant across all human situations, but their different contexts result in different definitions and assertions of *needs*. In this context, to impose a single set of universal human needs on all people would count as oppressive and dictatorial, and does not allow for diversity. But a relativist approach to needs, linked to a universal understanding of rights, is an invitation for fundamental human rights to be met in different ways in different contexts. The important thing is that the rights be met for all people, but they do not have to be met in the same ways, and indeed in a world that values cultural diversity there should also be maximum diversity in the ways in which human rights are realised.

There will still be instances, however, when a human right cannot be realised within a particular culture, despite different possible definitions of need. For example a culture that reinforces the oppression of women and denies women full participation in society, access to education or the right to self-determination is contravening human rights, and no amount of relative need definition will stop that. The point is that a human rights perspective requires that all societies meet human rights obligations; it does not matter how they do this, and it is precisely because societies will do it in different ways that we can learn from each other's experiences and can maintain a rich cultural diversity. But if a particular cultural tradition does not and cannot meet those human rights objectives, then people from outside that culture are fully justified in criticising and seeking to persuade people from within that cultural tradition to change. This does not mean that one solution is being imposed on them, as it must be recognised that human rights can be realised and guaranteed in different ways.

Another result of this perspective on rights and needs is that, within multicultural societies, there are likely to be different ways in which human rights can be met and guaranteed, for different cultural communities. Educational needs, for example, may vary significantly within a society because of cultural variations. There is an obvious value in diversity, and it is important that a human rights practice not seek to impose a uniform system on the entire society, or even on the entire world. To do so amounts to colonialist practice, which a human rights perspective must, by definition, avoid, as colonialism represents a significant violation of people's human rights.

Needs and rights, means and ends

Much of the above discussion has focused on needs as always being means, rather than ends in their own right. The word 'need', deriving from the idea of being necessary, carries with it the idea of something being needed in order to do, have or be something else. Rights have been seen as the ends, and human needs are seen as having to be met so that human rights can be realised. The distinction between means and ends, however, is not as clear-cut as this. One example used above was the idea that I may need new clothes in order to look smart. But looking smart was not the end (or right), it was only another means – I need to look smart so that people will trust and respect me in my work. And that too is a means – I need people to trust and respect me so that my work with them can be more effective. It is not so easy to separate means and ends, and similarly it is not always easy to separate needs and rights. I may *need* food (in order to survive), but we also talk about a human *right* to food. Often needs are talked about as ends in themselves, without great thought being given to why the particular provision in question is needed, and often that 'need' is defined instead as a 'right'.

It is perhaps naïve to seek more clarity in language, since the relationship between needs and rights is so complex, and the two so deeply enmeshed, that such clear linguistic separation is often quite artificial. From the point of view of rights-based practice, it is important, however, that a discourse of needs not be allowed to dominate the social work profession, to the exclusion of a discourse of rights. It is important that whenever the word 'need' is used, social workers stop to assess what are the implied rights behind the claim of need, and examine the link between the two. And whenever human rights are claimed, social workers will often have to translate this into some statement of needs; it is one thing to talk about the right to housing, for example, but it is also necessary to identify what that right means in terms of needs within the specific cultural, social, political and economic context of practice. One family or community's 'needs' will be very different from another's, if the human right to housing is to be met adequately for all.

The distinction between rights and needs is thus important, and despite some of the conceptual difficulties it throws up, including the problematic relationship between means and ends, it is nevertheless a significant part of human rights-based practice.

Who defines needs and rights

The focus of this chapter has been on both rights and needs as being defined, and as only attaining meaning in the act of definition. As outlined in Chapter 1, the approach to human rights taken in this book is that they are discursive: they are constantly constructed and reconstructed through dialogue, rather than existing in any objective positivist sense. And needs are clearly the same: they cannot be said to 'exist' objectively, but are the result of somebody deciding what is 'needed' in order to achieve some rights-based goal.

If the focus of both rights and needs is on the act of definition, this raises the question of whose definitions are to count and whose voices will be heard most strongly in the ongoing dialogue that establishes what is to count as a human right. This is a fundamentally important question for social workers who are concerned with human rights, and has significant implications for practice. It will not be dealt with here, as it deserves a chapter to itself (Chapter 8). In relation to need, however, it is worth remembering the argument of Illich (Illich et al. 1977) that social workers are to be counted among the 'disabling professions', whose enthusiasm for defining the needs of others acts only to 'disable' those whom the professionals claim to be helping. This is the opposite of empowerment-based practice, which many social workers claim is the basis of their work, and therefore the place of needs and need definition in social work discourse requires closer examination (Pease & Fook 1999). The important practice principle is that social workers have to give up their appropriation of the right to define people's needs for them, and find ways in which the people concerned can reclaim that right and define their own needs. This does not mean that the social worker has no role in need definition; in reality a social worker can assist the process considerably. People will not define a service or provision as 'needed' if they do not know that it exists or what it can achieve, and social workers are knowledgeable about a wide range of resources that may be unknown to the people or communities with which they are working. A person will not define him/herself as 'needing', for example, trauma counselling if they are unaware that such services are available or what they can accomplish. Similarly, social workers may well have expert knowledge of the effectiveness or otherwise of particular forms of provision, and this can be made available. A community troubled by an apparent rise in juvenile crime may argue that they 'need' more police, whereas a social worker is likely to realise that more police alone will do little to reduce juvenile crime and that other programs are likely to be much more effective in the long term.

A social worker therefore has an important role to play in *assisting* in the definition of need, but this does not mean that the social worker takes on that responsibility to the exclusion of the people with whom he/she is working, at whatever level. Rather, need definition must be seen as a *partnership* between the social worker and the person, family, group or community, where the expertise of each is shared and where the social worker assists and facilitates the need definition process *by the people most directly affected*. This approach to practice applies not only to the definition of needs but also the practice of human rights-based social work, and it will be described in more detail in Chapter 10.

Conclusion

The relationship between needs and rights, as discussed in this chapter, lies at the heart of social work. In making the connection between needs, which social workers consider every day, and rights, social workers can move towards developing a human rights basis for practice as advocated in previous chapters. The connection between needs and rights is critical. It provides a stronger moral reference point for the meeting of need, it grounds human rights in the day-to-day practice of social work, it contextualises human rights within particular cultural and organisational locations, and it helps to establish a social work praxis which incorporates both relativist and universal themes. It is therefore a key component of human rights-based social work practice, which will be more fully developed in Chapter 10.

CHAPTER 6

Human Rights and Obligations

This chapter examines the link between rights and responsibilities, duties or obligations. If people are assumed to have rights, these can be seen as implying certain corresponding obligations, on the part of both the state and individuals, to ensure that those rights are protected and realised. These need to be examined in some detail as they have significant implications for a social work practice that assumes a human rights perspective. We will first examine the idea of the responsibilities of the state, or of some other civic body, which result from the acknowledgement and affirmation of human rights.

The erosion of the state

It is clear that human rights impose some obligation on the state to ensure that those rights are respected, protected and realised. But before examining how this can be achieved, and its implications for social work, we need to examine the problematic role of the state in contemporary society. The 'crisis in the state' is a recurring theme in the social policy literature, and there is a substantial literature on the more specific 'crisis in the welfare state', which is particularly significant as it is the welfare state that has been seen as having the primary responsibility for ensuring the meeting of human rights, especially second-generation rights (Bryson 1992; Burrows & Loader 1994; Saunders 1994; Goodin et al. 1999; Mishra 1999; Rodger 2000).

The crisis in the state, and the state's potential inability to guarantee human rights to the extent to which many social workers would expect, can be seen as having two aspects. The first is the inherent contradictions of the welfare state in modern society, which has been the subject of considerable analysis. Because of its contradictory nature, the state is not able to meet all the social needs demanded of it while at the same time supporting continued economic growth and development. The welfare state plays a dual role of *maintaining* the health of the economy (by ensuring a healthy, well-educated workforce and by stimulating demand) and *undermining* the health of the economy (through loss of incentive and through an ever-increasing demand for public expenditure that cannot be met) (George & Wilding 1984; Mishra 1984). Thus the welfare state is contradictory and works against itself. Governments can no longer afford the welfare state, but neither can they afford to do without it (Offe 1984). The result is impasse in the capacity of the state to respond to the needs of either the citizens or the economy in a fully adequate way.

The other cause of the crisis in the state is globalisation, as was discussed in Chapter 1. The increasing power of global market forces has meant that governments have limited autonomy in the making of economic policy choices, and that even if a government wished to spend large amounts of money on public services to guarantee human rights (especially the expensive second-generation rights) it would be unable to do so for fear of economic collapse as markets lose confidence in the economy and seek investment and profits elsewhere.

One cannot have a human rights regime, however, without some agency – traditionally this has been the state – with the resources and the mandate to guarantee those rights. So, at a time of the erosion of the state, the question arises whether it is possible to talk about some other kind of public body that may be able to fill, at least in part, the function of guarantor of human rights, as currently expected of the state. In the context of global change there has been some attention paid to the role of non-state bodies as human rights *violators* (Bröhmer 1997; Rees & Wright 2000), but less attention has been paid to non-state bodies as human rights *protectors*. There are four possible alternatives that one might consider.

The first is the possibility of some form of global guarantor of human rights. Already the United Nations, through its Human Rights Commission and several other agencies, plays this role to some extent, though its influence is not always as recognised or as effective as one would hope, and many nations choose to ignore or undermine the influence of the United Nations in this regard. In an era of declining state power it becomes increasingly important that the human rights institutions of the United Nations be strengthened, and this is an important agenda for those interested in the promotion and protection of human rights. The other significant global human rights bodies are the human rights NGOs, most notably Amnesty International and Human Rights Watch. These of course have no formal mandate to ensure human rights standards, but internationally they do have strong moral authority, and by issuing research reports and media statements on human rights violations they play an important global role. However, they have neither the legal mandate nor the resources to assume 'state' obligations to protect and realise human rights. The United Nations does to some extent have such a legal mandate through the various conventions to which nations are signatories (see Appendix II), and it is also able to provide some resources (e.g. through UNESCO, UNICEF) to meet second-generation rights. But both its legal base and its resource base would need to be massively strengthened if it is to take over from the nation state the primary responsibility for meeting the public obligations required by a commitment to human rights.

There is also, at the international level, the real possibility of regional rather than global structures meeting human rights obligations. This is particularly seen in the case of the European Union (EU), which has a number of conventions guaranteeing certain human rights within its member states (Duparc 1993). These have had significant impact in a number of situations and have effectively provided the citizens of EU countries with an extra layer of human rights protection not available to people in other countries. It remains to be seen whether such regional structures will increase in economic and political importance with globalisation – that is only one possible globalisation scenario – but if they do, they also have the potential to play an important role in meeting the public obligation to ensure that human rights are met and safeguarded. The relative lack of similar human rights guarantees in other regional groupings, especially in Asia where regional human rights treaties are virtually non-existent, is a matter of some concern and forms an important agenda for human rights activists from non-European regions.

As was suggested in Chapter 1, one of the consequences of globalisation has been a counter-tendency towards localisation, and hence we need to ask whether it is possible for local community-based structures to have a role in meeting the obligations previously ascribed to states. In terms of second-generation rights, it can be argued that the future of the community services through which such rights are largely met lies in community-based structures and processes (Ife 1995). If indeed the welfare state is in decline, it seems likely that 'the community', in whatever form, will be required to pick up more of the responsibility for doing the things the welfare state has done in the past. In this case there will be an obligation on community-based structures to ensure that second-generation rights are met, and this can be extended to first and third-generation rights (Rodger 2000). This strongly suggests that community development is an important role for social workers and others concerned with human rights. The problem is that, in western societies in particular, human community has been under sustained attack from the forces of industrial (and more recently post-industrial) capitalism, and so the very community structures that we are now turning to for help are themselves substantially weakened. There is no point in talking about community-based human services unless there is a strong community in which to base them, and hence the building, or rebuilding, of strong communities becomes a priority. From a social work perspective, this is particularly important, as it suggests that community development should be a high priority for social workers.

Local community structures, however strong, cannot provide the only mechanisms through which human rights obligations are met. An exclusively community-based system would leave individual communities free to be self-determining, and some would inevitably choose directions that violated human rights. For this reason it is essential that there should be some structure at a higher level – national, regional or global – which can hold communities to account and require them to meet certain human rights standards. This can be done in different ways by different communities, as was discussed in Chapter 5 in relation to universal rights and contextualised needs. The concern of any central body should be that human rights standards are met, rather than specifying how this should be achieved. Indeed, because of the different community contexts in which human rights must be articulated, some degree of community autonomy would always be necessary. The picture that emerges is one of both local and higher-level structures working in partnership towards the guaranteeing and the realisation of human rights.

Another possibility, given the global trend towards privatisation and the increased power of the private sector of the economy, is to ask whether the private sector might bear some of the 'public' responsibility for the protection and realisation of human rights. Such a proposition is problematic, if only because the profit motive (which must be the overriding motivation for the private sector) can at times conflict directly with human rights. For example, profit can be maximised by exploiting the workforce, by preventing the formation of trade unions, by keeping wages below the poverty line, and by externalising environmental costs. All these are human rights violations, and they are naturally encouraged by the need for corporate profit (Rees & Wright 2000). For this reason, it is untenable to suggest that the private sector *alone* should be responsible for protecting and maintaining human rights. There are, however, other circumstances where the private sector really has nothing to gain by a poor human rights record, and in such circumstances it can be argued that in a pluralist society it does have some role to play. It must be remembered that historically some of the most progressive social programs were derived from the initiatives of the more public-minded and philanthropic entrepreneurs providing for their employees and deciding that the welfare of their employees was both socially responsible and in the company's interest. To deny a role or responsibility for the private sector, at a time when the private sector plays such an important part in all aspects of life, is to 'let it off the hook'. A more realistic approach would seek ways in which the private sector might be involved in the protection and realisation of human rights, while never expecting it to take on this role in its entirety.

The important thing is that human rights do require an obligation on the part of some public structure, whether it is the nation state or some other body with a clear mandate to act in the public good, to provide the resources and the mechanisms for both the protection and the realisation of the full range of human rights. The changing role of the state in contemporary society suggests that the state may no longer be able to fulfil this function alone, if it ever could. But if it cannot be done by the state, it has to be done by something else, if human rights are to have any meaning. And given the universal nature of human rights, it becomes essential that at the global level there should be some degree of recognised and effective responsibility for human rights – through the United Nations for want of any other obvious alternative.

The protection of human rights

In the previous section the protection and the realisation of human rights were discussed together. But the mechanisms and structures for achieving these two goals are characteristically different. The protection or safeguarding of human rights is the arena that has received most attention because of the dominance of first-generation views of human rights, and as we have already seen in Chapter 2, these are typically viewed as 'negative' rights that need to be protected and safeguarded by the state. They are not rights that need to be 'given' or 'provided' in such a way that they require major public sector expenditure or activity. Second-generation rights to health or housing, on the other hand, require that somebody has to provide health services and physical shelter, whereas the right to freedom of expression or freedom of assembly does not cost much to *grant*. It does, however, cost money to *protect* such rights. In their important book *The Cost of Rights*, Holmes and Sunstein (1999) argue that protecting basic civil and political rights does cost money, and hence that such rights are not after all totally compatible with an ideology of individualism and minimal government spending, as right-wing rhetoric would have us believe. First-generation rights, if they are to be protected and guaranteed, require substantial investment in legal and justice structures: police, courts, tribunals, training of lawyers and judges, funding of access to the legal system (through legal aid, community legal centres, etc.) and public education about rights and about mechanisms of appeal if one feels one's rights have been violated. States that do not invest adequately in such structures and processes cannot be said to be meeting their human rights obligations, even in the narrower first-generation sense, and many states in fact do not. The inadequacy of legal aid or community law centres in many countries makes a mockery of any notion of equality before the law and prevents low-income people from realising many of their first-generation rights. As long as the law and the legal system are seen as the primary mechanism for protecting an individual's or a group's human rights, the question of equality of access to the law becomes a primary human rights question. Access to the law is not equal; the rich have effectively many more legal rights than the poor, simply because they can afford more and 'better' lawyers to work for longer (Wilhelmsson & Hurri 1999). This has been a continuing theme in the western legal tradition and is not of recent origin; indeed the idea that the legal system exists primarily for the benefit of lawyers is found not only in Dickens' *Bleak House* but many centuries earlier in Aristophanes' *The Wasps*. The legal system remains fundamentally inequitable, and in terms of first-generation civil and political rights, the profession which claims to be the fundamental human rights profession denies and violates those rights in its day-to-day practice. Reform of western legal structures and the legal profession must be one of the main objectives of anyone really interested in the protection of first-generation human rights, and yet it is an issue not often talked about in the public arena or seen as a major human rights issue by the mainstream media. This only serves to underline the power of the legal profession to affect the dominant discourse in its own self-interest.

Social work practice, if it is to be concerned with the protection of first-generation rights, needs to address a number of issues. First, it can seek to ensure that people have complete access to legal services and that full use is made of legal aid and community legal centres. Second, social workers are also able to play advocacy roles at some level on behalf of their clients. They may not be able to represent their clients in court but they can nonetheless make sure that their clients' individual or collective concerns are made widely known and that the voices of the marginalised are not silenced (see Chapter 8). Third, social workers can be working in support of those seeking to reform the legal system, including those from within the legal profession who are committed to such change. Fourth, social workers can be publicly advocating for the adequate resourcing of appropriate legal services, most especially for the most vulnerable and marginalised in the community. Fifth, in the face of the inadequacy of the legal system in its present form in dealing equitably with human rights issues, social workers can be supporting those other organisations, such as Amnesty International and Human Rights Watch, that play important roles in helping to safeguard first-generation rights. Underlying all of this is the fundamental point that first-generation rights cannot be assumed. There is a public responsibility to provide adequate structures and resources for their effective protection for all citizens (especially the most disadvantaged and marginalised), and this at present is not being fully achieved in any of the world's nations. No society can call itself truly civilised, or truly committed to human rights, until this minimal protection of first-generation rights is effectively achieved. A social work that is committed to human rights must also be committed to work towards such a goal.

The realisation of human rights

Second and third-generation rights require not merely protection but also that action be taken by governments (or some other public body) to meet those human rights. It is not enough simply to have a law guaranteeing, for example, the right to education. Unlike, say, the right to free speech, the right to education requires that education be *provided*, and for that reason it requires a more proactive role for the state, or whatever may replace it in the globalised world. Protecting first-generation human rights may require public resources, as described above, but meeting second-generation human rights requires a far greater investment on the part of the state. Schools, hospitals, clinics, public housing, welfare agencies, social security, indeed the whole range of welfare state services and programs are part of the agenda of securing second-generation rights for all. And third-generation rights require substantial investment in environmental programs and in ensuring that economic and social development occurs in more disadvantaged communities, regions and nations.

First-generation human rights may not be provided for all, but that failure pales into insignificance beside the monumental failure of the global economic and political system to provide any realistic meeting of second and third-generation human rights for more than a small minority of the world's population (UNDP 2000). Famine, preventable disease, starvation, illiteracy, homelessness, poverty, and environmental degradation, all on a massive scale, are indictments of the global economic and political orthodoxy, and a powerful reason for action by social workers and all people concerned about human rights. Even in the most 'advanced' western societies, significant sections of the population have these rights daily denied, while the rich and powerful are profiting from the 'health' of the economy (the USA is perhaps the extreme example, but it is far from alone). If we are concerned with human rights, and if we include second and third-generation rights within our definition, this is an obscenity of immense proportions.

Framing poverty, exclusion, inadequate education, hunger, preventable disease, homelessness and environmental degradation as human rights abuses can be helpful in providing an extra moral imperative that these problems be effectively addressed. A discourse of rights, as opposed to a discourse of needs, suggests that there is indeed a public obligation, a moral imperative, to act. It puts the social worker, or anyone else advocating for adequate provision of public services, in the position of arguing for them on the basis of human rights, and implicitly accusing a public authority that does not provide them of human rights abuse. Advocating for better public services is hardly new for social workers – it has always been an important part of social work practice (Woodroofe 1962; Younghusband 1964) – but a human rights approach strengthens this. Social workers, from this perspective, are actually required to take such action if they are to accept their role as human rights workers. This means that a social work that sees itself as merely providing services, but no more than that, is failing in its responsibility. It also means that social workers are arguing for better services not just because they are a good idea, or would make people healthier, better educated, better housed, and so on. Rather, they are also arguing for them because it is people's human right to receive adequate services in order to realise their full humanity.

There are different ways in which social workers can work for the meeting of second and third-generation rights. Many will choose to do so from within their particular agency or bureaucracy. This may be done by policy development, by suggesting alternatives within the agency, or by researching the inadequacies of the system in meeting people's human rights and using this research as a basis for advocating change. Alternatively, social workers may choose to work externally, through an action group of some kind, putting pressure on the political process or involving themselves in party politics. In many formulations of social work, social action is seen as a fully legitimate method (Fisher & Karger 1997; Mullaly 1997), and social workers should not hesitate to adopt a social action perspective in seeking to further the cause of human rights. Using a rights-based rhetoric can often add a degree of moral suasion to the cause the social worker is seeking to advance.

Policy development and social action strategies are well documented in the social work literature (Yeatman 1998), and it is unnecessary to discuss in more detail here the methods that might be used. There are, however, two important points that need to be made in relation to such social work. The first is the importance of not falling into the 'advocacy trap' discussed earlier in Chapter 2, by confidently speaking on behalf of a disadvantaged or marginalised group without allowing them to speak for themselves. Social policy advocacy and social action can easily be disempowering and serve only to reinforce the powerless position of the group we are concerned with if we simply take it on ourselves to speak on their behalf. If they are to be consistent with the empowerment-based principles of social work, policy advocacy and social action must seek maximum involvement and control by the people who are themselves affected; they are the ones who own the struggle, not the social workers, and they should where possible be the ones to control, direct and participate in it, with social workers acting as support and in solidarity rather than taking control of the process (Freire 1985). This issue is central to social work as human rights work, and is the subject of Chapter 8.

The other point that needs to be made is the global nature of social disadvantage and human rights. If social workers concentrate only on their own 'patch' as the location for policy development and activism, they lose sight of the human rights violations in other parts of the world, where there may not be many social workers or other activists to take up the cause. As has already been identified (Chapter 4), social workers need to understand their problems on a global as well as a local level and to engage in policy advocacy and social action from this perspective. Social workers cannot afford the parochialism of concentrating only on their immediate context; they need to work in solidarity with their colleagues throughout the world in confronting the global aspects of human rights abuse. Charity may begin at home but it cannot afford to stay there and never venture outdoors.

Citizenship obligations

An understanding of human rights imposes obligations on the state to protect and realise those rights, but in a different way it also imposes obligations on the citizens who claim and benefit from those rights. The language of citizenship obligations has at times been used by politicians of the right to justify punitive attitudes towards those receiving state assistance: work for benefits, repayment of benefits, and the expectation that the recipients of state assistance should feel suitably grateful and should prove themselves 'deserving' by not making a fuss or engaging in deviant behaviour. Because of this it is all the more important to examine the citizenship obligations that do go with human rights, and to construct them not in this conservative, judgemental social control framework (which is in effect counter to human rights principles), but rather as a way of understanding the role of the citizen in relation to her/his human rights, and the citizenship obligations that are necessary for a system based on human rights to work in practice (Twine 1994). There are significant implications for social work from such an examination.

Respecting the rights of others

If human rights are universal, it follows not only that an individual is entitled to exercise those rights but also that he/she respects the similar rights held by others and allows others to exercise those rights as they choose.

Accepting a framework of rights cannot imply simply a selfish attitude on the part of the individual, claiming her/his own rights while remaining indifferent to the rights of others. There is a corresponding obligation on every member of the society to respect and support other people's rights. In this sense, human rights are not only individualistic but also form the basis for collectivism: a society held together by mutual respect for the human rights of all citizens and based on notions of interdependence, mutual support and collective well-being. Often, however, the language of rights is couched in individualistic, almost selfish, terms – I demand my rights, we demand our rights – without any corresponding consideration of the rights of others. A classic case is the gun lobby: people demand their 'right' to bear arms without due consideration of how this demand might affect the rights of others to a society free of threat and violence. Any claim of right, to be consistent with a universal rights framework, should include with it a consideration of how that claim affects the rights of others. The 'others' may be other members of one's family or local community, but they may also be much further removed. For example, the supposed 'right' of people in the affluent west to pursue wealthy lifestyles of high material consumption and waste, and to accumulate wealth indefinitely if they are clever or lucky enough, demonstrably affects the human rights of many millions in the 'developing' world, denying them basic living standards and causing poverty, hunger, environmental degradation, homelessness and a lack of basic health and education services (Chomsky 1998). It also affects the rights of future generations because of the long-term environmental impact of such lifestyles. These arguments significantly lessen the moral case of such a claim. Indeed when they are taken into account it is clear that the 'right' to accumulate limitless wealth cannot be justified from a human rights perspective, though this is seldom acknowledged when the rights of the rich – and of those who so desperately want to be rich – are advocated.

This collectivist understanding of the implication of human rights is often missing from human rights discourse. At best there is a liberal discussion about tolerance of the rights of others, for example the need to respect people's right to be different (in such matters as dress, sexuality or religious belief) and to respect others' right to freedom of speech even if one disagrees, as expressed in that famous Enlightenment statement of Voltaire: 'I disapprove of what you say, but I will defend to the death your right to say it'. Such tolerance of different views and defence of the rights of others to hold them are, of course, very important; it is one of the characteristics of a genuinely free and democratic society, and the infringement of this first-generation right in many parts of the world remains a human rights scandal. But while it is important, it is also necessary to understand that the collectivist obligations of human rights extend much further (Howard 1995).

If one incorporates the broader three-generation approach to human rights outlined in Chapter 2, and similarly if one takes seriously the claim that human rights impose obligations on the citizen to ensure that the rights of others are met, then this implies that citizens also have an obligation to do something about preventing the denial of human rights to others. And in a globalised world, where we are all subject to the same global forces and where materialist lifestyles in one place affect the human rights of those on the other side of the world, this implies an obligation to global understanding and global action. There is, in other words, an obligation on people in the west to seek to do something effective about human rights abuses of those who live in less affluent countries, where poverty and inadequate health, education, housing and food supply amount to gross human rights violations on a massive scale. The idea that we can only legitimately claim rights if they do not unduly impose on the rights of others may sound like a fairly uncontroversial idea inherent in liberalism, but in a globalised world where we are all connected, and where the lifestyles of some amount to human rights abuse for others, it is profoundly radical. In this sense a human rights perspective places an obligation on the citizen – and on communities and nations – to be an active participant in working towards a fairer world.

Seen in this way, human rights practice represents a radical position, and if social workers are to see themselves as human rights workers they must accept the radical implications of their profession. Activism that seeks a more socially just and environmentally sustainable world order, a radical questioning of the unsustainable lifestyles of the developed west, and an insistence on a significant redistribution of wealth, resources and land, becomes part of human rights practice. It is therefore not only legitimate for social workers, as human rights workers, to be engaged in such practice, but it is a necessary obligation. And an important component of social work practice is encouraging and supporting others to become actively engaged in this way, as part and parcel of their citizenship responsibilities.

Exercising one's rights

Human rights are, in many instances, hard won. Whether first, second or third-generation human rights, our accepted rights did not just suddenly materialise. There have been many long, hard and difficult struggles to establish the legitimacy of various human rights, and also to have them realised. And these struggles continue, as human rights are regularly denied to many. In such circumstances, one can make a moral case to the effect that there is an obligation on the citizen to take full advantage of those rights.

This can be illustrated by the case of the right to vote. Despite the heroic struggles of those who fought for universal suffrage, and who achieved it in many nations that now proudly call themselves democracies, many people in those countries simply do not bother to vote (except of course in those few nations where voting is compulsory). To feel a sense of personal responsibility to exercise the right to vote, one only needs to ponder what those who struggled for universal suffrage would think if they knew that often a majority of the population do not bother voting. Of course one can make the case that the right to vote should also imply the right to choose not to vote, and one can justify a choice not to vote as a carefully considered political act (e.g. as a protest against an election where two parties are offering the same policies and neither is dealing with the important issues). But this is very different from not voting simply because one cannot be bothered. That amounts, one might claim, to a betrayal of the often revolutionary struggles in earlier times to establish rights (Bobbio 1996), though one could also argue that the person who simply does not bother to vote is also making a political statement about the relevance of party politics to his/her particular needs and lifestyle. Another example is the right to form a trade union, for which in previous generations many people struggled in the face of intimidation, imprisonment, poverty and death. In the current climate we see trade union membership declining, and again we might wonder whether the people who are now not joining trade unions have any idea of the historical legacy they are effectively betraying, or of what working conditions would be like if it were not for the earlier struggles of unionists. Again, the issues are more complex than this, but the important point at issue is that there is, in some sense, an obligation to exercise one's rights – otherwise what is the point of having them? In terms of civil and political rights, it is clear that one can only have a vibrant and healthy civil and democratic society if significant numbers of people do in fact exercise their civil and political rights. And a similar case can be made for economic, social and cultural rights; the society will surely be much healthier if people make the most of the opportunities afforded by the possession of those rights (Giroux 1989). Human rights therefore are not only what is necessary to make *a person* fully human, they are also necessary to make *a society* fully human. We do not only have human rights for our own benefit but for the benefit of the society in which we live and for humanity as a whole.

Such a view of human rights carrying an *obligation to participate* also has significant implications for social work, if it is to call itself a human rights profession. It means that social workers should be working to develop a more *participatory* society, where people are encouraged to meet the citizenship obligations that go along with citizenship rights. The power of individualism and consumerism, which are inevitable products of the dominant economic and political orthodoxy of industrial and post-industrial capitalism, militate against such a participatory society. There is an acceptance of passive consumerism, and a degree of mistrust of those who do choose to exercise their rights; it is often 'better' not to be seen to be too controversial, or to be 'rocking the boat'. The 1970s protest graffito 'consume, be silent and die' is an eloquent statement of this norm of passive consumerism and non-participation. While people in totalitarian nations may struggle valiantly to achieve human rights, in western 'democracies', where many human rights are taken for granted, those rights are seldom exercised. This applies not only to the first-generation rights of freedom of speech, assembly and so on, but also to second-generation rights, perhaps most notably the right to education. Many people choose not to take advantage of educational opportunities, both formal (through schools, colleges, training institutions and universities) and informal (through libraries, educational radio and television, the Internet, and informal learning groups). This can be seen as being to the detriment of the society at large, as well as of the individuals concerned, and is a case of the obligation to exercise one's second-generation rights not being met.

Of course there are reasons for people not meeting these citizenship obligations to participate actively in the society, and it would be a mistake to use the above argument simply to blame the individuals concerned. The people who choose not to vote, to withdraw from union membership or not to take opportunities for self-education do so for a variety of reasons, many of them to do with the dominant ideology, the messages of the media, and real or perceived threats to someone who steps outside the norm of passive, silent consumer (Herman & Chomsky 1988). It is necessary, as always, to understand the situation in its broader structural context. Not the least reason for non-participation is the devaluing of the study of history and of understanding the present in a historical perspective. In a world divorced from its historical antecedents, where people are encouraged to live for the present and to dismiss the past as irrelevant, it is quite understandable that there is, for example, little awareness of a sense of betrayal by someone who withdraws from membership of a trade union, or who decides he/she cannot be bothered to vote. The role of social workers as human rights workers, therefore, is to seek ways to contextualise human actions such as voting, attending school or trade union membership within a historical perspective of the struggle for human rights. This is perhaps one step towards helping to develop a more genuinely participatory society.

If a human rights perspective implies an obligation to exercise our rights and to participate, maximising participation is an important part of human rights work. Increasing citizen participation has long been a goal of social workers, especially those working in community development.

Participation itself is a complex and contested idea, and there is not space here for a detailed examination of the issue. We can note, however, the problems of cooptation, of pseudo-participation, of tokenism, and similar instances where the 'participation' is more apparent than real (Ife 1995). We can also note the tendency to frame 'participation' in western patri-archal middle-class terms (e.g. going to committee meetings), thereby devaluing other forms of participation. There are, however, a number of principles that can be identified for encouraging citizen participation in community affairs and which have been used consistently by social work-ers. Elsewhere I have identified these as:

- people will participate if they feel the issue is important
- people must feel that their action will make a difference
- different forms of participation must be acknowledged
- people must be enabled to participate and supported in their partici-pation
- structures and processes must not be alienating (Ife 1995: 113–15).

Such material is familiar to community workers, and to social workers who know the community development literature. The important point of the present discussion, however, is that such community work can be seen as a significant, indeed essential, component of human rights work, and if social work is to be defined as a human rights profession, commu-nity development work needs to be seen as an important part of social work and not marginalised as it is in some contexts. The link between human rights and citizenship obligations is paralleled by the link between individualised service (or 'casework') and community development work. Each implies the other, and each is incomplete without the other.

Conclusion

This chapter has demonstrated how a concern for human rights as a cen-tral concept for social work leads both to a more collectivist view, where human rights are seen as good for the society as well as for the individual, and to a necessary link between a concern for the individual private world of the 'client' and a concern for a healthy, participatory society. Human rights practice belongs in both and is required to link both in a holistic understanding which breaks down the conventional macro/micro dual-ism that characterises much of the social work discourse. Social work which is committed to human rights must incorporate community devel-opment and social action approaches alongside individualised service provision; it must see each as a necessary complement to the other if human rights are to be protected and realised.

CHAPTER 7

Ethics and Human Rights

One of the important characteristics of a profession is that it should have a code of ethics (Corey et al. 1998). Social workers have long considered ethics an indispensable aspect of their practice, and many national social work associations have codes of ethics to which their members are required to adhere. Social work is no different here from many other professions, except that the importance it gives to values means that social workers are probably more immediately conscious of the ethical aspects of their practice than some other professionals. Certainly social workers spend a good deal of time talking about ethics, establishing and revising codes of ethics, and consciously dealing with ethical issues confronted in practice. The very nature of social work practice, dealing as it does with conflicting values and the making of difficult moral choices on behalf of society, means that ethical dilemmas will be part of the practice of every social worker (Clark 2000).

Codes of ethics are not only used to encourage 'ethical' behaviour on the part of social workers and to assist social workers who are confronted by difficult ethical dilemmas. They also perform a controlling function by seeking to prevent deliberately 'unethical' behaviour on the part of social workers. There is usually some form of sanction associated with the operation of a code of ethics: a mechanism for steps to be taken against unethical social workers, such as expulsion from the professional association, relinquishment of their right to practise, or a requirement to undertake further training (Gaha 1997). A code of ethics is therefore a significant part of the profession's formal mechanisms of control.

In the following pages, a critique of the conventional approach to social work ethics is outlined. It must not be assumed, however, that all social work codes of ethics, or ethical boards, are blind to these problems. Some social work codes of ethics have sought to express professional ethics differently, through, for example, linking ethical codes to clear statements of value positions and statements of human rights. It must therefore be emphasised that the following critique applies to a *conventional* framing of professional ethics, and that many social workers are creatively seeking alternative framings. The position argued here is that human rights can offer such an alternative.

Rights and ethics

Obviously there is a clear link between ethics and the idea of human rights (Baier 1994). Indeed at one level a code of ethics might be seen as equivalent to a statement of rights. The various principles and practices laid down in a social work code of ethics imply the assertion of rights: the rights of the client or client group, the rights of the social worker's employer, and the rights of the social worker's professional colleagues. The 'ethics' are therefore statements of the importance of those rights and prescriptions of how those rights are to be realised and protected. Conversely, a social work practice based on notions of fundamental and inalienable human rights requires ethical behaviour on the part of social workers.

Rights and ethics might therefore be seen, in the context of professional practice, as two sides of the same coin. Each implies the other, and the two are necessarily linked. Indeed it might seem as if they are two different ways of doing the same thing. But there are some important differences in emphasis. One of these has already been indicated, namely the control function of a professional code of ethics and an 'ethics' discourse. There is less of a strong control function attached to a discourse of rights, and the assumption is that one follows a rights perspective as a result of moral suasion rather than from fear of sanctions. Certainly there are possibilities of legal action against human rights abusers, through courts, human rights commissions, and so on, but not through the internal regulatory mechanisms of a professional association, and not with the stigma attached to being found 'guilty of unethical conduct'. It will also be demonstrated in the following paragraphs that there is a tendency towards modernist certainty in a conventional discourse of ethics, which renders it less likely to meet the needs of a social worker engaged in the messy and contradictory world of practice than is the case with a discourse of human rights, at least if the latter is discursively constructed.

Ethics as a conservative individualist discourse

A discourse of ethics is essentially individualist. It is about individuals making ethical choices in specific situations. In this sense it fits readily with many of the realities of social work practice, as social work is mostly described in terms of the individual practitioner making individual choices (Clark 2000). The emphasis is on the worker and the decision that worker has to take. A human rights discourse, on the other hand, is more readily directed to collective issues, as rights can attach to groups, whereas ethical decision-making remains framed in terms of individual choice. A human rights discourse also shifts attention from the worker to the person or group with which the social worker is interacting. Put in simple terms, ethical decision-making attaches to the worker, whereas rights attach to the 'client'(or however else we want to define the people with whom the social worker is interacting). While ethics and rights may in effect be dealing with the same issues, the two different discourses encourage us to construct them in quite different ways: one is introspective and self-reflective, while the other is more outwardly focused. A social work dilemma, framed in 'ethical' terms, sees the social worker as the actor with decision-making discretion; there is no clear role for the client in the social worker's ethical decision. On the other hand, a human rights perspective, as argued elsewhere in this book, allows the possibility for the client to be an active participant in the decision-making process. There is therefore a different construction of practice inherent in each discourse. In a discourse of ethics it is the practice of the professional with specific insight and expertise, with the potential of reinforcing the powerlessness of the person or people in the client role. In a discourse of rights there is a stronger capacity for empowerment-based practice; the emphasis is on realising and protecting the rights of the client, rather than facilitating the professional decision-making of a social worker.

From this perspective, a concentration on ethics can be seen as consistent with, and reinforcing, some of the more conservative manifestations of social work practice. As Foucault has argued (1991), the discourse we use defines and reinforces relationships of power and domination. While at one level nobody could object to the idea of professional ethics – after all we all want professionals acting 'ethically' rather than 'unethically' – it does represent a way of safeguarding the interests of the client which also reinforces relationships of professional power and domination. The client is normally given no role in ethical decision-making, and hence the very construction of decision-making in social work becomes one where the client is passive object rather than active subject. This is not to say that those social workers who concern themselves with developing and enforcing codes of ethics are not acting from the best of motives, but simply to identify that such practice can often subtly reinforce conservative and disempowering constructions of practice, in ways that are probably not intended by the social workers so involved.

Ethics as modernist

A code of ethics sets out to establish the rules for 'proper' ethical professional practice by prescribing what a social worker will try to do and
what actions are unacceptable. One of the dangers of such an approach
is that it can be seen as suggesting that there is one 'right' way to do social
work. The code of ethics is likely to project a single ideal model of professional practice, and social workers are to be encouraged (by a mix of
moral suasion and threat of sanction) to follow this model. As such, it
represents an attempt to encompass the varied and complex roles and
actions of social workers into a single ideal way of practising. This is
heroic modernism at its best; the attempt to incorporate complexity and
diversity into a single narrative in order to 'make sense' of it is characteristic of the modernist project and has been the implicit aim of much
western philosophy and social science (Touraine 1995; Griffin 1996;
Jenkins 1999). If somehow we can bring everything together into one system, it makes it easier to understand and to act. This was so embedded in
the modernist world-view that it was scarcely questioned, except for a few
philosophers easily marginalised as deviant, until the advent of the series
of critiques which called the modernist project into question, namely
postmodernism (Harvey 1989; Seidman 1994; Kumar 1995). Postmodernism suggests that the search for a single authoritative account of anything is unachievable and simply results in the marginalisation of
different voices by those who control the dominant world-view. The postmodernist critique, in its various forms (because from a postmodernist
perspective there cannot ever be a *single* postmodernism – that would be
a contradiction), may have become well recognised in philosophy and
the social sciences, but it has not always penetrated mainstream constructions of social phenomena. Social policy, for example, is still largely
intent on finding the one *best* way to run a social security system, a health
system, an education system, and so on. From a postmodernist perspective such a quest is doomed to eternal failure, since postmodernism
would allow for a multiplicity of 'right' ways to do those things, depending on context, culture, history, and the continually changing constructions and reconstructions of 'reality' (or 'realities') by the people
involved. That ethics is still largely caught up in a modernist paradigm is,
therefore, barely surprising. Social work is, however, beginning to come
to terms with postmodernism (Howe 1994; Ife 1997b; Leonard 1997;
Pease & Fook 1999; Healy 2000), though how this might be incorporated
into social work is still contested. There is a challenge to reformulate the
idea of social work ethics into something more consistent with a postmodern philosophy and with a postmodern world characterised by a lack
of certainty and assurance, by diversity and multiple realities, rather than

the confident categorical assertions of right and wrong implied in many social work codes of ethics.

Another way in which conventional codes of ethics are essentially modernist is in their attempt to cover all eventualities and provide a 'manual' for social workers that will help them in any potentially difficult situation. Social work students are often given the code of ethics and asked to use it to 'solve' a series of difficult problems. The assumption seems to be that the code of ethics will, if used properly, provide you with all the answers. Again, such confidence is quintessential modernism. The assumption that a code of ethics could provide 'the answer' to every possible practice predicament is, from the point of view of postmodernism, absurd. And indeed the practice experience of social workers often bears this out – most social workers seem to be able to provide anecdotal evidence of circumstances where the code of ethics either could not provide a clear 'answer' or could be read as implying two conflicting 'answers'. The real world of practice is much more complicated and messy than can possibly be contained in a modernist code of ethics, or for that matter in a modernist social work textbook that seeks to tie everything up into neat prescriptions (Parton & O'Byrne 2000).

A further critique that can be made of the use of codes of ethics is that they can play a controlling role within the profession. A code of ethics, inevitably, amounts to something written by a small group of social workers (e.g. an 'ethics committee') who have set themselves up to tell other social workers how they should and should not practise. Hence by its very nature the code of ethics becomes an instrument of control. This raises the questions of who wrote the code of ethics, who approved it, who applies it and how; all these are essentially political acts, which will portray a particular form of social work practice as preferred and which will reflect certain assumptions about the ideology of practice. This is indeed tacitly acknowledged by the establishment of alternative codes of ethics: codes of ethics for radical social workers, for indigenous social workers, for social workers of colour, and so on (Loewenberg et al. 2000). The existence of such alternative codes suggests that all of 'social work' cannot be encompassed by a single code of ethics, and that any suggestion that it can do so results in the inevitable marginalisation of less powerful voices within the profession. The existence of alternative codes represents an acknowledgement of the postmodern critique of the impossibility of a single code, but while there remains a 'mainstream' modernist code of ethics, with the others held up as 'alternatives' in opposition to it, the hegemony of modernism remains. A truly postmodern answer might lie in the legitimation of a multiplicity of codes of ethics, being continually constructed and reconstructed by different groups of social workers as the need arises. This might better reflect the reality of practice, but it also becomes of limited use in protecting the vulnerable and discouraging 'unethical' behaviour by social workers. Such a multiplicity of codes of ethics, without a moral reference point, would allow, for example, a self-defined code of ethics for racist social workers, one for paedophile social workers, one for anti-Semitic social workers, and so on. There seems to be a need, then, for reconstructing the idea of social work ethics so that it takes more account of the postmodern critique, but at the same time does not leave social workers drowning in a sea of moral relativism. It will be argued below that a human rights perspective has the potential to meet this challenge.

Before such an exploration, however, it is necessary to explore the postmodernist critique of ethics more closely. Of course one may choose to reject postmodernism completely and remain operating in a purely modernist framework, despite its evident limitations. It is the position of this book, however, that the postmodern critique must be taken seriously. While one may not wish to embrace an extreme sceptical postmodernist position (Rosenau 1992), postmodernism represents an important critique of the environment in which social work is practised, and it has much to contribute to social work theory and practice (Howe 1994; Ife 1997b, 1999; Leonard 1997; Pease & Fook 1999; Healy 2000). It values voices from the marginalised, moves away from the obsession with finding the one 'right' answer, and legitimates (indeed celebrates) diversity. It accepts the messiness of the reality of social work practice and of daily life, and does not insist on imposing a false order on natural chaos. In so doing, it provides opportunities for a critique of the dominant social, economic and political order, with its patriarchal capitalist western assumptions, and therefore provides the means for creating the alternatives that are so clearly needed in the blatantly unjust and unsustainable world in which social workers live and work. The extent to which one can accept such a critique is contested; in other contexts I have argued that acceptance of an extreme postmodernism is incompatible with social work's commitment to social justice, and that it simply reinforces a dominant conservatism and the ideology of the market by removing the very tools and conceptual frameworks needed to critique them (Ife 1997b, 1999). Other writers (Pease & Fook 1999) are more comfortable with postmodernism, emphasising its transformative potential. I would agree completely with Pease and Fook, however, that the postmodern critique demands to be taken seriously by social workers, and that to reject it out of hand is not only to turn one's back on potentially powerful and liberating scholarship but to confine oneself to the increasingly sterile and ultimately irrelevant paradigm of modernism.

To return to the subject of ethics, perhaps the most significant writer on postmodern reconstructions of ethics is Zygmunt Bauman (1993,

1995). Bauman's ideas are far removed indeed from the confident certainty of the conventional formulation of a social work code of ethics. He sees the breakdown of modernism as resulting in the breakdown of ethical codes, for the reasons outlined in the paragraphs above. But he does not accept that this also means the end of morality. Indeed he suggests that the end of the 'era of ethics' can also be the beginning of the era of morality. Ethics may be defined as rule-based morality, but if we reject the 'rules' we do not necessarily also reject the morality. Bauman sees people as being forced to make moral decisions about what is good and bad, right and wrong, that arise out of everyday life experience. Life, indeed, is a constant engagement with moral decisions, and this, according to Bauman, has not changed in the era of postmodernity. What has changed is the reliance on an external codified morality in the form of ethics; such grand formulations are no longer of relevance in the postmodern world. This has some resonance with Ulrich Beck's ideas of the reinvention of politics (Beck 1997; see also Bauman 1999). Beck sees a 'new' politics emerging which is not grounded in the traditional structures of the party and the state but is the result of ordinary people trying to make sense of their lives. Such politics no longer needs the grand narratives of traditional political discourse as its reference point; rather it finds its reference in the everyday world and people's lived experience. It is wrong therefore to say that people are no longer interested in politics just because they do not vote or join political parties; instead people are reinventing politics out of their daily struggle to make sense of life. Bauman's understanding of morality is similarly grounded in the local and the everyday.

According to Bauman, we cannot know the full consequences of our actions, and therefore all we can do is to try to do what we see as the 'right' thing, driven by some form of morality that is inherent in the human condition. This, it could be suggested, is a morality that might find its expression in some idea of human rights (defined discursively rather than as objective natural rights), and hence human rights may be a construction in which ethics can be reformulated.

Bauman raises another point about ethics which sounds a warning to those who might rush to reject any idea of a code of ethics as outmoded modernism. Codes of ethics, he argues, have been used as constraints on the powerful, rather than a means to regulate the powerless. Historically, it has been the powerful who have been persuaded to consider ethics, morality and moral reasoning, and to agonise about the 'rightness' of a particular decision. The poor and the powerless, however, make decisions out of necessity, and they do not have the option of engaging in moral reasoning and ethical debate. Moreover they have few decisions to make, since their power to control their own lives is limited by their domination at the hands of the powerful – codes of ethics are not for them.

Thus codes of ethics are about controlling the excesses of the powerful, and historically it has been the poor and disadvantaged who have called for such constraints, and for rules through which the powerful can be held to account (Bauman 1995). When we think about who is constrained by codes of ethics in contemporary society, it is indeed the powerful: the professions (medicine, law, social work, psychology), other people in positions of power (as in the call for ethical behaviour by politicians), and perhaps most significant of all, the move to establish 'business ethics' and to require 'ethical' behaviour by corporations (such as international pharmaceutical or tobacco companies). By contrast, there is little talk of the need for a code of ethics for prisoners, Indigenous People, residents of nursing homes, families in poverty, people with disabilities, and other less powerful groups. 'Ethics' is therefore a discourse about the behaviour of the powerful and is an attempt to circumscribe such behaviour in the interests of the less powerful. For this reason we should be wary of any attempt, however philosophically sophisticated, to dismiss ethics as redundant in the postmodern age; it can simply serve to remove what limits there may have been on the behaviour of the powerful, and thereby further to disadvantage the already disadvantaged.

This is an example of one of the problems with postmodernism. It can invalidate or at least devalue some of the discourses which have been most important in acting in the interests of the least powerful, thereby reinforcing relationships of domination and oppression. Simply abandoning the idea of ethical behaviour, and codes of ethics, may thus be counter-productive to the social justice aims of social work. This raises a significant question about the claims of some postmodernists that postmodernism is progressive and liberating. There are certainly some aspects of postmodernism that support emancipatory practice (Pease & Fook 1999) but there are others that can reinforce oppression, and social work needs to be cautious in embracing postmodernism uncritically.

A complete rejection of a discourse of ethics, then, may not be in the best interests either of social work or the social justice aims it espouses. It is equally clear that the simplistic modernist construction of ethics is of limited value (Bauman 1993; Griffin 1996; Jenkins 1999). In the following section we will explore the potential for a human rights perspective to inform a reframing of social work ethics as based on human rights.

Ethics and human rights

The important thing about professional codes of ethics is not the ethical codes themselves but the morality that lies behind them. It is the *morality* of social work and social workers' actions that is at issue; ethical codes are merely a yardstick by which that morality can be measured and evaluated.

This is the point of Bauman's claim that morality and ethics need to be separated, and that the end of the era of ethics does not imply the end of morality. Ethics are an expression of morality, but they need not be the only one, and in a postmodern era we need to look for other moral discourses, such as human rights (Hershock 2000). But the purely existential approach to morality, which is the logical outcome of Bauman's position, will not suffice for social workers, who have to live not only with their personal evaluations of right and wrong but with publicly constructed (and often contradictory) statements of morality. In addition, social workers will claim an accountability not only to their own values and moral principles but also to those of their clients, whether at individual, family, group, community or societal levels (Clark 2000). This requires not merely a personal morality but also a shared morality that is discursively constructed, involving the social worker and others with whom she/he interacts. For social workers, morality, whether expressed through ethical codes or in some other way, is interactive, and cannot be just a matter for lonely existential decisions.

The question then is to what extent a human rights discourse enables that discursive morality to be constructed. As was discussed in Chapter 1, the approach to human rights taken in this book is discursive; human rights do not exist in an objective positive sense but are constructed through an ongoing discourse. The same, it appears, can be true of morality, if it is divorced from the modernist construction of a code of ethics. Thus it may well be that human rights can provide an alternative moral space for the making of practice decisions, rather than by recourse to a formal code of ethics. A human rights discourse, as previously noted, is concerned with ideas of what it means to be human – what is the nature of our common humanity that transcends culture, race, gender, age, class. Human rights are the way in which we seek to define that common humanity and to provide the environment for people to realise their full human potential (Czerny 1993). From this perspective, moral principles for a social work based on human rights might be expressed simply in this way:

- Act so as always to affirm and realise the human rights of all people.
- Do nothing to restrict, deny or violate the human rights of anyone.

Such principles, of course, beg the question of what *are* the human rights that must be affirmed, realised and protected. A social worker cannot act in accordance with such principles unless he/she has an understanding of what those human rights might be. And as human rights are discursive, no single written statement will ever quite suffice. Written statements, such as the Universal Declaration of Human Rights, are nevertheless important because they represent an attempt at consensus and are well known as powerful statements of human rights. It is the working out of the meaning of human rights in any particular context, however, that is important, especially in terms of the contextualisation of rights as statements of needs (see Chapter 5). This is an active process, involving social worker, clients, colleagues, policy-makers and members of the wider community, which will be discussed further in Chapter 9. To try to define human rights as a static authoritative statement is as futile and as modernist as a fixed code of ethics. But the idea of rights, discursively constructed, can form the basis of an alternative and powerful approach to morality in social work practice.

Practising ethically

Even though the use of a formal ethical code may seem irrelevant in a postmodern age, the idea of ethics is not one that need necessarily be discarded. As was seen above, the use of ethical codes tends to imply a constraint on the powerful, and hence it has particular importance for a profession such as social work, which is so concerned with issues of power and empowerment and which should wholeheartedly support curbs on the powerful to prevent them taking undue advantage of those with less power. In particular, for social workers, the idea of 'professional ethics' implies a constraint on the power of professionals to practise oppressively. It can therefore make sense to talk about *practising ethically*, which we can understand in terms of practising morally, using an understanding of human rights as a reference point for what that morality might be. The principles suggested above, about always seeking to maximise the realisation and protection of human rights and never violating another's human rights, can form the basis of such a framing of ethical practice.

This puts a somewhat broader construction on professional ethics than is common with formalised ethical codes. A major emphasis in codes of ethics is the social worker respecting the human rights of the person or people with whom she/he is working. For example, the worker is required to respect and ensure confidentiality, and not to take advantage of the client financially, sexually, or in any other way. The worker is further required to provide the best possible service to all people, and not to discriminate on the basis of sex, age, race or ethnicity. These are obviously important principles and they are where codes of ethics have the strongest impact; social workers who consistently (or even once) do not meet such obligations are likely to have formal action taken against them for breach of professional ethics. These issues can all clearly be included within the idea of the worker respecting the human rights of the client.

But there are further levels of ethical practice involved in a human rights perspective, arising from the principles above. The first is the requirement to ensure that the human rights of the client are maximised

(Czerny 1993); this goes beyond simply providing the best service available within the social worker's agency; it also necessitates looking at all the person's human rights and making sure they are realised and protected. Thus a social worker in a hospital can be seen as having a responsibility to work for a patient's second-generation human rights not only to health but also to education, adequate housing, employment, social security, and so on. Most social workers would accept this as part of their role, and it would be common for a social worker to be concerned for all these aspects of a person's second-generation rights. However, it would not usually be thought of in terms of a social worker's *ethical* responsibilities, and few social workers would be subject to complaints of *unethical* practice if they did not pursue all these rights with every person they see; it might be regarded as something to be covered in supervision, but hardly for complaint to an ethics board, except in extreme circumstances where a client's obviously urgent and pressing needs were ignored by a social worker.

Moving into the other generations of human rights, however, opens up new arenas for the application of ideas of 'ethics'. A client's first-generation human rights are obviously central to an 'ethics' discourse when they relate to the social worker–client relationship directly, for example in terms of discrimination on the part of the social worker. When we come to first-generation rights in the broader sense, however, the connection is much weaker. A client's right to join a trade union, for example, would be unlikely to be a major focus of a hospital social worker's work with that client, and failure to ensure that client's right to join a union would hardly be considered 'unethical' behaviour on the part of the social worker, in the traditional sense. Issues of first-generation rights are often part of day-to-day social work practice. For example when a client is the subject of discrimination in the workplace a social worker is likely to take this issue up with the client, employer or union. Failure to do so is unlikely to be construed as 'unethical' behaviour on the part of the worker, but from a human rights perspective this would be the case.

Third-generation rights are even less likely to be seen as matters for ethical consideration. This is partly because they only emerge at a collective level, and social work (at least in most western countries) remains largely focused on the individual client or the family. A concern for third-generation rights and an ethical obligation to ensure that one's client's third-generation rights are realised and protected require that a social worker take the step from the individual to the collective. Denial of the third-generation right to economic development may have implications for individual clients in the form of poverty, but it can only be addressed as a third-generation right at the level of the community or the society. Again, many social workers will make this connection and will involve themselves in policy advocacy, or social or political action, to ensure that third-generation rights are met. Other social workers will not, choosing to concentrate only on individualised service ('casework') practice. While such practice might be condemned as conservative by social workers with a broader human rights perspective, it is, again, unlikely to be classed as *unethical* and result in formal complaints to an ethics board. And if we extend third-generation rights still further to include environmental rights, one can suggest that therefore social workers have an obligation also to be concerned about the environment. This is an important argument and points the way to a very different formulation of the central concerns of social work, but it is unlikely that anyone would seriously wish to make a complaint against a social worker for unethical conduct simply because that social worker was not an environmental activist.

The question, then, is whether a human rights perspective is simply too broad in its implications to be useful as a reframing for what counts as 'ethical' and 'unethical' practice. Or is it precisely *because* human rights provide such a broad frame of reference that it represents a radical challenge to social work to reconstruct its morality in a way that removes it from the conservatising individualism that has dominated so much of social work discourse? Such a move to a broad human rights framework for ethics takes social work into relatively uncharted waters, but at a time of the crisis of the state, globalisation, and the many threats to social work as traditionally understood, it is necessary to take such new and bold steps. At this stage we can make some tentative identification of what might constitute such an approach to practice, though this will not be fully developed until Chapter 10 as it also needs to draw on the discussion in other chapters.

One of the significant implications of this approach is that it moves social work's construction of ethical and unethical practice away from the focus only on the individual worker acting in isolation and requires that the resolution of an 'ethical issue' be one that involves other actors. The question for the worker then is not 'what should I do?', but first 'whom should I talk to?', and then 'what should we do?' This is part of moving towards seeing the social worker as being connected with many other actors in a common undertaking – a reflection of the community orientation that I believe is necessary for all social work (see Ife 1997b). The question 'whom should I talk to?' does not simply imply that a social worker needs to discuss an ethical issue with a supervisor (though this can be very useful). It involves others who are important actors in the drama, including the client, the client's family, community members, colleagues, and other professionals. This starts to define the 'we' implied in the second question, 'what should we do?', because again no action taken by a social worker is taken in isolation. If we are really interested in human rights we should have some commitment to ensuring that all those likely to be affected by a decision can have some effective input into it. Indeed not to follow such a prescription is not respectful of human rights, and therefore in the terms of this discussion becomes unethical. Hence the framing of ethics purely in terms of the individual social worker making a lonely moral choice (with or without the help of a formal ethical code) is itself unethical practice – a radical notion indeed.

Another important implication of social work moving to a human rights perspective on ethics, as suggested above, is that it inevitably moves social workers away from purely individualising practice. Human rights (across the three generations) cannot be realised and safeguarded through individualised practice alone. A concentration on 'casework', 'direct practice' or 'therapy' alone therefore does not meet the aim of social work practice based on human rights. Social workers thus have a clear responsibility to link their interpersonal practice with community work, policy development, social action and other 'macro' forms of practice. As was argued in Chapter 6, the traditional split between 'macro' and 'micro' social work practice simply does not hold up if a human rights perspective is consistently applied, and indeed is counter to the human rights aims of social work. The human rights approach to ethical practice suggests that a social worker who insists on maintaining the division between macro and micro practice, and only operates within one of them, is also practising unethically, and the same criticism could be made of university departments which perpetuate the macro/micro divide in their curricula. Again, this is a significant and radical departure from our understanding of what counts as professional ethics.

The above discussion should not be interpreted as advocating that all specialist caseworkers, specialist community workers, therapists, and heads of social work schools which use the terms 'macro' and 'micro' should be brought before a board and charged with ethical misconduct. Boards of this nature are really only useful for holding particular individuals to account for the more extreme and blatant cases of unethical practice. Ethical practice, in the human rights sense, can be much more readily achieved using more positive and constructive means, by encouraging critical debate and providing structures and opportunities for social workers to talk to each other, to clients, to other professionals and to community members about a human rights perspective and what it means in the real world of practice. There can therefore be no quick and easy prescription; one of the consequences of the decline of modernist certainty is the decline of the neat, packaged simple solution, and this applies to ethics and to all aspects of social work practice.

The rejection of neat 'how to do it' instruction books has been an ongoing theme of social work. Any social worker who tries to set down such clear 'cookbook' prescriptions for practice is heading for irrelevance. Social work practice changes with each worker (style, personality, age, sex, race), with each context (cultural, organisational, political, community) and with each situation (client, family, community), to such an extent that what 'works' for one worker in one context will not necessarily work for another worker, or in a different context. Social work practice is not predictable; it is messy, chaotic, and infinitely changeable. This is the reason that most social work texts refuse to lay out specific prescriptions for practice, and instead rely on theory, principles of practice, and case studies, much to the frustration of students, who are frequently under the misapprehension that in a social work course they will be 'taught how to do it'. It is also why the texts that do try to follow the 'how to do it' approach are often seen as irrelevant and ignored in the world of practice, and why every social worker has to develop her/his own practice model. So it is interesting that in the field of ethics, if nowhere else, there has been a continuing attempt to be prescriptive and to impose a world-view of certainty. Perhaps this needs to change.

Yet the chaos and the unpredictability of practice do not mean we should give up any notion of guiding principles and leave social workers to a series of individualised nihilistic existential encounters with specific situations, to be dealt with in the best way they can. This, indeed, would be to condone the nihilistic individualism on which the forces of inequality and injustice thrive. Human rights do provide a framework for universal and universalising themes within the reality of practice, and this means that the phrase 'practising ethically' still has some relevance and that it opens up possibilities for more collective and progressive practice.

Conclusion

This chapter has raised some of the problematic aspects of a traditional framing of social work ethics. While it might be suggested that in the era of postmodernity a modernist discourse such as conventional 'ethics' has little relevance, it would be a mistake to reject entirely any understanding of ethics and ethical practice. Clearly ideas of ethics and human rights are closely linked, and it is suggested that by pursuing this link a human rights perspective can provide a more robust framing of 'practising ethically' which has application to contemporary social work.

CHAPTER 8

Participation in the Human Rights Discourse

The discursive view of human rights, emphasised throughout this book, suggests that human rights must be understood as an ongoing and ever-changing discourse about what it means to be human and about what should comprise the rights of common global citizenship. If this is the case, it is most important to examine the nature of that global dialogue. Who is responsible for maintaining that discourse, who contributes, who does not, and whose voices are the most powerful in defining what is to count as 'human rights'?

As discussed in Chapter 1, one of the consequences of globalisation has been localisation, and this has led to the identification of the *global* and the *local* as the sites of significant change and praxis. For this reason the discussion in this chapter will be divided into a consideration of global and local dialogues around human rights.

The global discourse of human rights

While not wanting to underemphasise the disproportionate role that western voices have had in framing the human rights discourse, it is also clear that this concern is now being vigorously addressed. Even a cursory glance at the human rights literature shows that the issue of cultural relativism and the western domination of the discourse has received substantial attention and that a significant number of non-western writers are now talking about human rights (Schmale 1993; Aziz 1999; Bauer & Bell 1999; Parekh, B. 1999; Van Ness 1999). This fully justifiable concern for the need to have different cultural voices heard in the human rights discourse has diverted attention from another perhaps more fundamental exclusion. That is that *the human rights discourse remains dominated by the voices of the privileged*, and it is rare for the disadvantaged, the powerless, and the victims of human rights abuses to be heard in the debate. The discourse reflects the voices of lawyers, academics, politicians, diplomats, religious leaders, philosophers, theologians, journalists and middle-class activists (Beetham 1999). It is true that the discourse has opened up to include those from non-western cultures, but it is the privileged from within those cultures, just as it is the privileged from the west, who dominate the debate. Thus *the human rights discourse remains a discourse of the powerful about the powerless*, and therefore becomes part of the discourse of domination and disempowerment. This must be of fundamental concern for social workers and suggests some important priorities for social work practice.

The concentration on cultural difference and the corresponding underemphasis on class and other dimensions of oppression underline a serious problem with much of the literature concerned with social change, namely the tendency to emphasise one dimension of difference or disadvantage (in this case culture) to the exclusion of others. Thus the Marxist critique, by emphasising class as the primary dimension of oppression, has been criticised for not taking adequate account of gender issues (hooks 1981), while feminism has been accused of ignoring the importance of class (Lee 1996). Both can be criticised for a tendency to devalue the importance of race and culture, and sexuality is often ignored in all these discourses. It is important to maintain a view that incorporates the multiple dimensions of oppression, but this is very difficult when fundamentalists of whatever variety claim one dimension of difference or disadvantage as more important (or 'fundamental') than the others and insist on viewing the world through a single lens. Of course there have been many writers within these different traditions who have sought to broaden their analysis; arguably feminist writers have been the most successful at this, as some forms of feminism have emphasised the importance of inclusion, difference and holistic understandings (Plumwood 1993). Social workers, given the necessarily holistic nature of a profession that links the personal and the political, need to allow for the inclusion of differing framings of disadvantage. In the human rights field, however, the continuing emphasis on issues of culture and cultural relativism has tended to blind us to the fact that the voices of the disadvantaged remain largely excluded from the human rights discourse, even while issues of culture are being addressed.

This is hardly surprising. The disadvantaged and the marginalised tend to be excluded from all discourses of power, and human rights are in this sense no different from economics, politics, culture, law, business, higher education, and professionalism. Human rights are a special case, however. *The exclusion of the disadvantaged from the human rights discourse is itself a denial of human rights*, and so the human rights discourse, in its dominant privileged form, is self-contradictory. This contradiction in the dominant discursive framing of human rights has received very little attention, yet for social workers as human rights practitioners it must be of central concern.

Understood discursively, the ideal of human rights can only be realised in a genuinely participatory society. Otherwise the voices of the disadvantaged are excluded in the very construction of human rights and what they mean, and thus human rights are violated in a fundamental sense. Some form of participatory democracy is therefore a *precondition* for human rights. The advocates of liberal American values often claim that human rights and democracy belong together. While such claims are usually made with very limited and circumscribed understandings of both democracy and human rights, and are confused with ideas of free-market capitalism, which is seen by its proponents as synonymous with freedom, human rights and democracy all at once, there is nevertheless a necessary connection between democracy and human rights that deserves further exploration. In this sense, both 'democracy' and 'human rights' need to be understood in a much broader sense than would be assumed by, for example, a mainstream American political commentator advocating human rights and democracy as twin pillars of 'the American way'. The broader construction of human rights has been outlined in earlier chapters, but it is now necessary to consider the idea of democracy, which is necessarily associated with the idea of human rights.

Participatory democracy

Democracy, like human rights, is a complex and contested concept (Held 1987). While there is obvious positive value attached to the idea of democracy, or 'rule of the people', it is far from clear how that rule should be exercised, and even who 'the people' are. In classical Greek democracy, where the idea of democracy is commonly seen as having originated, women, children and slaves were omitted from the construction of 'the people' (Sinclair 1988); it was actually a very limited form of democracy that excluded more than it included. And in modern democracies, too, not everyone is included in the decision-making process – children do not have the right to vote, nor do aliens or 'non-citizens'. And in reality many more people are excluded from access to the decision-making of so-called 'democratic' governments, through poverty, gender, social class, educational background, or race (Martin & Schumann 1997). Indeed, for many people, 'democracy' is a myth that hides the reality of their effective powerlessness.

Modern societies are so complex, and there are so many decisions that need to be taken, that direct democratic participation by all the people in all the decision-making is impossible (Rayner 1998). Hence we have some form of *representative* democracy, where the role of the people is not to make democratic decisions but to elect or appoint representatives to a parliament or some other assembly, trusting those they have elected to make decisions of which they will approve. But the mechanisms of modern government are so complex that this also does not work, and many decisions are further delegated to the civil service – people who are not elected but are paid to carry out the work of government. Hence the decision-making power of the citizen in a democracy is twice delegated, first to the politicians then to the civil service, and the input of the citizen is limited indeed. The role of the citizen in such a 'democracy' is to vote every few years, and even this can be a largely symbolic gesture, given the media manipulation of public opinion, and especially if the voter lives in a 'safe' constituency. In any case, a sizeable proportion of the population (sometimes a majority, given the vagaries of electoral systems) will not have voted for the party that won government and can justifiably complain that the government does not represent their views in any way.

Representative democracy, therefore, has moved a long way from the romantic notion of 'government of the people, by the people, for the people'. The role of the individual citizen is minimal and has been further eroded by the complexity and the mystification of modern government (Martin & Schumann 1997). Increasingly policy is defined, and accepted, as so complex that only trained experts can understand it, and hence 'public' policy is removed from the realm of democratic debate and becomes the exclusive domain of the expert (Fay 1975; Rayner 1998; Held 1999). The most significant example of this is, of course, economics. Economics, and the direction of economic policy, are of vital importance to us all; they affect our living standard, quality of life, and overall life chances. Yet economics is constructed in such a way that very few people are considered 'competent' to understand it. Economic policy is something best left to the economic experts, and in any case the language of economics effectively excludes the uninitiated. This is also, effectively, an erosion of democratic control and is paralleled in other policy areas; the choices left to the voting citizen are few, and the contribution that the citizen can make is limited by her/his lack of 'expertise'. In the case of economics the erosion of democratic control goes even further: in most western countries the central bank, which makes crucial decisions regarding economic policy, has been established as independent of government. The democratically elected leaders of the nation are evidently not considered sufficiently competent or reliable to make key economic decisions, and the lack of public concern at this alarming state of affairs only serves to underline the level of public acceptance of this effective disenfranchisement in relation to some of the most important public policy decisions.

For these reasons, there have been attempts to find other ways in which democracy can be more *participatory*. The idea of participatory democracy, as opposed to representative democracy, is that it maximises the extent to which 'the people' can participate in the actual decision-making process. Obviously it is impossible to have all the people participating in all the decisions that need to be taken; and indeed who would want to be part of every decision of government? Many decisions that are taken are reasonably uncontroversial, and most people would presumably be happy not to be involved in them. However, the form of representative democracy characteristic of most self-styled 'democracies' is clearly disempowering and tokenistic, and as a result more participatory models have been proposed. And in the interests of human rights, such a quest is of considerable importance (Beetham 1999). Four common proposals can be termed *citizens' initiated referendums, deliberative democracy, electronic democracy* and *decentralised democracy*.

There have been regular calls for *citizens' initiated referendums* on issues of concern to people, as a reaction against the feelings of disempowerment that characterise the modern western experience of 'democracy' (Setälä 1999). The idea of a citizens' initiated referendum is that if a sufficient number of citizens were to sign a petition requesting such a referendum, it would have to be put to the people and the result would be binding on the government. Referendums have an obvious superficial appeal, as they clearly increase the ability of ordinary people to be involved in the decision-making process. They are used in a number of American states, and commonly in Switzerland. There are, however, problems with referendums, and the introduction of a system of referendums is a simplistic answer to the problems of modern democracy. To be suitable for a referendum, a policy issue has to be expressed in a simple, preferably yes/no, form. But most policy issues are rather more complex than that, and to reduce them to a simple referendum question means that they can become issues for populist sloganeering rather than careful thought. The main problem, however, is that most people have neither the time nor the inclination to become well informed about an issue before voting in a referendum. Unless it is a question in which they have a particular interest, their vote will be a superficially informed one, made on the basis of reaction to campaign slogans and twenty-second commercials – hardly a basis for sound judgement. The result of the referendum is therefore unlikely to represent the pooled *wisdom* of the population, but rather pooled *sentiment* and pooled *prejudice* (Setälä 1999, Roemer 1999). This is especially true in societies where there is no tradition of referendums – in Switzerland one would expect people to be more used to thinking issues through and becoming well informed before voting. For referendums to be useful as a democratic tool would require a major cultural shift, in many western countries in particular, where political apathy and ignorance are a cultural norm (Bauman 1993).

In addition, there is no guarantee that the results of citizens' referendums would enhance the cause of human rights. While it may assist in the exercising of rights to self-determination and to participation in decision-making, a citizens' referendum can produce an oppressive result. The 'tyranny of the majority' can very easily override the human rights of a minority of the population. A referendum may, for example, result in the adoption of more racist or exclusionary policies towards minority ethnic and cultural groups, or, as was the case in California in 1996 (Proposition 209), the outlawing of positive discrimination programs based on race. Such outcomes are especially likely in a climate of perceived threat and instability, when scapegoating can be anticipated. This is an example of the exercise of one claimed 'human right' that actually results in the denial of other human rights; on the basis of the definition of human rights developed in earlier chapters, this would not be acceptable as a human rights outcome.

The introduction of citizens' referendums would only be an effective tool for increasing participatory democracy if there were adequate and effective education programs as well, to enable the population to cast an *informed* vote. This is a much harder program than simply introducing referendums, but it would significantly change the results of referendums on many issues. A good example is the case of the death penalty, a major human rights issue. In many countries, opinion polls suggest that a popular referendum would result in a majority favouring the death penalty, and its proponents have called for such referendums in countries where capital punishment has been abolished. But the experience of people who have worked with community groups on death penalty issues is that if people are exposed to all arguments on both sides, and given a chance (and the time and space) to examine the results of research and to think through the issues in more detail, a significant majority will decide against the death penalty (Roberts & Stalans 1997). The results of a referendum on the death penalty, therefore, will largely be determined by the extent to which the population has been exposed to the arguments (not just the slogans) and been given an opportunity to come to an informed opinion. This relates to the discussion in Chapter 6 about rights and obligations: with the 'right' to participate in decision-making goes the 'responsibility' to do so in an informed rather than an uninformed way. Expanding people's democratic rights also requires an expansion of the capacity for them realistically to meet their citizenship obligations to be *informed* contributors to democratic decisions.

In 1999 the people of Australia voted in a referendum that sought to change the constitution to make Australia a republic rather than maintaining traditional ties to the British monarch. The issues, inevitably, were more complex than that, and the campaign by both sides (but particularly the opponents to the proposal) served to confuse rather than clarify the issue. On voting day, a significant majority of Australians voted to maintain the status quo, to the puzzlement of the rest of the world, who could not see what possible relevance a British monarch had for Australians in the twenty-first century (Li 1999). While the campaign was being undertaken, however, an interesting experiment was taking place. A number of Australians, drawn from all walks of life, were brought together for several days of intensive study of the issues. They had the opportunity to hear and question advocates of both sides, to talk the issues through, to read relevant information, and so on. At the beginning of the program the group included some republicans, some monarchists, and some who were undecided; at that stage their stated voting intentions were roughly the same as those of the Australian population as a whole. After the process of being exposed to the arguments and examining the issues, however, a significant majority said they would now vote for the republican proposal, a reversal of the views of the whole electorate as expressed on the day of the vote. This was similar to the experience with the death penalty and shows the importance of democratic decision-making being well informed. The process that took place with that group of Australians is a good example of *deliberative democracy*, the idea that people can make a wise decision if they are given full access to all relevant information and the time to study and debate the issues in some depth, amounting to an extension of the jury system into the public policy arena. There is now considerable interest worldwide in the possibilities of deliberative democracy as a means of increasing participatory forms of democracy and getting over the problems associated with citizens' referendums (Saward 1998; Uhr 1998, 2000; Roemer 1999). Deliberative democracy concentrates on process; it suggests that it is in the integrity of the process and the opportunity for people to have genuine input into deliberative processes that effective democracy can be realised. People are often prepared to accept a decision that goes against their particular preferences, as long as they can be satisfied that they have had an opportunity to have effective input (i.e. their voice has been heard), and that the decision-making process has been open and fair. The jury system, as outlined in the above example, is one form of deliberative democracy; other forms include widespread community consultation (before rather than after a specific proposal has been made) and the implementation of consensus decision-making, where people may not agree with the outcome but agree with the participatory process and so are prepared to accept the result. The key element of deliberative democracy, however, is that citizens are enabled to be part of the process of studying alternatives, researching possible outcomes and formulating proposals; they are asked to contribute to the process rather than simply react to a proposal.

Electronic democracy seeks to use the new power of the Internet to increase levels of citizen participation. Through the Internet, people who may never meet face to face are able to discuss issues and even come to a consensus. This is currently happening in a largely unplanned and anarchistic way, and even so it has brought about some spectacular results. The defeat of the proposed Multilateral Agreement on Investment was a triumph of citizen groups communicating via the Internet, sharing information and expertise, and combining to effect significant global power. This would not have been possible in the pre-computer era. More organised use of the Internet to facilitate participatory democracy might include ongoing discussion groups, computer voting on issues, and the use of websites to provide people with the information necessary to make informed decisions – a kind of virtual deliberative democracy. Such ideas are only in their infancy, and while there are many exciting possibilities for the use of the Internet to increase participatory democracy (Wheeler 1997), it is also worth remembering the disadvantages of using the computer in this way. It is still the case that computers are only available to a minority of the world's population (and that is the most advantaged minority), so any democratic process that relies exclusively on the Internet will exclude the majority of humanity. And there are many others who, while they may have access to a computer, do not have the level of computer skills to make full and effective use of the Internet. Moreover, electronic democracy will undoubtedly favour the voices of not merely the computer-literate but in particular the voices of the computer-obsessives. New technologies can certainly assist with a project of increasing participatory democracy, but they cannot be assumed to be the magic answer.

Decentralised democracy suggests that the most effective way to have people actively involved in decision-making over issues that directly affect them is to decentralise decision-making as much as possible, so that decisions are made in more local community-based structures which enable people to have much more direct input (Rayner 1998). This can be achieved through more accessible local government structures, with local governments taking increasing responsibility for a wide range of issues. It can also make use of other community-based structures, local precinct groups, resident groups, and so on. This has been a major thrust of community development theory and practice, which has seen the maximisation of citizen participation as one of its central aims. But even at this level, where there is considerably more practice experience than is the case with deliberative or electronic democracy, the idea of participation is problematic, and genuine ongoing citizen participation has proved extremely difficult to achieve. This is because democratic participation actually conflicts with a number of powerful vested interests, which seek to maintain the existing structures and processes of power and exclusion and to ensure that the level of citizen participation remains largely token. Community workers have successfully identified strategies for increasing effective participation, often not through grand gestures but through day-to-day engagement with issues on a micro level. There is a good deal of social work expertise in maximising participation at local community level, and this is important in human rights-based social work, which will be taken up below when the local arena for participation is discussed. For the present discussion, this form of practice is seen as contributing to an overall national or global strategy of encouraging local participation and decentralising decision-making wherever possible. This is supported particularly by Green political theory (Goodin 1992; Dobson 1995), which has emphasised the ecological principles of diversity and sustainability; these can best be achieved, according to many Green writers (e.g. Bookchin 1990), from a highly decentralised system. It is also consistent with anarchist ideology (Marshall 1992) and chaos theory (Kellert 1993), which sees effective order as emerging spontaneously from below rather than needing to be imposed from above.

In the newly globalising world, with increasingly powerful global economic forces and the increasing possibilities of global communications, is it now possible to contemplate some form of global participatory democracy (Holden 2000)? It is perhaps too soon to answer such a question with any certainty, and there are varying views on the likelihood of such a project or how it might work (Falk 2000b; Galtung 2000; Held 2000; Hirst & Thompson 2000), but it is nonetheless an issue of critical importance for the future of human rights. Human rights, as we have seen, are the consequence of some notion of global citizenship, implying that we are all citizens of a global society and that despite our many cultural and other differences there is a shared humanity that we hold in common. If human rights are indeed global citizenship rights, one of the more important of these rights is the right to participation in the body politic, in this case at the global level. Yet there is little opportunity for formalised citizen input into global decisions. The opportunities do exist, however, in less formalised ways, using the more fluid structures of civil society. In the case of the global opposition to the Multilateral Agreement on Investment, people took matters into their own hands and created the opportunities for change despite a lack of formal structures. Such cases are important, and it is likely to be through struggles of this kind that citizen participation at the global level might ultimately be legitimised.

At present the existing embryonic global democratic structures that exist are federal, through the United Nations: people elect national governments, and those governments in turn are represented at the UN. There is little possibility of direct involvement by individuals (except in certain circumstances such as the right of an individual to appeal to the UN Human Rights Commission). A genuine global participatory democracy would need to be much more powerful and effective than the UN, despite the best efforts of many of those involved in establishing and maintaining the UN and its various agencies. This is most likely to be achieved, however, not through the formal structures of the UN but through the strength of global civil society (Galtung 2000). Civil society has been much better able to replicate itself at global level than have formal state structures, as can be seen in the power and the effectiveness of a multitude of global NGOs (Fox & Brown 1998), as well as the more spontaneous coalitions that emerge in reaction to the excesses of global capital (such as the 1999 protest against the World Trade Organisation in Seattle).

What are the implications of the global democracy movement for social workers? The above discussion of strategies to develop more participatory democracy at the global level is important, from a human rights point of view, for two reasons. First, such participation helps to realise human rights: rights to participate fully as a citizen, rights of self-determination, and so on. And second, given the discursive nature of human rights, such participation is actually necessary for there to be adequate debate about what count as human rights, in order to counter the elitist nature of the human rights discourse already noted. Human rights workers (i.e. social workers) therefore have a considerable interest in working towards some form of global democracy and a more participatory global regime than that of the present. This relates back to the idea of 'globalisation from below' (Falk 1993; Brecher & Costello 1994), as discussed initially in Chapter 1. This idea, it will be recalled, does not oppose globalisation per se but rather seeks a form of globalisation that is genuinely democratic and in the interests of a broader humanity rather than a small number of controllers of global capital. And as we have already seen, this can often be more effectively achieved informally through citizen action within civil society, rather than formally through governmental structures. Social workers have many opportunities in their day-to-day work to help establish globalisation from below, and this is one reason why the link between the local and the global is now so important for social workers in all settings. Such social work need not be particularly elaborate or grandiose. Examples would include linking a local community group to similar groups in other countries through the

Internet, linking a person not only to local agencies that can assist him/her but also to global networks and organisations that are dealing with the issue, supporting and publicising global campaigns for social justice and human rights, supporting the work of global NGOs and working towards more democratic structures within them, helping to make clients and colleagues aware of the global aspects of their experiences, and applying well-known community work principles of encouraging participation, but in a global context (Keck & Sikkink 1998). Most particularly, social workers can work with groups of disadvantaged or marginalised people to encourage them to make their voices heard in international debates about human rights, for example in the decision-making bodies of Amnesty International, in preparing submissions for the UN Human Rights Commission, and in articulating through the media what human rights mean for them.

The local discourse of human rights

Thus far the discussion has been focused on increasing the voices of the disadvantaged in the global discourse of human rights. But it is also important to consider the more local dimension of a human rights discourse and the ways in which this might also be made more inclusive. Although human rights, by their very nature, are universal, they are often articulated, and met, in a more local context. Hence the issue of the involvement of the disadvantaged, and the victims of human rights abuse, in the construction of human rights also has important implications for social workers working locally (Mahoney & Mahoney 1993).

As was shown in Chapter 5, the way in which universal human *rights* are often contextualised locally is through the definition of human *needs*. The universal right to education can be redefined as the need for more teachers, the right to shelter as the need for a refuge for the homeless, an individual's right to personal mobility as the need for a wheelchair. It is therefore in the definition of needs that individuals at the local level can participate in and contribute to the discourse that defines human rights, and so the definition of needs becomes important ground for framing the human rights discourse. And, as pointed out in Chapter 5, social workers are among those professionals who stand accused of appropriating the authority to define people's needs (and hence their rights) for them. In this light, the questions around need definition must be of particular concern for this discussion because it is in struggles over the definition of need at the local individual or community level that people can seek to regain control over the definition of their human rights.

For this reason, social workers should be very reluctant to accept uncritically the role of need definer, which includes undertaking needs studies – a familiar process for any community worker – and, at the case-work level, 'doing an assessment'. When a social worker performs such an assessment, with a view to identifying what is 'needed', he/she is effec-tively controlling the human rights discourse by defining what human rights are to count. While there may be a case for a social worker to apply professional expertise to help determine how a human right might best be translated into a need, there is surely no case for a social worker to take over the responsibility of determining what the 'right' is that will be satisfied by the meeting of the contextualised need. It is therefore essen-tial that social work practice involve a dialogue with the individual, fam-ily, group or community around the issue of rights: what people might perceive as their rights, how those rights impact on the rights of others, whether they really can count as human rights in terms of the definition offered in Chapter 1, and lastly (not first as is normally the case) how those rights might be translated into 'needs' which can then be 'met'.

Of course a social worker would in most cases not use such language in framing the discussion about rights. The language of rights as used by professionals can be alienating to many people, as it is typically the lan-guage of the middle-class intellectual. Social workers are typically such middle-class intellectuals, so it is a language that comes easily to them. As long as the discourse of human rights remains the exclusive property of middle-class intellectuals it perpetuates structures of disadvantage and inequality and can never realise the goal of universal human rights. Social workers therefore face the challenge of reframing the language of human rights so that others can join the debate. This reframing, which is simply the ability to find another set of words with which to discuss something, is a task in which social workers are well practised. To cite some simple examples, the right to free speech might be reframed in terms of 'letting everyone have their say'; the right to benefit from eco-nomic development might be talked about in terms such as 'we hear a lot about how prosperous the country is, how about finding ways we can all share it?'; the right to shelter and adequate physical care might become a discussion of what sort of nursing home would best meet the needs of a frail elderly relative with dementia; and the right to education could be reframed as 'how can we make sure children get the chance to learn the things they need to know?'. In each case this reframing leads to other questions: what are the things children need to know and what sort of school might provide them for this child? how can we make sure every-one has a say? how do we make a decision about a nursing home? These are the kinds of questions with which social workers and the people they work with deal in their everyday practice, but it is important to remem-ber that at heart they are questions about human rights. The social worker is, in effect, having a discussion with an individual, a family or a community about what they understand by basic human rights and how these can best be realised and protected, even if such words are not used. The important thing for the social worker to realise is that the way in which the discussion is constructed can either facilitate or inhibit the client's defining what she/he means by human rights and how they can be met. The micro-level activity of social work practice thus can be seen as located within a broader societal discourse about human rights, and the social worker who enables and facilitates other people to engage in and with that discourse is broadening the basis on which a human rights consensus might be developed.

Unfortunately many of the conventional professional constructions of social work practice militate against such an approach. The reader may have noticed that the above discussion did not use the word 'interview' in describing the interaction between worker and client; this was a deliberate choice because the very idea of an 'interview' assumes certain power relations between the two people involved, which can easily work against empowerment-based practice. In the professional interview it is assumed that the worker is in control, sets the agenda, manages the timing, sets the boundaries, and so on. Of course some of these are often negotiated with the client, but usually on the worker's terms. This will be further discussed in Chapter 11, where other familiar social work constructions such as 'client', 'intervention', 'supervision' and 'profession' are also shown to be potentially disempowering. Of course these can be otherwise framed to incorporate a perspective that is more emancipatory and more geared to human rights, but the conservatising and disempowering associations of these terms suggest that any time a social worker uses any of them, she/he should carefully examine the way in which they are constructed, and whether by using them the social worker is simply acquiescing to a discourse of disempowerment and professional privilege.

Perhaps the important question to ask is *who translates the assumed rights to statements of need.* In other words, whose definition of need is accepted as legitimate? If needs are the contextualisation of human rights, the main point at issue is who assumes responsibility for the definition of need. It is, however, not a simple matter of saying it is the client alone who should have that responsibility; as pointed out in Chapter 5, a judgement of need contains not only a value (human rights) component but also a component of expertise about the effectiveness of the apparently 'needed' provision. For example, the problem of violence and the right to personal security could be translated into the 'need' for harsher sentences for juvenile offenders. Here a social worker may well be in a better position than a client or community group to judge whether the proposed need will in fact address the rights question at issue; it is an area in which social workers can claim some expertise, and indeed a social worker in such an instance would be right to point out that tougher sentences may have no effect on levels of personal security. This is a case where the human right is not at issue but the means to realise it are contested, and the social worker has some expertise to contribute to the determination of what is 'needed' to secure the right to personal security. Thus it is too simple to say that the responsibility for need definition should rest solely with the 'client', just as it is to say that it should rest solely with the professional expertise of the social worker. What is needed instead is a *dialogue* between the two, where each will recognise, value and learn from the expertise of the other, so that together they can work towards effective action. This will be taken up and further developed in Chapter 10.

The discussion thus far has concentrated on how the disadvantaged and marginalised can be helped to contribute to the human rights discourse through social work practice at the most micro, casework, or individual level. But social workers are also engaged at community level, and it is often in community development roles that there are additional opportunities for the human rights discourse to be broadened to include voices that are commonly excluded. Some of these were dealt with in the previous section, but here it is worth emphasising the role of community workers in encouraging and facilitating community participation. In doing so, community workers can have a major impact on the inclusiveness of the human rights discourse. One of the important aspects of such work is a questioning of the traditional framing of 'participation' (Parker et al. 1999) and the inclusion of a wider range of activities through which people can be active in identifying what they understand by their human rights and what is needed for these rights to be met and protected. Mention has already been made of the western, patriarchal, middle-class assumptions behind 'participation' and the need for finding other ways by which people can participate in the processes of their community and in the making of decisions. The reframing of 'participation' is thus a major agenda item for social workers, especially those concerned with community development. Some of the ways in which this can be achieved include exploring alternative ways of organising meetings, models of consensus decision-making, use of theatre, art or story-telling, and using the opportunities created by informal everyday interaction. Participation does not have to take place in a formal meeting, and in a postmodern age one could suggest that the formal meeting is increasingly irrelevant as a site for meaningful participation. In many ways the 'meeting' is to the community worker what the 'interview' is to the caseworker. Each needs to be deconstructed and reconstructed from a more inclusive perspective that takes account of the discourses of power inherent in the traditional form. These ideas are not new for community workers and have been discussed at some length in the community work literature (Craig & Mayo 1995; Ife 1995; McIntyre 1995; Kenny 1999). Community workers are familiar with the problems and contradictions of citizen participation, and much of their practice is focused on finding alternative and diverse mechanisms for participation to be facilitated and for the voices of the marginalised to be validated and heard. This can be strongly identified as human rights work, and in the terms within which human rights are understood in this book, such participation-focused community work is fundamental to the realisation of human rights.

Conclusion

The discursive nature of human rights emphasises the importance of the question of who participates in the human rights discourse. Hence the encouragement of more participatory forms of democracy, incorporating the voices of the marginalised and the victims of human rights abuse, is of central concern. This is an essential component of human rights work, and if social workers are to be understood as human rights workers the aspects of practice that deal with the encouragement of participatory democracy, whether at global or local level, become of primary importance. Social workers have particular skills and expertise in this arena, both through community development and also through the negotiation of human rights definitions with clients. The latter is the subject of the next chapter.

CHAPTER 9

Constructing Human Rights for Social Work Practice

Thus far there has been no discussion about how we construct, define or accept human rights. What rights should actually count as human rights for social work practice? Do we simply accept the Universal Declaration, do we add to it, do we subtract from it, or do we reformulate it? Reading the Universal Declaration (see Appendix I) one is struck by how many of the rights contained in it are violated daily for millions of people. This applies not only to developing nations or nations with a 'human rights record' that is seen as 'poor'. It also applies to the so-called 'developed' world, where the rights outlined in the Universal Declaration are certainly not all adequately met for the whole population. What country, for example, can clearly demonstrate the full realisation of the right to equality before the law, the right to work and to free choice of work, higher education equally accessible to all on the basis of ability alone, and so on?

There are also many other statements of human rights – international treaties and conventions, regional declarations and national constitutions and bills of rights – which can be useful for social workers. Social workers cannot work as human rights workers without a clear idea of what are the human rights on which their practice should be based, and so there is a need to refer to, or construct, some formulation of what human rights are to count.

It is not, however, a simple matter of finding some appropriate statement like the Universal Declaration and then adopting it. Human rights, as discussed in earlier chapters, are seen discursively, and while formal written statements are an important part of the discourse of human rights, they are by no means the entire discourse. An important characteristic of any discourse is that it is contested and that it is constantly being constructed, challenged and reconstructed. We therefore need to look at the continuing construction of human rights as well as the inevitably static formal statements from the UN and other bodies. And the statements themselves are open to different interpretations and emphases: people will see some articles of the Universal Declaration as more important or significant in their context than others. Social workers need to see themselves as active participants in this discursive process, and indeed social work practice itself can be seen as part of the ongoing process of the reconstruction of human rights. It is partly through social work practice that human rights are operationalised, and hence defined.

For practising social workers, human rights are not simply a case of academic or political definition as outlined in something like the Universal Declaration. Rather, they are grounded in practice, and it is the relationship between the discursive construction of human rights and the practice of human rights that is critical. There are two ways in which social workers might go about making this important connection, namely the *deductive* and the *inductive*. The deductive approach starts with a statement or understanding of particular rights and then asks 'what does this mean for practice?' A child welfare worker, for example, may start with a statement on children's rights (such as the UN Convention on the Rights of the Child, together with its Optional Protocols) and then deduce from it certain principles of practice. The inductive approach, on the other hand, starts with the reality of a practice situation and then asks what are the human rights issues at stake, as a way towards informed practice. Thus the child welfare worker, faced with a conflict between the wishes of a parent and the safety of a child, may engage in an analysis of rights along the lines suggested in Chapter 3. In summary, the deductive approach starts with rights and applies them to a practice issue, while the inductive approach starts with the practice issue and then moves to rights.

This is a useful distinction for the benefit of discussion, but it should not be thought of as an exclusive dichotomy, in other words that social workers will only do one or the other. The reality is that social workers will normally work both inductively and deductively. Indeed it would be impossible for a social worker to work in only one of these ways. The idea of *praxis*, as outlined in Chapter 10, requires that a worker be working in both modes constantly, using each to inform the other. The distinction between deductive and inductive approaches is therefore made for the purposes of analysis and thinking about human rights practice, rather than as advocating that social workers maintain a clear distinction in their work. The discussion below should be read from that perspective.

Deductive approaches to human rights practice

The deductive approach starts with one or more texts of human rights and then derives practice from them. These texts can have two forms: formal documents and informal understandings.

Formal documents

As already indicated, there is a vast range of formal statements of human rights. The Universal Declaration of Human Rights is reproduced in Appendix I. Other important statements are the International Covenants on Civil and Political Rights, and on Economic, Social and Cultural Rights, together with other important international declarations, protocols and conventions (these are listed in Appendix II). There are also important regional statements and national declarations of rights, usually enshrined in national constitutions or in Bills of Rights. All these statements can be important for social work practice, though they are not without their problems. The texts of these statements are now readily available from the Internet, the most useful site being that of the UN Human Rights website (www.unhchr.ch).

One problem is that, like any written text, these documents can become outdated. The Universal Declaration itself reads as somewhat dated (e.g. through the use of gendered language, which many would now see as against human rights principles), and the discursive nature of human rights means that by the time such a declaration is published and disseminated it will be under challenge.

A second problem is that these statements are drawn up and approved not by a participatory process but by an elite, and are then published as in the interests of all of humanity. The Universal Declaration has been criticised for the dominant role western interests had in its creation in 1948 (Chomsky 1998; Aziz 1999). And even though other declarations and protocols have been drawn up by people from diverse cultural backgrounds, the criticism of Chapter 8 remains important, namely that despite cultural diversity it is still the privileged of the world – politicians, academics, lawyers and leading human rights activists – who have taken on themselves the responsibility of defining the rights of the world's people, and thus the human rights discourse remains a privileged one. It is perhaps analogous to social workers acting 'in the best interests of' some vulnerable person or group; it is undoubtedly well intentioned, but the process can readily reinforce structures of disadvantage and oppression and is itself counter to human rights principles.

A third problem is that such conventions and protocols need to be understood as political documents to which governments may have acceded for reasons of image rather than necessarily because of any intention to follow the principles laid down in them. The articles of the Universal Declaration and many other human rights agreements are frequently ignored or violated by governments, and in many cases the formal mechanisms for enforcement are such that governments are effectively free to ignore them if they so choose. The Universal Declaration is, after all, a *declaration* of principle or intent rather than a firm undertaking or a legally binding contract.

Despite these evident problems, there are also some important ways in which these conventions can be useful for social workers, and therefore they should not be ignored. First, they do carry a strong moral force, which should not be underestimated. The Universal Declaration is a powerful and inspirational document, and simply to quote it as part of the advocacy for a particular policy position or as part of an activist campaign can have a strong impact. To demonstrate to a government, an agency board or a social work manager that they are acting counter to the Universal Declaration of Human Rights can be a powerful argument, quite apart from the legal impotence such a position may have in reality. It can also be useful at client or community level to discuss the issues involved in a particular problem in the context of charters, conventions and so on. For a client or community group to realise that the agency they are in conflict with may actually be violating the Universal Declaration of Human Rights may be enough to maintain energy for an ongoing struggle which otherwise might be seen as not worth the effort. There is no reason why discussion of human rights conventions with clients or communities should not be a regular part of a social worker's practice. Copies of the Universal Declaration could, for example, be prominently displayed on the wall of a community centre or in an agency waiting room.

In many instances it is also true that human rights treaties and conventions do have legal force, and this can be used in particular cases. Countries that have ratified the First Optional Protocol to the International Covenant on Civil and Political Rights have given their citizens the right to appeal to the UN Human Rights Commission if their human rights have been violated and they have not received redress from their government and the legal system of their country. National governments are then bound by treaty obligations to respect the rulings of the Commission. This can be used to assist particular cases where there has been demonstrable human rights abuse, and also to force governments to overturn laws which may contravene human rights principles. For example, in Australia it was as a result of a case being taken to the Commission that the Australian Government was able effectively to overturn state legislation that discriminated against gays and lesbians (HREOC 1996). It is important for social workers to know the availability of such mechanisms, which will vary from country to country – for example the government of a country that has not ratified the First Optional Protocol is not bound by the above obligations.

Some regional human rights treaties and conventions have more legal force, most especially those of the European Union, where national laws have been overturned on the grounds that they contravene European human rights standards (Neuwahl & Rosas 1995). Those in other regions of the world could study the European example and lobby their governments for the establishment of similarly strong regional human rights regimes elsewhere. However, there is usually more scope for legal challenge to legislation, or for case-based advocacy, through human rights statements at national level such as bills of rights and constitutions. This is simply because the national legal system has been in place for longer, and has more effective power, than the international legal system. Obviously the situation will vary from nation to nation, but it is an important area in which social workers should be well informed, and it is important for basic and continuing social work education programs to include material about the formal protection of the rights of citizens within the nation concerned, and the ways in which citizens either individually or in groups can take action if they feel these rights have been violated.

The link between rights and needs, as discussed in Chapter 5, is important in the deductive move from rights definition to practice. For example, for the right to shelter to become operationalised for practice, it is necessary to determine what housing 'needs' derive from that right in a particular context. A need is couched in the language of implementation; it stipulates what has to be done if a right is to be met, and so it is in need definition, that most characteristic social work activity, that the deductive process moves from principles to practice. The way in which this can be achieved, using a dialogical process that is itself consistent with human rights principles, is discussed in the next chapter.

Defining rights

Formal documents, of course, are only one aspect of the human rights discourse. If we are to take seriously the criticism that human rights definition has remained in the hands of the privileged, it is important in practice to look for ways in which there might be broader participation in the process of defining human rights. This means that while still working deductively, social workers can involve communities, groups and individual clients in a dialogue about human rights. This would mean engaging in a process of helping such groups to define human rights (in terms of what it means to be human and what all humans have a right to claim as their birthright) from their own perspective. In doing so, the social worker needs to be aware of the five definitional criteria for human rights as set out in Chapter 1 (pages 10–11); this is necessary in order to prevent the people concerned from infringing on the rights of others by their own definition of their rights (e.g. it means the worker cannot accept a group defining human rights in exclusionary or racist terms). But there can be great potential created for liberating practice by the worker framing human rights as something that people themselves can be involved in defining, rather than something they need to sit back and accept. This dialogue may of course make use of formal documents such as the Universal Declaration, but in an empowering sense so that people could be encouraged to think about what it says, what it doesn't say, and how from their perspective such a statement may need additions, deletions or amendments.

If such a dialogical approach has been taken to human rights definition, it becomes natural for the next step of the deductive process, namely moving from rights to needs and hence to action, also to take place in dialogue with the community, group or client. This makes the client an active partner in the process of need definition as described in Chapter 5, through reflection on what the human rights perspective implies in relation to the full range of social work practice options.

Inductive approaches to human rights practice

While the deductive approach starts with a construction of human rights and then sees how that can be applied in social work practice, the inductive approach does the reverse, starting rather with the grounded and 'real' world of practice, identifying issues, needs or problems, and then seeing what human rights issues lie behind them. While social workers will inevitably operate in both ways, it is probably true that the inductive is the more usual or dominant way in which practitioners will relate practice to human rights. Academics, writing from within a university environment rather than a practice environment, are more likely to think in the deductive mode. Hence there is a need for dialogue between practitioner and academic to maintain some level of balance between the two: to ensure that academics do not become so absorbed with principles that they forget the reality of practice, and that practitioners are not so immersed in the world of practice with its competing demands that academic principles are seen as a luxury rather than a necessity.

The essence of the inductive approach is that it starts with the immediate practice concern, which is usually framed in terms of a private trouble rather than a public issue (Mills 1970). Making the step to articulating this in human rights terms requires the acceptance of a political dimension of the problem (see Chapter 10) and seeing the personal problem in a structural framework. Thus if a person seeks social work assistance because she/he is unemployed, this needs to be framed in human rights terms, most obviously the right to meaningful and rewarding work. But there may be other rights involved as well: for an unemployed person from a racial or ethnic minority there may be issues of the right to be free from discrimination; if the person has a disability there may be another

set of discrimination rights; or it may be that the person's right to education has been denied and that this is a contributory factor to his/her
unemployment. At another level, the reason the person has no job may
be partly because local industry has been relocated in search of maximum
profits in the global marketplace, and the right of the individual and the
local community to have some say in larger economic and business decisions may also be an important issue. Competing claims of rights may also
be a concern and may be used as a framework for understanding why a
particular case or community issue is problematic. The example of child
welfare, with competing claims of parental rights and the 'best interests'
of the child, has been discussed in earlier chapters in this regard.

The same kind of approach can be used when working at community
level. The difficulties people may be having with mobility and access to
services raise the issue of public transport, which involves a number of
issues of rights: not just a right to mobility, but the rights that mobility
allows us to exercise, such as rights to education, rights to health services,
rights to exercise freedoms of speech and of assembly by attending community meetings. There is, to take just one instance, no effective right to
freedom of assembly if one is prevented from attending the assembly of
one's choice through lack of adequate, affordable and safe transport.
Lack of transport, therefore, can affect a number of human rights in a
community, and a community work process that can frame, for example,
a poor bus service as an issue of human rights can be energising and
empowering for local action. It provides a focus and a purpose for a campaign that goes well beyond the simple matter of improving a bus service.

The inductive approach means that the human rights questions are
not asked in the abstract (e.g. what are important human rights?) but are
focused and concrete (e.g. what rights issues does this specific situation
pose?). This makes it easier for there to be a dialogical approach involving worker and client(s), as it is usually easier to engage in a dialogue
where there is a specific situation in which the dialogue can be
grounded. This is the essence of Freire's approach to critical pedagogy
(1996), which will be discussed in the next chapter. The context makes
the human rights issue come alive and allows it to be defined in such a
way that it is directly relevant to the client's experience and opens up the
possibility of action and change (Fay 1975, 1987). This linking of dialogue with action is at the heart of the idea of praxis, involving an active
process of learning/theorising and acting/changing at the same time.

The inductive approach means that rather than relying on previously
determined human rights ideas, it is the definition of human rights that
itself emerges from praxis. Thus the process of social work becomes a
part of the discourse of human rights, and at a fundamental level social
work helps to articulate and define human rights. The particular value of

this is that it means the human rights discourse is informed by *praxis* rather than only by ideas and debate, and it becomes a discourse that is more firmly grounded and informed by people's struggles against oppression and disadvantage.

Conclusion

This chapter has identified some of the key issues in the construction of human rights for social work practice, and in the linking of the definition of rights with practice reality. This is commonly achieved through a combination of deductive and inductive approaches, the former relying on constructions of human rights (whether formalised or not) that inform practice, while the latter requires that the human rights issues inherent in the world of practice be identified and analysed. Such processes are a necessary prelude to the development of a human rights-based praxis, as explored in the next chapter.

CHAPTER 10

Achieving Human Rights through Social Work Practice

The previous chapters, in exploring various aspects of human rights and the implications of seeing social work as a human rights profession, have touched on many important practice issues in relation to social work. The issues are not new. Ethics, social control, the place of policy and advocacy, professionalism, the role of expertise, linking the personal and the political, cultural relativism, need definition, empowerment, and so on are all familiar and are frequently contested within social work. In the preceding chapters, however, they have arisen not out of a consideration of social work per se but rather out of a discussion of human rights and the possible implications of a human rights approach to practice. Various social work practice principles emerged from these discussions, and the purpose of this chapter is to bring these together in order to derive an overall picture of human rights-based social work. This will be done around three organising themes: *foundations, empowerment* and *contextual/universal issues.*

Foundations

Before moving to more directly practice-oriented aspects of social work, it is important to examine some other more 'theoretical' issues which are implied by the discussions of earlier chapters. These represent important foundations for human rights practice.

Praxis

The idea of 'praxis' (Freire 1996) is that theory and practice, or learning and doing, cannot be separated. It is through theory/reflection that we develop practice/action, and *at the same time* it is through practice/action that we develop theory/reflection. We learn by doing and we do by learning. Praxis is therefore about both knowledge and action; knowledge without action would be sterile, ungrounded and irrelevant, and action without knowledge is anti-intellectual, uninformed and usually dangerous. Social work, however, has frequently seen theory and practice as separate (Pease & Fook 1999), as is seen in lengthy and tortuous discussions about how the two can be linked; such discussions would be unnecessary in a truly praxis-based understanding of social work. The discussion of human rights in earlier chapters showed a clear and necessary link between theory and practice: to talk about human rights means to talk both theory and practice at the same time and to be constantly weighing each in terms of the other. This is one of the important contributions that social work can make; because of its grounding in the real world of day-to-day practice, it cannot afford theoretical formulations that are not similarly grounded in lived reality. A human rights perspective allows for, and indeed requires, such a praxis formulation. It is for that reason that this book has not attempted to separate theoretical exploration from discussion of practice; one can only be true to a praxis perspective by talking about the two together.

The praxis orientation also means that there can be no clear separation between social work education and social work practice. Social work education can only occur effectively if the student is able to ground her/his learning in practice and to develop both 'practice skills' and 'theoretical understanding' at the same time, as effectively the same process. And similarly, social work practice can only occur in an environment of ongoing learning that does not stop on graduation day. Social workers are constantly learning and reformulating their world-views and approaches to practice, as a direct consequence of their day-to-day work. They are formulating theories ('grounded theories' in research terminology; see Strauss & Corbin 1990) and acting as researcher/practitioners, not in the social engineering sense in which that term is sometimes used but in the sense of collaborative inquiry. How this is achieved will be discussed in later sections of this chapter.

Morality

Social work is an essentially moral activity, as it is based on values and on conceptions of right and wrong (though social workers will not often use these terms). Social workers make difficult moral judgements, which are often couched in terms of 'ethics' or 'values' but which require some form of moral reasoning. Hence it is necessary for social workers to have some capacity to engage with difficult moral dilemmas, to undertake some form of moral argument, and to make essentially moral decisions.

A human rights perspective provides a framework within which such moral reasoning and decision-making can take place. The discursive nature of human rights enables a social worker to move away from the traps of moral absolutism, where 'right' and 'wrong' are clearly spelled out in an unchangeable moral code, and to feel more comfortable in the less certain world of postmodernity. This does not mean, however, that such decision-making by social workers is not strong and robust. One of the characteristics of a human rights discourse is that the values of human rights are strongly and passionately felt, and framing values in terms of human rights provides a more powerful base for action than mere abstract 'armchair' moral reasoning. A human rights perspective also requires that a social worker not just make decisions in isolation purely on the basis of 'what seems right at the time' – this is the lonely existential decision of Bauman's postmodern ethics (Bauman 1993). Rather it requires that the worker be able to think through issues of morality, and more importantly be able to do so collaboratively with those with whom he/she has contact. The social worker is a moral agent, but because of the very nature of social work, not a lonely, isolated one. It is in a social worker's capacity to engage other actors in moral decision-making that the social worker's effectiveness as a human rights worker can be judged.

Passion

As suggested above, human rights-based social work is not simply a case of careful and sterile 'thinking through' of moral issues, in a disinterested academic way. Human rights are something to get passionate about, and indeed they are worth getting passionate about. Social work is driven not only by careful analysis (important and necessary though that is) but also by a passion to make the world a better place, an outrage at injustice and oppression, and a commitment to change. Human rights are important, and historically have been important enough for people to die for; they cannot be classified simply as an academic or philosophical problem. Social work that is based on human rights must thus find a place for the passion that inevitably goes with ideas of human rights. The idea therefore of a social worker as a detached professional 'intervening in systems' (Pincus & Minahan 1976; Compton & Galaway 1999) on the basis of research-generated knowledge is not enough. Social work need not apologise that it is driven by some of the noblest ideals of a common humanity; indeed it should pride itself on this heritage. Social workers need not feel guilty about feeling passionate about the cause of human rights, or outraged at the continued violation of human rights that is evident to them every day in their practice. The task for social workers is not to deny the passion and the rage but to channel them into effective action that makes a difference. It is often by maintaining their rage, and their vision of a better world, that social workers are able to keep working in oppressive and dehumanising structures.

Maintaining a passion is therefore an important part of human rights-based social work. But it is often too easy for the passion to fade, as the task seems just too hard and as the organisational demands of social work practice take over more of the worker's available energy. For this reason it is important for a social worker to remind her/himself of the reasons for choosing social work as a profession, and to find ways of maintaining a sense of vision, purpose and passion. Different workers will go about this in different ways, but it is often through the inspiration of the example of others that this can be achieved. The struggles of people such as Aung San Suu Kyi, Nelson Mandela, Vaclav Havel, Xanana Gusmao and Martin Luther King have served as a continuing inspiration for many people committed to social change, including many social workers. Such examples are compelling and powerful motivators, as is the work of poets, artists, writers, musicians and film-makers. For anyone concerned with human rights there are many such sources of inspiration, waiting to be tapped. But for social workers, in addition, there is the example of many of the people with whom they come into contact in the course of their day-to-day work: the parents who are struggling against all the odds in a severely disadvantaged environment to bring up their children with values of caring, sharing and social justice; the carers of people with disabilities – from young children with severe intellectual disability to elderly relatives with worsening dementia – who are sacrificing so much; the community activists who are committing all their spare time to make their local neighbourhood a safe, friendly and caring environment; the refugee family that has battled persecution in one country and persistent racism in another; the parents who work long hours for low wages to ensure a good education for their children. One of the privileges of being a social worker is that it brings one constantly into contact with people whose commitment, determination and self-sacrifice provide a daily lesson in human rights and their importance; from such people one can learn about human rights in a way that will never come simply from reading or academic discussions.

Ideology

The human rights perspective outlined in earlier chapters clearly has ideological implications. The notion of citizenship obligations, which goes alongside citizenship rights, implies a form of collectivism: we not only have rights we can claim and exercise, but we have an obligation to exercise those rights and to ensure that the rights of others are fully realised (Stapleton 1995). Thus there is an imperative to see oneself not as an isolated individual seeking to maximise personal gain, if necessary at the expense of others, but rather as someone who is in a relationship of interdependency with others, through a series of mutual obligations implied by the rights we hold in common as global citizens. A rugged and selfish individualism, the assumed foundation of orthodox economic theory and neo-liberal policies, is therefore incompatible with human rights. A human rights perspective implies at the very least a social democratic ideological position, if not some form of socialism. Human rights therefore, at least in the sense outlined in this book, are not politically neutral. It is true that a narrow interpretation of civil and political rights can be seen as compatible with individualism and laissez-faire economics, though even that limited commitment to human rights involves a level of state intervention which is incompatible with a pure free-market liberalism (Holmes & Sunstein 1999). However, once second-generation economic, social and cultural rights and third-generation collective rights are included in the definition, it becomes necessary for there to be a strong measure of public provision, which the free market has proved quite unable to provide in a comprehensive and equitable way. To adopt a human rights perspective (at least as described in this book) is thus to take a position that has certain ideological consequences. Human rights-based social work is therefore inevitably *political* social work, committing a social worker to an ideological position that incorporates at least some degree of collectivism and a strong role for the public sector, in whatever form this sector may take as a result of globalisation. It seems likely that, in time, at least some of the functions carried out by the state will move to either the global or the local level, but in either case a strong collectivist approach will be necessary if the full range of human rights is to be realised and achieved.

Many formulations of social work are still constructed within an apolitical context, with the assumption that social workers may occupy a full range of ideological positions, or indeed may have no articulated political position at all. A human rights perspective, however, specifically rejects this. It sees social work as being about enhancing human rights; as such it is about power relationships and is therefore inevitably political. Further, it to some extent determines what political positions are compatible with social work, and it identifies individualism and a pure reliance on the free market as being incompatible with human rights-based practice. Human rights workers are political workers, and human rights, in the broad sense, require a political commitment. Politics and ideological critique therefore need to be part and parcel of social work practice.

History

Because human rights are discursively constructed, and therefore change over time, it is important to have some understanding of the history of the struggle for human rights – not only in the west, it should be emphasised – and to place one's own human rights work into a historical context. In this sense, the move away from a positivist framing to a discursive understanding makes human rights more powerful; rights are not simply 'things' waiting to be discovered and measured, but rather are the result of ongoing historical struggles in which every social worker, in his/her role as human rights worker, plays a part. Human rights can therefore not be properly understood in a static, ahistorical sense. This suggests that the study of history is important for social workers, and from the discussion in earlier chapters such an assertion of the value of history can be further justified on four grounds.

First, a historical perspective is important for emphasising that things can and do change. Without a sense of history it is easy to think that the existing order is somehow 'natural' and immutable. It is easy for those concerned with progressive social change to become disheartened at a system of inequality and disadvantage that seems intractable, to accept the conservative argument that the way things are is the 'natural' order of things that cannot be altered, and hence to believe that the way people behave in the modern world is 'human nature' and therefore unchangeable. A historical perspective suggests otherwise. It recognises that many of the things commonly taken for granted are of recent historical origin, and that in the past there have been very different ways of organising society, when people behaved very differently towards each other. A historical perspective also shows that what may seem impossible today can become feasible tomorrow; the examples of people such as Nelson Mandela (1994) and Vaclav Havel (1991, 1992), who dared to envision a different future at a time when no such future seemed 'realistically' possible, are a clear example of the need to think beyond the limits of the present. Indeed it can be suggested that the existing global social, economic, political and ecological order is so blatantly unsustainable that the one thing of which we *can* be certain is that the future will not be a simple extension of the present. Seeing ourselves as in an ongoing process of historical change is much more empowering than seeing ourselves trapped in an ahistorical present, and the study of history can only help in this regard.

Second, the study of history can be seen as the study of the struggle for human rights, which gives an extra immediacy to the human rights issues of the present. It was suggested in Chapter 6 that lack of a historical understanding can leave people uncommitted to exercising the human rights for which people in previous generations fought and died; the right to vote, the right to form a trade union and the right to education were cited as three examples of cases where people often forgo their rights, with apparent disregard for, or ignorance of, the struggles of previous generations to establish those rights. The history of the human rights movement, including struggles for the right to vote, the right to form a union, women's rights, the right to political self-determination, the right to education, the right to economic development and the right to a clean environment, is an important part of our heritage, whatever our national or cultural background. It is a very important history for any social worker who identifies as a human rights worker, and it can thus be seen as a central component of social work education.

The third reason a study of history is important relates to the need to deconstruct the western Enlightenment tradition within which the human rights discourse was framed and which, as was pointed out in Chapter 4, has so limited the understanding of human rights and has led to the criticism of a human rights discourse as being a discourse of western domination. One of the key elements of the Enlightenment was the view of history as necessarily progressive, moving towards greater 'enlightenment', each era being somehow superior to those that have gone before. The assumption is that through the achievements of western science, art, philosophy, industry, technology and military adventures, the west has shown itself as superior or more 'advanced' than other cultures and traditions, and this has provided the rationale for the imposition of western cultural values and practices on the rest of the world (Said 1993, 1995). This view is deeply embedded in the consciousness not only of the west but of many other cultures, where people have been socialised into thinking that the more 'advanced' societies of the west have more to offer in terms of education, science, art, music, philosophy, technology. Such a view, it has been argued, severely limits the understanding of human rights (Touraine 1995) and has been responsible for the narrow emphasis on civil and political rights and the resultant critique of human rights being little more than a colonialist discourse of western domination. The study of history is one way in which such cultural blindness can be overcome, through a study of the 'history of ideas' that moves beyond the boundaries of the western intellectual tradition and that incorporates a history of western imperialism and colonialism and the struggles against it.

The fourth reason for the importance of history is the extension of the idea of human rights to issues of intergenerational justice, as discussed in Chapter 1. If the present generation is seen as being responsible for addressing human rights violations in the past (e.g. the 'stolen generations' of Indigenous People), and preventing human rights abuse of future generations (e.g. through protection of the environment and conservation of resources), it is necessary to include a historical perspective in human rights work. Social work with any individual, family or community must include an understanding of their history, including if necessary (and with Indigenous People in particular it is absolutely essential) a history extending back several generations, so that human rights issues can be adequately addressed in their historical context.

The study of history, therefore, can be seen as of central importance to an understanding of human rights. Human rights must be historically understood and contextualised, and ahistorical practice can itself be seen as a continuation of human rights abuse by not acknowledging the importance of historical patterns of human rights violations.

Structural disadvantage

Understanding why human rights are not defined, realised or protected for many people requires an analysis of structural oppression or disadvantage. This must be at the basis of all human rights-based social work. Individual accounts of disadvantage, though an important part of social workers' understandings of particular people and their problems, are insufficient to explain, for example, why many people are in poverty, why women remain disadvantaged in both the public and the private spheres, why women and children remain the main victims of violence, why Indigenous People continue to suffer massive disadvantage and discrimination, why there are some rich countries and some poor countries (significantly affecting the life chances of their citizens), why the colour of one's skin still determines how one is treated, why globalisation is affecting everybody (but advantaging some and disadvantaging others), and so on. It is necessary to have strong analyses of oppression on the basis of class, race, gender, sexuality, nationality, disability, culture and age. The people with whom social workers work are victims of such oppressions, however much they may or may not be aware of these forces, and we cannot hope to understand, let alone help, them without a sound understanding of the nature and pervasiveness of structures of oppression and disadvantage (Mullaly 1997).

It is these oppressive structures that serve to deny many people basic human rights, and so if social workers are human rights workers, their practice must address these issues of structural disadvantage. Indeed a practice that does not specifically incorporate structural analyses of oppression is most likely, unintentionally, to reinforce oppressive structures. Just as the activism of many earlier Marxists served to reinforce the oppression of women because these Marxists were blind to a gender analysis, and conversely the activism of liberal feminists has, by ignoring a class analysis, done little to address the needs of working-class women, so any social work practice that does not take due account of all dimensions of structural oppression will only serve to reinforce some oppressive structures while addressing others. An important contemporary example is the tendency for many social activists in wealthier nations to fight for stronger economic development within their own countries (often using a rhetoric of opposition to globalisation) so that standards of living can be raised and human rights protected, while the result of such activism is the even greater exploitation of people in poorer countries, since the desired economic development is achieved at the cost of human rights elsewhere, and of increasing global inequalities.

All social work must therefore incorporate multidimensional analyses of structural disadvantage, and this must be at the forefront of social work thinking, at whatever level the social worker is practising. Structural inequality and oppression are the context within which social workers practise, and if they do not deliberately seek to be part of the solution, their practice will inevitably become part of the problem.

Holism

The deconstruction of the western view of human rights requires a rejection of the restricted linear thinking that is characteristic of the western Enlightenment view of progress and the embracing of a more holistic understanding. This is reflected in the idea of human rights implying, and being implied by, citizen obligations, and in the need to contextualise the articulation of human rights through the definition of human needs; these can only properly be understood in a more ecological, holistic framework. Holism is not new for social workers, and it is important in a number of formulations of social work practice (e.g. in the ecological model of Germaine [1991]). But moving beyond linear thinking is not easy for a social worker educated within the western tradition because this tradition has consistently emphasised linear causal relationships, following a single line of inquiry, and research that 'discovers more and more about less and less' by studying a small part of the overall picture instead of trying to understand how all the different components interact and contribute to a whole that is 'greater than the sum of its parts'. Social work actually presents opportunities to do this; for example in trying to understand a family, a community or an organisation, social workers will usually try to see it as a complex whole rather than split it up into its constituent parts and study them in detail.

One important source of a more holistic and systemic paradigm, from within the western context, has been the Green movement (Goodin 1992; Dobson 1995; Carter 1999; Torgerson 1999). This has emphasised the essential interconnectedness of everything as part of an ecological approach and has shown how the pursuit of purely linear thinking can lead to ecological disaster. The fact that the Green movement has a strong basis in the physical sciences has lent holism an extra degree of scientific respectability, and writing from within the Green movement over the last decade represents a significant challenge to traditional western ways of thinking. This is also important for social workers: the environmental movement has in many ways been pursuing similar ends (e.g. the building of sustainable communities), and with the inclusion of third-generation environmental rights within the field of human rights, the environment becomes a legitimate, and indeed important, concern for social workers.

The other source of a more holistic and systemic world-view is to be found in non-western intellectual traditions, such as Buddhist or Confucian traditions (De Bary & Weiming 1998; Hershock 2000), which have emphasised harmony and balance (naturally systemic) rather than growth and progress (naturally linear). Indigenous People have also emphasised oneness with the natural world and the importance of wholeness and interconnection. Indeed a good case can be made that the western tradition of linear thinking is really the deviant tradition and is out of line with the intellectual norms of other cultural traditions. For a western social worker to accept such a view requires a modesty and a humility not generally compatible with western confidence and arrogance. But such traditions are important for progressive social work, and the contributions to social work that are now being made from various indigenous traditions in particular represent some of the most exciting developments in the social work profession.

Postmodernism and post-structuralism

One of the themes in the preceding chapters was the inadequacy of a purely modernist account of human rights and hence of human rights-based social work. A postmodern understanding is therefore important for social workers, and as I have argued elsewhere (Ife 1997b, 1999), is an essential component of critical social work practice. Postmodernism helps social work to move away from the single narrative and the obsession with one 'right' answer for any problem, towards a view that values multiple voices and allows for the construction of different meanings and multiple realities. As suggested in Chapter 7, there is danger in an extreme postmodernism, and indeed there are inevitably different views of what postmodernism means for social work (Pease & Fook 1999). The point of view elaborated below suggests that postmodernism, while a necessary component of human rights-based social work, is not sufficient by itself but needs to be located within an overall critical paradigm that accepts and incorporates analyses of oppression and disadvantage.

The insistence throughout this book on human rights being discursively constructed, and the emphasis on the discourses of human rights as changing discourses of power, suggest that a post-structuralist perspective, drawing on the work of Foucault (1970, 1972, 1986, 1991), underlies much of the approach taken in this book (Parton & O'Byrne 2000). Foucault's work on discourses of power and Habermas' view of discursive rationality (Habermas 1984) are therefore important reference points for anyone interested in developing a strong human rights-based social work practice. The importance of such approaches to social and political theory for the development of a conceptually sound social work is not always recognised in social work education programs, whether at the level of entry to the profession or as part of continuing professional education. This is partly because of the difficulty many social workers find in accessing these writers, and one of the contradictions of much of this literature is that while it is concerned with liberation and transformation it remains inaccessible to many of the people who might most benefit from such an agenda.

An important role for social workers is to take many of the ideas contained in such literature and help to make them accessible to a wider audience, through an empowerment-based practice as outlined below. Empowerment is not simply enabling people to take action to have their needs met; it is also about making accessible the theoretical basis of an analysis of power, discourse and narrative, so that social theory can become useful as a way of helping people to contextualise their own situation and develop strategies to bring about change (Clegg 1989). Social work, therefore, requires intellectual effort. It is not simply a case of learning how to do it and then applying principles in a mechanistic manner, nor is it a case of rejecting theory as 'not part of the real world' and therefore adopting an atheoretical (and anti-intellectual) stance. Rather, it requires a constant engagement with both the intellectual and the practical, testing each against the other in a constant process of action/reflection, or praxis.

Empowerment

Following the consideration of a number of foundational or theoretical issues, it is now necessary to move to issues of praxis, which can be discussed around the idea of empowerment. This has been inherent in much that has been discussed so far in this and earlier chapters. While space does not allow a detailed examination of the concept of empowerment, it is worth noting that it has been of central concern to social workers for some considerable time (Benn 1981; Rees 1991). Yet it is also a word that has been overused and is in danger of losing any substantive meaning. Despite this, the idea of empowerment remains attractive to social workers, and for good reason: the simple idea of enabling the powerless to achieve more power is, for many social workers, exactly what their practice is all about. And human rights-based practice, as described thus far, implies a strong element of empowerment; ideas of enabling people to define their rights and to act in order to have them realised and protected are the very essence of empowerment.

It makes no sense to talk about empowerment without some under-standing of the nature of power and the different theoretical and politi-cal perspectives on power, including pluralist, elitist, structural and post-structural accounts (Clegg 1989). In the approach to social work described here, the post-structural account, where power is located within discourse, and relationships of power are constantly being constructed and reconstructed within an ongoing and changing discourse, has been of particular importance. However, structural accounts of power, under-stood in terms of structural disadvantage on the basis of class, race, gen-der and so on, are equally important, and a social work understanding of power (from which empowerment practice must derive) needs to incor-porate both the structural and the post-structural perspectives (Healy 2000). There are a number of aspects to empowerment-based practice inherent in the human rights approach, and these are outlined below.

Dialogical praxis

The idea of dialogical praxis draws particularly on the work of Paulo Freire (1972, 1985, 1996) and others who have sought ways to put his work into practice (McLaren & Leonard 1993; McLaren & Lankshear 1994). A key element of dialogical praxis is 'conscientisation', which can be described as the raising of consciousness through dialogue linking the personal and the political, in such a way that it opens up possibilities for action as people become more aware of the structures and the discourses that define and perpetuate oppression. This is consistent with the critical social science paradigm as described by Brian Fay (1975, 1987). However, such an approach to social science, and the very use of the idea of consciousness-raising, can be itself patronising and oppressive. It can easily sound as if the worker arrogantly assumes that he/she has superior consciousness and seeks to impose this consciousness on the people with whom she/he is working. For this reason, the idea of *dialogue* is crucial. This requires that both the worker and those with whom she/he is working are seen as hav-ing equivalent wisdom and expertise, rather than the more conventional privileging of professional expertise over the expertise of others. While it is true that the worker will have specialised knowledge and skills which the client may not, it is equally true that the client has a range of knowledge, skills and expertise that the worker does not, namely the expertise that comes from lived experience and the survival skills developed out of neces-sity. The notion of dialogical praxis requires that both worker and client engage in praxis (i.e. both knowledge/theory-building and action) together. Each learns from the other in a relationship of shared knowledge and expertise which does not privilege one above the other. And as a result of that sharing of expertise, they then act together towards the goal of achieving human rights. This is a form of practice that aims to achieve human rights and that also respects and affirms human rights within the actual methodology that is employed (Narayan 2000).

To engage in dialogical praxis, a social worker has to reject many of the trappings of professionalism, including the idea of professional 'status' as somehow implying privilege, and the idea that knowledge acquired through professional education is somehow superior to knowledge acquired through life experience (Freire 1996). This is not to devalue professionally acquired knowledge – it is important and has a vital role to play in dialogical praxis – but rather to refuse to privilege such knowledge above other forms of human knowledge and understanding, in which the client may well be much more 'qualified' than the worker.

Given this, the 'worker' and the 'client' need to establish a dialogue where the goal is for each to share and learn from each other's experience. To do this the worker needs to be able to establish empathy and rapport – an important part of the traditional 'social work interview' (Kadushin & Kadushin 1997) – but beyond this the idea of 'dialogue' and the idea of 'interview' are very different. An interview is deliberately designed as an interaction of unequal power, with one person 'doing' the interview while the other is 'interviewed'. In a dialogue, however, the aim is for an equal exchange, with each party learning from the other. Hence the social worker has to be able to give up the need to be (or to be seen to be) in control, and instead must allow the interaction to develop in a way that is determined by both parties. Obviously the social worker, because of employment and organisational constraints, will have certain interests in the dialogue achieving certain ends. But this does not mean the social worker should seek to dominate or control; it should be just as obvious that the client also has certain interests in the outcome of the dialogue, and these are ultimately more important than the interests of the social worker, since the client's needs are the reason for social work in the first place.

As well as equality within the dialogical relationship (which can be reframed as respecting each other's human rights), there is a need to work towards shared understandings, so that the relationship is a genuinely educational one for both worker and client. This means a concentration on communication, and a social worker's interpersonal skills are therefore crucial in the facilitation of dialogical praxis. But simply reaching shared understandings is not enough. It is also necessary to work towards action, since one of the important characteristics of human rights is that they must be not merely understood and defined but also realised. Social work practice is about action and change, and hence a social science that only leads to communication and understanding, while necessary, is not sufficient. It is for this reason that much social theory, which is strong on analysis but weak on action, can be frustratingly limiting for social workers, and hence the emphasis needs to be not on dialogue alone but on *dialogical praxis*. Ultimately social work leads to action, taken by worker and client working together in partnership, each having benefited from the other's experience and wisdom. True, the worker and the client will often have different roles in that action – there are some things the client can do that the worker cannot, and vice versa – but they will be acting as part of a joint undertaking arising out of their shared wisdom and dialogue, and each can have her/his humanity enhanced as a consequence. And the goal of that shared action is, ultimately, the enhancement and protection of human rights.

The above discussion has used the traditional terms 'worker' and 'client' to illustrate the nature of dialogical praxis within a direct-service 'casework' form of practice, but it applies equally in working with families, groups, organisations or communities. The idea of shared expertise, mutual learning, not privileging professional knowledge over life experience, dialogue so all can learn, and joint action towards human rights is applicable to all social work settings except on those occasions where a social worker is required to act 'in the best interests' of a dependent person in order to safeguard his/her human rights (see Chapter 3). A human rights perspective, however, warns such a social worker that to 'act in the best interests of' another person can easily become itself a human rights violation, and that such social work must be undertaken only with a sense of deep unease and moral questioning.

The other occasion when it may seem that dialogical praxis is impossible is when the organisational context is such that the client is not free to engage in such a relationship with a social worker, for example when the client is a prisoner or a person on probation, and the social worker represents the 'authority of society' (Barber 1991; Rooney 1992). Here, however, it is imperative for a social worker to ask whether it is truly impossible to develop a dialogical praxis relationship, at least to some degree. If it is indeed impossible, then one can argue that the client's human rights are actually being denied or violated. In this case, the task for a human rights-based social work is clear: not to collude with demonstrably oppressive structures and practices but to work towards their reform as a matter of human rights.

Participatory democracy

A recurring theme throughout the earlier chapters has been the idea that a society that respects and realises human rights is a participatory society. This is partly because the discursive nature of human rights means that it is necessary for all sections of the global society to be heard in shaping the discourse of human rights, not merely the voices of academics, lawyers, politicians and activists. But it is also because of the idea of citizenship rights implying citizenship obligations, in the sense described in Chapter 6: the obligation for people to exercise their rights as citizens in a strong, active society, and the obligation to create the conditions in which others are able to do the same.

Therefore social work that is based on the idea of human rights must aim to maximise citizen participation in all aspects of life. This can be done at one level by working with individuals: encouraging community participation by valuing the contribution people can make, maximising their opportunities to do so, and facilitating participation using a whole range of skills that are familiar to community workers. But it is not only in traditional community work that social workers have the opportunity to encourage participation. Social workers working individually with clients also have many opportunities to do so, for example by putting people in touch with action groups, by simply bringing together groups of people with a common problem, by talking with people about how they might actually be able to make a difference, or by encouraging them to become part of some program, action or organisation.

This, however, is only one side of encouraging participation. To see the lack of citizen participation as a result of people's reluctance to become involved and to work on 'motivating' them is simply to individualise the problem and to blame the victim. It is necessary to understand the lack of participation as being a result of structures and processes that militate against participation and that encourage a society of passive individual consumerism (Beck 1997; Bauman 1999). Such structures and processes can thus be seen as working against the establishment and realisation of human rights because they prevent the formation of a healthy participatory society. Human rights-based social work must therefore seek ways to confront these structural barriers and change or reform them. This again has been a recurring agenda within social work, through social work's concern for institutional change and reform, policy advocacy and social activism.

Ideas of participation, and of participatory democracy, are of course contested, and this has always been a difficult and contradictory area of practice for social workers (Clark 2000). There is no space here to discuss all the dilemmas and contradictions of participation and of ideas of democracy; what is important in the present context is to identify it as a significant location for social work practice and for continued struggle by social workers to practise in such a way that honours these ideals and therefore furthers the cause of human rights.

Anti-colonialist practice

One of the main criticisms of the western domination of the human rights discourse, and its association with Enlightenment thinking, has been that human rights thus constructed have been used to reinforce colonialism and the continued colonising of the non-western world by western economic, political and cultural norms. This was discussed in Chapter 4, where it was shown how a reconstruction of human rights using the three generations, and an understanding of the discursive nature of human rights, can to some extent overcome some of these difficulties. But this reframing is not of itself sufficient to overcome the problems of western colonialism in social work, and colonialist practice remains a significant problem. In this context, colonialist practice implies any form of practice that assumes the practitioner is coming from a position of superiority, where the world-view of the practitioner is thereby imposed on others, and where practice serves to promote the interests and needs of the practitioner rather than those with whom the practitioner is working. Colonialism in social work can be subtle and insidious, and many practitioners are not aware of the colonialist implications of their practice. Other groups, however, are well aware of such colonialism; this is especially the case with Indigenous People, who have clearly pointed out the way in which many conventional practices of professions like social work have effectively colonised and disempowered Indigenous People and their communities. Similarly, people with disabilities, people from cultural, ethnic and racial minorities, and almost any other 'client group' have found their genuine lived experiences 'colonised' and devalued by mainstream professional practice (whether of social workers or others). The colonising effect of mainstream social work has been seen historically in the often quite inappropriate imposition of social work formulations from the USA and UK in other cultural and national contexts, denying the validity of the local experience (Healy et al. 1986). From this point of view the lack of awareness by social workers of the processes and experience of colonialism (Said 1993, 1995) is a major weakness in most social work education. Social workers who are concerned with practising from a human rights perspective need therefore to work consciously to counter the effects of colonialism, and not to practise from a colonialist position.

A key element in anti-colonialist practice is to listen particularly to the voices of the most oppressed victims of colonialism, namely Indigenous

People. Precisely because of their experience of colonisation, Indigenous People are in an especially important position to argue the critique of colonialism and to articulate alternatives based on forms of wisdom and knowledge that western colonialism has both devalued and suppressed (Knudston & Suzuki 1992). For this reason the voices of Indigenous People must be an important part of the education (both basic and ongoing) of every social worker, as it is only by listening to the stories and the wisdom of Indigenous People that non-indigenous social workers can begin to understand the enormous damage that has been (and continues to be) done by colonialist practice, and the subtle ways in which colonialism can influence the most well-intentioned social work. Further, an important part of social work practice must be to make sure that the voices of Indigenous People are validated and heard not only in human rights and social work discourse but in the broader society, so that the issue of colonialism remains firmly on the public agenda (Hazlehurst 1995). This is important not only in societies where there are significant indigenous populations but in all societies, since with globalisation the continuing colonisation of Indigenous Peoples crosses national boundaries and implicates the global economic and political system in some of the most devastating cases of human rights violation.

Feminism

Another key element in human rights-based practice, as discussed in Chapter 3, is feminism. A structural or post-structural feminism is a necessary component of the critique of the dominating and oppressive patriarchal structures that deny human rights and yet are so much part of the organisations and the societies in which social workers practise. Patriarchy represents a major human rights abuse, across all three generations of human rights, and so challenging patriarchal structures and processes must be a significant component of social work practice. Hence a social work informed by feminism is not an optional extra only for self-declared feminists or for social workers working with women; it must be a central component of all social work. Such feminism helps to challenge some of the assumptions behind social policies and practices and points to social work practice that is based on more inclusive, holistic, non-violent and consensus principles.

Feminism is thus an essential component of social work education and praxis, if social work is to be based on a human rights perspective. A social worker should therefore ensure that a feminist analysis is part of the process of assessment and analysis (undertaken in partnership with the client as part of dialogical praxis), and that feminist forms of practice, challenging patriarchal structures and processes, are applied in all social work settings. This should in any case be natural for social workers; social work and feminism have a common concern with linking the personal and the political – making the personal political, and the political personal – and hence social work's incorporation of feminism is both natural and inevitable (Van Den Bergh & Cooper 1986; Dominelli & McLeod 1989; Lee 1994).

The above paragraphs have outlined the case for including feminism as an essential part of social work, quite apart from any acknowledgement of gender and the importance of working with women and men around issues of gender oppression. For obvious reasons, this is another important justification for an incorporation of feminism into social work and only adds to the strength of the argument that human rights-based social work must be informed by feminism. As pointed out earlier in this chapter, however, it is important that the incorporation of feminism in this way should not diminish the importance given to other dimensions of oppression, such as class and race. Discussion of whether any of these dimensions of structural oppression is more 'fundamental' than the others is both complicated and counter-productive, and can lead to a dangerous fundamentalism. A much more useful and holistic way to think about it is to see all of them as centrally important and to realise that each can serve to reinforce and compound the effects of the others.

Non-violence

Much of the preceding discussion can also be understood in terms of the principle of non-violence. Non-violence rests on a rejection of the distinction between means and ends, and a refusal to accept that violent means can be justified in order to meet non-violent ends. The principle of non-violence is that means and ends cannot be separated in this way, and that to use violent means to reach non-violent ends will corrupt the ends and will not achieve the desired outcome (Fay 1975). The idea of violence in this context extends beyond the simple idea of physical violence to include structures of violence, and indeed it sees the denial of human rights as being a form of violence. The education system, for example, can be seen as a violent system, even if no physical violence is used, if it is seen to deny people equal access, to dehumanise those involved in it, to restrict rather than open up opportunities, or to reinforce competition and aggression.

Gandhi, the best-known advocate and practitioner of non-violence, sought always to value the humanity of those who opposed him, to allow them to exit from a conflict situation with their dignity intact, to be inclusive rather than exclusive, and to use methods which were non-violent in the broadest sense of the term (Gandhi 1964). This involved opposing ideas rather than people, respecting the human rights of his opponents, and refusing to react to violence with violence; in that way he sought to break the cycle of violence and to move towards non-violent inclusive solutions. The theory of non-violence is that such solutions are likely to last and be sustainable in a way that solutions reached through violence can never be.

Non-violence, understood in this sense, might be seen as another way of framing the human rights perspective advocated throughout this book. It certainly involves an absolute respect for the human rights of others, including those with whom one may be in conflict. It involves, above all, the intrinsic valuing of other human beings, and this is inherent in a praxis founded on human rights. Non-violence has had an important impact on some aspects of social work, most notably community develop-ment through the work of Indian community workers who have been influenced by the Gandhian tradition (Gaikwad 1981). Its application across all aspects of social work, however, is obviously both desirable and necessary from the point of view of a human rights perspective.

In order to practise non-violence, a social worker needs to be aware of structures and processes that can be described as violent and must pre-vent her/his praxis being appropriated by them, as well as seeking to confront those violent structures and processes to establish non-violent alternatives. This can apply across the full range of social work, whether dealing with violent individuals, violence in families, violence in organi-sations, violence in communities, or the valuing and perpetuating of vio-lent 'solutions' to social problems. Challenging such violence is an important aspect of social work and of human rights praxis.

Needs

The definition of need as the way in which human rights are often con-textualised was discussed at some length in Chapter 5, where the idea of social workers exercising power by assuming the right to define needs for others was seen as counter to human rights principles. One of the impor-tant aspects of human rights-based practice identified there was to allow, and indeed facilitate, people being able to define their own needs within a context of dialogical praxis that is a result of genuine dialogue drawing on the expertise of both the social worker and the people directly affected. Human rights are implicit in the definition of needs, and one of the problems with a discourse of human needs is that the human rights that lie behind assertions of need remain hidden.

The definition of needs is therefore a central component of human rights-based social work. Social workers, especially when undertaking 'need assessments', should be able to identify the human rights implicit in any statement of need and should seek to make those rights explicit so they can be openly acknowledged and if necessary contested and debated.

Social workers should also be ready to take a long, hard look at the rights implications whenever anybody (client, colleague, supervisor, manager or community member) uses the word 'need'. But above all, social workers should be working to find ways whereby people can have a genuine role in the definition of their own needs, in the appreciation of the rights that lie behind them, and in determining what action is required so that those needs can best be met. Power over definition of need is one of the most important aspects of human rights practice, since any practice that does not allow people to exercise such power is inevitably a denial of their human rights. Need definition may be seen in the literature as essentially a technical activity, with its own methods (McKillip 1987), but from a human rights perspective it is also a moral activity and has to be undertaken as such.

Research

Research has long been an important part of social work, and social work research has encompassed a wide variety of designs and methodologies: assessing needs, evaluating practice, documenting the inadequacies of the welfare state, collecting data about social problems, seeking to understand the experiences of the people with whom social workers work, exploring the dilemmas and contradictions of practice, and so on (Fook 1996). From a human rights perspective, social work research needs to address a human rights agenda, and this can involve a number of different research approaches:

- specifically identifying individuals and groups whose rights have been violated or denied
- documenting the nature and extent of human rights abuses
- providing information for people to be able to articulate the need for various human rights to be met
- providing a mechanism for the voices of the disadvantaged (i.e. those whose human rights have been denied) to be heard
- evaluating policies and programs in terms of their adequacy in meeting human rights.

All the above imply that the research process is oriented towards empowerment in human rights terms. It cannot therefore be neutral, positivist, value-free research, but rather research with a clearly articulated value position. It is aimed at some form of empowerment, and at the realisation and protection of human rights (Fisher & Karger 1997). Within that overall perspective, however, different designs and methodologies will be appropriate, depending on the specific issue being researched. At times, for example, empirical research can be particularly important in documenting the extent of human rights abuses for all three generations. More qualitative methodologies, aimed at providing a space for people to tell their stories, can also be important in furthering the cause of human rights.

One of the important aspects of human rights-oriented research is that it should, where possible, include the disadvantaged in the design, implementation, interpretation and presentation of the research. Social research can often simply reinforce power differentials by being something that is carried out by 'researchers' *on* 'subjects', so that the researcher can gain new knowledge (and credit, prestige, career advancement), while the benefit to the researched may be marginal (Kirby & McKenna 1989). The researched are seen as passive providers of data, and the researcher maintains a monopoly on the collection, analysis and presentation of the 'knowledge' derived from the research process. Such research, needless to say, is itself counter to human rights principles and does little to further the cause of human rights. Thus social workers who are researching from a human rights perspective need to be paying attention to models of research that challenge this orthodoxy in research methodology. There are many such approaches, to be found in feminist methodology, collaborative inquiry, participatory action research, grounded theory research, and so on (Smith et al. 1997). In recent years such methodologies have been of particular interest to social workers, and their potential to further the cause of human rights is significant. The same means–ends position, discussed above in relation to non-violence, applies also to research: research that aims to further the cause of human rights must itself respect human rights principles in its own methodologies.

Contextual/universal issues

A further set of praxis principles can be grouped under the heading of contextual/universal issues, as they deal with contextual/universal dualisms in various forms. The need to break down, transcend or cross those dualisms has been a recurring theme in earlier chapters, and these issues must now be considered together as important principles of social work practice. Human rights are, by their very nature, universal, and yet the era of postmodernity is seeing the increasing fragmentation and localisation of multiple narratives and an increasing emphasis on context and relativism. Confronting such universal/contextual dualisms is therefore a major challenge for human rights-based social work.

The personal and the political

The link between the personal and the political is central to social work: understanding the personal in terms of the political, understanding the political in terms of the personal, and acting to bring about change at both levels (Van Den Bergh & Cooper 1986; Dominelli & McLeod 1989; Fook 1993). This is particularly important within a human rights framework since human rights also need to be understood as both personal and political. They are personal because they affect personal well-being, security, survival, and self-actualisation, representing as they do a series of statements on what it means to be human. And they are political because human rights are about power and its distribution, about who has and should have the rights to exercise power, and in what circumstances. Human rights are therefore by their very nature both personal and political. They must be understood in both contexts, and one can only be an effective human rights worker if one can work with both the personal and the political. Because this link is central to social work, social workers are well equipped to be human rights workers. But if they are to fill that role, their praxis must constantly maintain both the personal and the political focuses. More significantly, social workers need to be able to link the two, insisting that each can only be fully understood in terms of the other. Human rights provide a solid foundation for such a link. This link is one of the most problematic for a society entering the era of postmodernity (Bauman 1999), and hence it is a very significant role for social workers to play.

In practice, this means that social workers must always be articulating the political aspects of the personal and the personal aspects of the political. The person who is unemployed, for example, must be understood both at the personal level of the implications for self-esteem and for income security and also at the political level of the reasons for high unemployment, the structure of the labour market, education and training opportunities, workplace relations, labour commodification, and so on. The human rights involved in such a case can be understood in terms of the individual's rights to meaningful work, to earn an income, to self-esteem, to social security, to participation in the economy. There may also, in particular cases of unemployment, be other rights in relation to freedom from discrimination on the basis of age, sex, race, disability, sexuality, religion. All these 'personal' rights have their political implications in terms of the obligations on the state and other actors to meet those rights: to provide work opportunities, to ensure adequate minimum wages, to prevent discrimination, and so on. To work for human rights requires that a social worker work both with the individual to ensure that his/her rights are adequately met and protected, and also with the institutions of the state and the labour market to ensure that the political obligations implied by human rights are adequately met. In doing so, it is inevitable that a social worker will seek to help the individual to see her/his rights in a political context, and to assist the structures of the state and private sector actors to see their actions in light of the impact on people's human rights and their obligation to meet and uphold those rights.

The linking of the personal and the political is itself a radical act, as it flies in the face of the dominant social and political order which seeks to divide the two, to see people's personal lives and concerns as 'no concern of the state', and to see politics as something that is engaged in only by a minority of people who are politically active, and which need not be the concern of the majority. Feminism has for a long time used the idea that the personal is political as a way to challenge this dominant ideology, through its questioning of patriarchy and through its framing of patriarchy as being responsible for the separation of the political from the personal. The radical, and some would say dangerous, act of linking the personal and the political is therefore not undertaken lightly. Neither is it a simple matter since it will involve social workers coming up against many vested interests and many structures and discourses of power. But this is a crucial arena for social work struggle, whether through the actions of individual social workers or through social workers working collectively through organised groups, unions or professional associations.

The private and the public

As was pointed out in Chapter 3, the traditional western understanding of human rights has concentrated on civil and political rights in the public sphere and has tended to overlook the human rights abuses, particularly of women and children, in the private or domestic sphere. By contrast, social work has often tended to define its primary activities as in the private or domestic sphere; it has been more concerned with domestic violence, child abuse and similar issues than it has with the more public face of civil and political human rights. This is perhaps why social work has not readily identified itself as a human rights profession, and why social workers have tended to identify a concern for human rights within their role as 'concerned citizen' rather than their role as professional social worker. But the approach to human rights described in earlier chapters requires that human rights be extended to cover the private domestic sphere, and similarly the concern discussed above that social work be about both the personal and the political brings the human rights and the social work discourses together and emphasises the important role social work can play in human rights, as well as the important position human rights can occupy in social work.

The practice implications of the linking of the private and the public are similar to those of linking the personal and the political. It is important that social workers insist on an understanding of human rights that extends to the private as well as the public arena, and that they seek to

break down the private/public dichotomy which has effectively prevented the pursuit of human rights in the private sphere, because it is
seen as 'no business of the state'. Indeed the construction of the public
and the private has been important in divorcing many areas of social policy from the realm of public debate, and also in marginalising the concerns of women and children as 'not really counting' in the forums that
are considered 'really important'. Breaking down this dualism, in dialogical partnership with those most affected, is therefore an important
task for social workers concerned for human rights.

Cultural relativism

Issues of cultural relativism and human rights have been addressed in
some detail in Chapter 4 and so need not be revisited at length here.
There are, however, very important implications for practice. For social
workers who are confronted with cultural practices that they feel contravene human rights, this is a very real and immediate practice concern.
The norms of cultural groups around issues of women's role, men's power
and authority, the raising of children, bodily mutilation, care of the aged,
gay and lesbian issues, education for girls, child labour, corporal punishment, distribution of labour within the family, and so on can all confront
the human rights values of a social worker from a different culture, yet
rights to self-determination and cultural integrity seem to cut across such
concerns. As described in Chapter 4, it is necessary to move away from a
world-view that reifies culture or that sees cultures as static and monolithic. Cultures are characteristically changing and pluralistic, and a broad
human rights framework allows social workers to understand that oppression and human rights abuses occur across cultural boundaries and that
the struggles for human rights and social justice transcend cultural difference. At the same time, abuses occur within cultural contexts, and the
way in which, for example, struggles for the liberation of women are
located in different cultures needs to be understood by social workers.

Practice in such contexts is always complex and involves difficult moral
choices for a social worker. But it is important also, as discussed earlier in
this chapter, to move away from the notion of an individual social worker
making a lonely moral choice and taking independent action, moving
instead towards a model of dialogical praxis where the moral decisions are
made in collaboration with the people concerned and where dialogue is
the vehicle whereby both worker and client can become more informed
and can seek common understandings and common action. In accordance with Bauman's postmodern critique of ethics (1993, 1995), there
cannot be a single authoritative 'answer' to such a practice dilemma; the
answer must be discovered through dialogue and mutual education.

Macro and micro practice

The discussion throughout this chapter suggests strongly that the traditional division between 'macro' and 'micro' social work practice is artificial and does not serve the ends of human rights-based praxis. Social work, from the perspective of this book, must always be concerned with both the personal and the political, and will inevitably operate at both macro and micro levels. A social caseworker simply cannot afford to see the 'case', whether an individual or a family, in isolation from the broader societal context, and she/he will need to engage in practice that moves beyond the simple counselling approach. Indeed, in most social work roles, the capacity of a social worker to help a person or family is determined far more by that social worker's ability to work in organisational systems, to operate in team meetings, to advocate with a range of community services, and to build strong community supports than it is by his/her capacity to work interpersonal magic in a counselling interview. And if a social worker is to avoid the conservatising and disempowering constructions of individualism (which is usually part of the problem rather than part of the solution) it is necessary to seek more collective forms of action, working in solidarity with consumer groups, colleagues, activists and other professionals.

Similarly, a macro social worker, working in community or policy work, cannot afford to ignore the understandings and skills of micro practice. The community worker, for example, constantly uses interpersonal skills in a wide variety of contexts, though these are unlikely to be constructed as interviews in the conventional sense. And if a policy worker or activist lacks the skills to communicate effectively with those he/she wishes to influence, that worker's effectiveness will be severely handicapped.

This may seem obvious, and it has indeed been reiterated by many social work writers over the years (Compton & Galaway 1999). Yet there is an apparent reluctance on the part of social workers, students or educators to abandon this macro/micro dichotomy, and a corresponding persistence in defining oneself as primarily in one or the other. A human rights perspective adds an extra impetus to breaking down this dichotomy. In order to do so, social workers perhaps need to stop using the terms 'macro', 'micro', 'casework' and 'community work', and to refuse to be so categorised. Certainly there is a need for social work education to take stronger steps to overcome this dichotomy and to encourage students to see themselves as necessarily practising at both macro and micro levels, whatever their field of practice. Working towards such a basic shift in the dominant social work discourse is therefore a major task facing social work. A human rights framework, by emphasising the connectedness of practice at all levels, should assist this process.

The global and the local

The above dualisms have been faced by social workers for a long time, and there is a significant social work literature about the need to transcend them. A new concern that has emerged only in recent years, with the advent of globalisation, involves social work practice in a globalised world. As was argued in Chapter 1, globalisation has lent a new urgency to the cause of human rights, as the form of globalisation currently experienced is seen as counter to human rights principles and as diminishing human rights. It was also suggested in Chapter 1 that one of the important reactions to globalisation has been localisation, and that with the 'hollowing out' of the state (Jessop 1994) there has been increasing activity at the more local level as people who feel that the global economy no longer meets their needs seek to establish their own community-based alternatives (Ife 2000). With this change, the important sites for resistance to globalisation and also for social work practice become the global and the local, since these are the locations where practice is more likely to bring about change. Practising at the local level is nothing new for social workers, but the global/local issue raises two important new areas for social work: practising globally, and linking the global and the local. If social work is to remain relevant in a globalised world, and especially if it is to see itself as a human rights profession, then practising globally and linking the global with the local in everyday practice are important priorities for the development of future social work.

Practising globally requires that social workers engage with new (and not so new) global structures, whether these be UN agencies, regional groupings such as the EU and ASEAN, economic organisations such as the World Bank, the International Monetary Fund and the World Trade Organisation, or NGOs such as Amnesty International, Greenpeace and Oxfam. Social work voices are, by and large, not well represented in these forums, yet it should be clear that social workers have a good deal of expertise to contribute, and these are crucial organisations in shaping the future of human rights. Further, global practice requires that social workers facilitate the input of the voices of the disadvantaged and the marginalised into these forums; such voices are conspicuously lacking, yet must be heard and validated if the goals of human rights are to be realised.

The other aspect of social work practice in the globalised world is to be able not only to operate at global and local levels but to link the two in a form of creative practice that transcends the local/global divide. This requires the capacity to see local problems also as global problems, to see that they can only be adequately addressed by action at both global and local levels, and to find ways to link the two. This of course cannot be done simply by a worker acting alone. It requires him/her to work cooperatively at two levels: first by working dialogically with the people most affected (client, community, etc.), and second by forming partnerships with other workers and clients or communities elsewhere in the world who are facing the same issues. In Chapter 4 the example of child welfare was used – the linking of child welfare and 'rights of the child' issues across national boundaries in an attempt to seek action solutions to common problems. In an increasingly globalising world, social work practice that does not do this but concentrates only on the local is likely to become increasingly irrelevant and ineffective. Social workers engaged in dialogue, partnerships and collective action now need to join Castells' 'network society' (1996, 1997, 1998) and to establish and use their own networks of power for furthering a human rights agenda. A human rights basis for social work, where human rights are by their very nature universal, requires such creative global/local practice (Lawson 2000).

Conclusion

This chapter has brought together many of the practice principles identified in earlier chapters, to provide an overall picture of what it means to think about achieving human rights through social work practice.

Many of these practice principles are not new and have been discussed by social workers in other contexts, for example feminist social work, radical social work, critical social work, postmodern social work, and counter-oppressive practice (Fook 1993; Fisher & Karger 1997; Ife 1997b; Mullaly 1997; Gil 1998; Pease & Fook 1999; Healy 2000). Similarly, most of the social work skills involved in such practice are not new. Human rights-based social work does not necessarily require social workers to be doing much that they are not already doing, though the emphasis on particular activities, the purpose of various practice methods, and the overall framing of the social work task may well be different.

Skills, of course, will vary with context, and hence in a book like this it would be both inappropriate and misleading to spell out specifically 'how to do' human rights-based social work. Practice principles, as discussed in this chapter, represent the limits to which one can be prescriptive, and the actual processes and methods to be used will vary with different workers, different organisational locations, and different cultural and political contexts.

There is another level, however, where human rights principles inform social work practice. The emphasis in this chapter has been on social work as a means to achieve the realisation of human rights. But as we have seen, means and ends cannot be so easily separated, and it is therefore important to examine the impact of human rights principles on the practice of social work itself. This is the subject of the next chapter.

CHAPTER 11

Respecting Human Rights in Social Work Practice

The previous chapter dealt with ways to realise and protect human rights through social work practice. This chapter, by contrast, focuses on social work practice itself – it is the processes, rather than the outcomes, of social work practice that are of concern here. If social work is a human rights profession and aims to meet human rights through its practice, it is essential that the profession itself operate in such a way that its own practices observe human rights principles and do not violate the human rights of others. As in the previous chapter, many of the principles identified here have already emerged from previous discussion, for example in Chapter 7, concerning ethics and human rights, though that chapter did not undertake an examination of social work practice per se from a human rights perspective. The important principle throughout this chapter is that *we respect other people's human rights by allowing them maximum self-determination and control over the situation in which they find themselves.* This principle can be applied to the practice of social work. While social workers have been always committed to the principle of client self-determination, this has often applied to the life of the client rather than to the practice of social work itself and to the way social work practice is constructed by social workers. To be consistent with a human rights perspective, however, the principle must also be applied to all those with whom a social worker interacts: clients, community members, colleagues, managers, supervisors, students, and other professionals.

The language of social work

In keeping with the idea of human rights as discursive, it is important to examine the language of social work. By using certain language – words such as 'supervision', 'profession', 'client', and so on – social workers construct their work in certain ways, and these frequently have human rights implications.

Labelling a client

Up to this point in our discussions, the word 'client' has been used without critique, though the word is problematic and contested. It is a word widely used in social work and implies that a special status is to be given to a particular person or group within the whole range of people with whom social workers interact. The question 'who is the client?' has been central to many case discussions in social work schools (Heron 1990). Why is the client status so special, why should someone be so singled out, and why is the identification of a client seen as such an important question? In its original meaning, 'client' referred to a person who voluntarily engaged the services of a professional to provide a service the client had requested, and the client controlled the nature and extent of the service provided. This is a long way from the reality of the client in most social work practice locations. In many cases the client has no choice over the selection of the worker, the nature of the service provided, the limits to the service provision, or the evaluation. Indeed the meaning of the word has changed so much in social work that the term 'involuntary client' is often used – in the original sense of 'client' there could be no such thing, and the term would be an oxymoron. Instead, the word 'client' has come to imply a dependent or relatively powerless position, and in some quarters it has been suggested that 'customer' be used instead as it is seen to imply more autonomy and freedom of choice by the person concerned. The word 'customer', however, has other connotations and is too identified with a market ideology to sit comfortably with many social workers.

In the current practice context in western societies, we can identify four competing discourses of human services: the managerial, the market, the professional and the community (for a fuller analysis see Ife 1997b). Each has its own term for the person receiving or benefiting from human services, respectively 'consumer', 'customer', 'client' and 'citizen'. The term 'client' is part of the professional discourse, which implies essentially a top-down approach to wisdom and expertise, motivated by human values, but with an assumption that the professional is in possession of superior knowledge and skills which are put at the service of the client. Such practice is compatible with human rights at one level, in that the value base of professional practice is likely to be founded on the importance of human rights, but at another level it actually works against human rights by devaluing the wisdom of the client and hence engaging in 'disabling' practice as described by Illich (Illich et al. 1977) and as discussed in Chapter 10.

Elsewhere I have advocated that social work seek to adopt the community discourse and aim to practise from such a perspective, since this is more consistent with the value base of social work and more likely to be effective in the long term (Ife 1997b). This would require abandoning the use of the word 'client' and with it the obsession with labelling a client for every social work situation. Such reframing would be more consistent with a human rights approach, given the construction of 'client' in professional discourse. Instead, social workers could talk about 'people' or 'citizens'; indeed the latter is particularly appropriate for a human rights-based practice, as it implies citizenship rights which need to be guaranteed. One way of working towards human rights within social work practice, therefore, is to abandon, or at least limit, the use of the word 'client' and all the associations that go with it.

Intervention

Another common social work term with worrying connotations from a human rights perspective is 'intervention'. The word became widely used in social work with the popularity of systems theory in the 1970s (Pincus & Minahan 1976). Individuals, families, agencies, communities and so on were all analysed as 'systems', and the role of the social worker was to 'intervene' in these systems to bring about change. Although systems theory has declined in influence (while the less grandiose 'systems perspective' is still popular), the term 'intervention' has remained. The idea of a social worker 'intervening' is problematic on two grounds. First, it locates the social worker outside the systems within which interactions occur. One cannot really 'intervene' from within; the word implies the action of an external agent coming in to fix things up and then departing. This weakens a social worker's identification with the people with whom she/he is working, and it does not see the social worker as part of the overall picture. Dialogical praxis becomes difficult because the social worker cannot be seen as a partner in an action process, but more as an outside expert. The second problem is that all the action is seen as belonging to the social worker, the one who is doing the intervening. The role of others in effecting change is minimised, and it is the social worker, acting alone through 'intervention', who is responsible for bringing about change. It therefore reinforces the individualist practitioner role ('what can I do?' rather than 'what can we do together?'). Thus the idea of 'intervention' serves to disempower, and to see people who are disadvantaged as passive recipients of the social worker's expert interference. There is, on reflection, an arrogance about the idea of 'intervention' which suggests that it is incompatible with a human rights perspective and does not really value the human rights of the client as an active participant in the change process.

For the human rights-based social worker, therefore, the word 'intervention' is, like 'client', one that should be discouraged. Indeed when a social worker finds him/herself using such a word, it is necessary to ask serious questions about its implications, and whether its use is in fact working against a human rights approach to practice.

Military metaphors

The use of military metaphors is widespread in social work, especially in community work, and is largely unnoticed and unacknowledged. It is not hard to come up with a substantial list of terms frequently used by social workers which have origins in or associations with military activity:

- strategy
- strategic
- tactics
- tactical
- campaign
- target
- join battle
- win the battle but lose the war
- fight a rearguard action
- withdrawal
- outflanking
- manoeuvring
- engagement
- disengagement
- alliance
- guerilla tactics
- join forces
- volunteer
- operational plan.

Such a list must surely raise the question of why a profession apparently committed to social justice and human rights should be so happy to borrow terms from an institution devoted to violence and which many social workers would regard as the antithesis of social work values. It certainly does not fit well with a profession built on ideas of non-violence. While it could be argued that many of the above terms have lost their military connotations over time and with repeated use in professional discourse (e.g. they are widely used in management terminology, possibly because they sit easily with notions of efficiency, competition and the importance of 'winning'), such an argument ignores the unconscious reinforcement of a particular world-view by the repeated use of language with certain connotations. It needs to be remembered that the impact of sexist language went unrecognised until feminist critics drew it to public attention; before that, gender-specific language had seemed harmless and benign, whereas now it is regarded as excluding and oppressive. Perhaps the same needs to be said for militaristic language. Such language leads us to construct practice (and indeed life) as if it were a war, with violence, conflict, confrontation, winners, losers and casualties all taken as given. It hardly seems compatible with the human rights perspective described in this book.

A human rights approach to social work therefore suggests that we seek deliberately not to use militaristic metaphors, and that it is necessary to be more aware of the implications of the language we do use in constructing social work practice. This applies particularly in the field of community work, where words such as 'strategy', 'tactics', 'campaign' and so on are very frequently used, and where the influence of Alinsky (1971) – who perhaps drew the military metaphor more strongly than any other community work writer – can still be felt.

Supervision

Supervision is seen as very important in social work. It is regarded as an essential component of professional development and competent practice, and has been given particular attention in the literature. The way in which professional supervision is carried out will be discussed later in this chapter, but here it is the use of the word itself that is at issue.

There can be no question that many of the goals of supervision are important and worthwhile. Social workers are (or should be) always learning, and the value of reflecting on one's practice with an experienced colleague is obvious. But the word 'supervision' has many more connotations than this. A 'supervisor' in the lay sense of the word is an overseer, a person who is in a position of superior power, who knows better than the supervisee how the job is to be done, and who should be telling the supervisee how to do it. There are strong elements here of control and surveillance: the worker's performance is to be closely scrutinised and if necessary corrected by the supervisor, whose wisdom is not to be questioned. In line with a Foucauldian analysis (Foucault 1991), the implied close observation and surveillance suggest the exercise of power, control and discipline. Given this, it is interesting that social workers should have become so attached to the word, even though it may be understood in an apparently more benign sense. One needs to ask whether the use of the word in professional discourse suggests more of a control agenda, and whether it is really just an apparently more respectable version of the panopticon described by Foucault, where more 'senior' and experienced social workers and educators exercise power and control over less experienced workers or students by keeping them under constant surveillance. Foucault's description of surveillance also emphasised the maintaining of those under surveillance in individual isolation, and this can also be paralleled in the conventional approach to supervision: usually supervision is individual, between a single worker and a single supervisor, with at least an implicit confidentiality about the exchange, rather than any notion of collective sharing of experience.

It must be reiterated that this is not to condemn everything that goes under the name of 'supervision' in social work. To do so would be absurd and naïve. Rather, it is to question the use of the word itself, to identify the potential human rights problems that such usage creates, and to suggest that it may be more appropriate to use other words to describe the process of 'professional supervision'. The process itself, as distinct from the word, will be further discussed below.

Profession

There has been considerable literature on professionalism in social work, and whether it is appropriate or not for social work to define itself as a profession (e.g. Ife 1997b; Pease & Fook 1999; Healy 2000). For the purposes of the present discussion, the focus is on the meaning of the word itself. Does the use of the term 'profession' in social work's self-definition have human rights implications for social workers? Professions have been criticised by a number of writers because of the inappropriate wielding of professional power as a form of control (Foucault 1970; Illich et al. 1977). If this is the case, professionalism has significant human rights implications, and indeed the term 'human rights profession' would be an oxymoron. If the very idea of a 'profession' carries with it disempowering practice, then it is incompatible with a human rights perspective as detailed elsewhere in this book. In that case, the sooner social workers stop thinking of themselves as professionals, the better.

The counter-argument is that professionalism has brought major benefits for social work, and that professional status enables social workers to be more effective in working towards change. It also enables them to be more independent and gives them a strong case as to why they should not always slavishly follow the commands of managers, bureaucrats and politicians. From this perspective, for social workers to give up their professional status would be to put themselves in a weaker position to achieve their objectives of social justice. As well as this, professionalism requires the adherence to certain standards of practice competence and ethical conduct, which are clearly important.

Using the word 'professional' to describe social work and social workers is therefore contentious and can be seen to have both advantages and problems. From a human rights perspective, it is important to be aware of the power relationship and the assumption of superior expertise on the part of the social worker that seem to be implied by professionalism. These are counter to human rights principles in that they privilege the worker over the client and can disempower the client through the professional relationship. If the term 'professional' is to be used to describe either social work or social workers, therefore, it is necessary to ensure that it is accompanied by an adequate power analysis to protect the human rights of the disadvantaged. It is also important to ask why, in any particular situation, the words 'profession' or 'professional' are used. There may well be good reasons for the use of these words, but it may also be that their unthinking and excessive use subtly but significantly erodes a human rights perspective.

There has only been space here to identify a few cases where the language of social work may counter the aims of human rights. The reader will undoubtedly be able to identify others. The simple point is that language is powerful, that language helps to define and reinforce power relationships, and that it is necessary to subject social work language to critical analysis if social workers are to be consistent in human rights practice.

The processes of social work

Social work employs a wide range of practice methods. While there is not enough space here to consider all of them, an examination of some of the more common social work practices will enable certain human rights principles to be identified.

Interviews

The interview has long been regarded as at the centre of social work methods, even though most social workers actually spend only a small proportion of their working day in formal interview contact with clients. In social work education courses interpersonal skills are often equated with interviewing skills, even though social workers use interpersonal skills in many other transactions than client interviews. Indeed the interview has been reified within social work and has achieved special status among the whole range of social work methodologies.

The social work interview has typically been constructed in unequal power terms. It is generally expected that the social worker, not the client, will be the one who 'controls' the interview. If the worker 'loses control' that is a sign of lack of competence, whereas if the client loses control this is simply seen as an extra challenge for the worker. It is the worker who is expected to be setting the limits, controlling the duration of the interview, and so on. The interview is constructed as being an unequal relationship where it is the needs of the client, not the social worker, that are the focus of discussion and action. While the interaction may be controlled by the social worker, it is meant to be entirely in the interests of the client. As discussed in Chapter 3, whenever social workers claim to be working 'in the best interests of' somebody else, human rights alarm bells should ring loudly. The traditional social work interview is structured in just such a way: it is a process controlled by one person but designed to be in the interests of the other. Despite the rhetoric of self-determination and empowerment, too often the social work interview will serve the opposite purpose and will simply reinforce an unequal power relationship between client and worker. This has implications for the human rights social worker, as such an approach to the interview can be seen as amounting to an infringement on the client's human rights – more so as it also involves an element of deception in that the language used by the social worker often implies the reverse.

This is not to suggest that all social work interviews are oppressive and a violation of clients' human rights. This would obviously be an exaggeration and would insult the many social workers who take a very different view of their role in the interview. Rather, it suggests that the traditional framing of the 'interview' within social work is not conducive to the pursuit of human rights-based practice, that this construction can reinforce oppressive practice by unthinking social workers, and that there are important human rights issues involved in the way an 'interview' is conducted. To address these issues, there is a need for an alternative construction of the interaction that takes place between a worker and a client. Instead of using the word 'interview', social workers could simply talk about 'talking with' or 'having a conversation with' the person concerned. This would remove the special status accorded the interview among the many interpersonal interactions in which a social worker engages; social workers talk with colleagues, supervisors, workers in other agencies, other professionals, students, and many others, yet it is only the interactions with 'the client' that are normally described as an 'interview', with all that this word implies. This identification of the interaction with the client, and its allocation of the precious title of 'interview', unnecessarily singles out and privileges this activity from the other conversations social workers hold in the course of their work, and it would be helpful to use other language to describe it.

Within the interview (or conversation, discussion, chat, or whatever we choose to call it) there are certain principles that would need to operate if a human rights perspective is to be maintained. Most importantly, the rights of the client need to be respected at all times during the exchange. This includes the right to free expression, the right to silence, the right to be treated with respect and dignity, and rights to have some control over the exchange: its duration, structure, tone, location, and so on. Given that often there will be an initial perception on the part of the client that the social worker is in the superior position of knowledge and power (this is unlikely to be the first time the person has been interviewed), it is necessary for the social worker to make a point of attempting to engage the client in a discussion of the way in which the exchange will be conducted, or at least the way it will start – for example, asking the client what he/she hopes to get from the conversation (and then seeking to dialogue about shared goals), asking him/her how much time she/he has, asking whether she/he would prefer to 'meet downstairs over a coffee', checking about how the client would like to be addressed, and so on. Such comments represent different ways in which a social worker can try to break away from the conventional construction of an interview and seek a more equal dialogical relationship. Of course none of this is new; such things have been part of the practice of many social workers, and some workers strongly maintain the importance of 'professional distance' in their interviews. But from a human rights perspective such actions on the part of the worker (though not necessarily in exactly the form described here – it depends on the context) are necessary in order to respect and further the client's human rights in the professional relationship.

Groups

All social workers work in groups, of one kind or another. Often what is referred to as 'group work' refers only to one kind of group, involving people who might be identified as clients or community members, with the social worker in a leadership or facilitation role. But social workers also work in many other group situations, for example team meetings, case conferences, action groups, management committees. The construction of 'group work' to apply only to one kind of group is similar to the construction of 'interview' as applying to only one form of interpersonal interaction. Both tend to limit the applicability of social work skills; just as interpersonal skills are often constructed only as applying to interviews, group work skills are often constructed as applying only to groups in which the social worker is the leader or facilitator.

From a human rights perspective, the important thing about working in groups is that it is important to work towards making the group democratic and participatory, rather than engaging in, or supporting, practices that limit participation and increase control of the group by one or a few members. Just as the social worker is expected to be 'in control' of the interview, so a group worker is often expected to be 'in control' of a group. This encouragement of a controlling function is, of course, counter to ideas of human rights and the replication within the group of rights to freedom of expression, self-determination, and so on. Just as in the larger society rights to freedom of expression carry with them obligations to allow that freedom to others, the same applies in a small group; someone who aggressively dominates the group in the name of her/his right to self-expression is ignoring the obligation to extend that same right to all other members of a group.

There are a number of ways in which participatory and democratic processes can be facilitated in small groups (Gastil 1993), and social workers, especially those with experience in group and community settings, are familiar with such practice principles as respect for others, allowing all members to speak, and consensus-based decision-making. Often, unfortunately, social workers seem able to apply such principles when working with clients but not when working with colleagues or other professionals. Such practice in all contexts, however, is an important part of human rights-based social work as it effectively protects and affirms the human rights of group members. If those rights cannot be adequately safeguarded and realised in social work groups, social workers are unlikely to be successful in achieving human rights goals in the wider society.

Community processes

Social work with community processes also needs to ensure that its practice respects human rights and includes adequate opportunities for people to exercise their human rights and to respect the rights of others. This has been a particular concern of the community work literature, especially the literature that seeks to incorporate non-violent methods, consensus decision-making and empowerment. There is no space here to discuss such methods in detail, and they are adequately dealt with in the community work literature (Shields 1991; Nozick 1992; Craig & Mayo 1995; Ife 1995; Kenny 1999).

There are some aspects of community work, however, which do not fit as well into a human rights framework. These include the conflict-oriented community work approaches of writers who are influenced by Alinsky (1971). As we have seen, these are approaches that incorporate militaristic metaphors, that define 'winners' and 'losers', and separate ends and means, assuming that it is the end that is important and that any means, violent or otherwise, is justified in order to achieve it. Such community work can easily ride roughshod over human rights and is incompatible with human rights-based social work. There is, however, a more subtle level at which human rights can be violated in community work. Often means can be seen as subservient to ends in less extreme or obvious forms than is the case with community organising in the Alinsky tradition. One example is the frequent call for community groups to be 'disciplined' in certain situations, for good 'strategic' reasons (note the militaristic language again). While such approaches are often advocated for good and apparently commonsense reasons (e.g. the need to keep the media and public opinion on side), they can also easily imply a denial of human rights for some of the participants, for example by not allowing everyone to speak at a meeting or a delegation because of the 'strategic' need to keep a focus to the action, or preventing people from taking extreme action because of the negative publicity that might ensue. The key to successful practice here is to ensure that, for example, a decision to restrict people's participation at a meeting is not one made in isolation by a worker or community leader and then issued to everyone else in the form of an order, but rather that such a decision is made democratically, through full consultation and consensus decision-making. The decision is then one that is made and owned by the whole group, and in that way a human rights perspective can be maintained, and indeed enhanced.

Planning

One of the consequences of the managerial approach to human service provision, which is so powerful in many western societies, is what amounts to an obsession with planning (Lawler 2000). Social workers spend many hours in planning: strategic planning, indicative planning, operational planning, business planning, corporate planning, defining goals, specifying objectives, defining outcomes, preparing work plans, and so on. In a postmodern world it is important to ask why so much time is spent in such a quintessentially modernist activity as planning, which assumes a rational, ordered and predictable world that postmodernists would see as a figment of modernist imagination. Unforeseen (and unforeseeable) events can instantly render the best of plans redundant, thereby wasting untold hours spent in the plan's preparation. Yet the managerial response is, characteristically, to impose yet more planning methods, planning courses and rationalist solutions that are simply irrelevant in a non-rationalist world. It is, in one sense, only natural to try to impose some form of order and predictability on the messy and chaotic world in which social workers practise; it represents a way of making an impossible task seem more manageable and controllable by the social worker and others in the organisation. But it is a classic western Enlightenment, patriarchal and modernist solution, seeking to impose control and order, and from the perspective developed in this book it is hardly likely to meet with great success. Indeed many social workers are highly sceptical about the value of such planning processes, and in some organisations in the author's experience employees have been so busily engaged with the planning process that they have virtually stopped doing the things they were actually employed to do. The experience of a client or colleague being unable to contact a worker 'because she is at a planning meeting' is all too familiar.

From a human rights perspective, the important thing about the obsession with planning is that it can erode the possibility for transformative human rights. The planning paradigm requires a clear definition of objectives or outcomes to be achieved, and indeed this is frequently required in order for a program to be funded. The problem is that this usually occurs before the social worker has even met the client or the community with whom she/he is to work. This is hardly conducive to dialogical praxis; in fact it directly negates it and denies the client or community the right to self-determination. It leads to a social work practice where the service is prepackaged and delivered to the recipient who has no say in its design or delivery.

This should not be taken as a total condemnation of planning. Clearly there is value for social workers, and those who work with them, in thinking about where they are going in their work, what they hope to achieve, and how they might be able to get there. But this need not be undertaken within the rigid constraints of the 'business plan' or the document where objectives are specified in minute detail. Most important, however, is the need to incorporate in the planning process the people who are most likely to be affected, in other words the clients. One might ask how many social work agencies involve clients in their planning days (and not just in a tokenistic way), and genuinely seek to ensure that clients' voices are fully heard when their plans are drawn up and their outcomes specified in funding applications. Yet this is surely a requirement of social work that is genuinely based on human rights principles; to do otherwise is to violate the clients' rights to self-determination (Fattore et al. 2000).

The metaphor of a journey can be used to describe two approaches to social work. One is the journey to a known destination, following a defined route, using a map, and keeping to a predetermined timetable. The other is the journey of discovery, where we do not know where we are going, or at best have only a vague idea, where the route is largely uncharted, and where we have no idea how long the journey will take. For the first journey, an unexpected detour is a nuisance that upsets our schedule, while for the second it is an opportunity to go somewhere new and learn or experience something different. For the first journey, the aim is to arrive, and the journey itself is a distraction to be dispensed with as quickly as possible, while for the second, arrival is almost secondary: the aim is to explore, to experience, to learn, and the journey itself is to be enjoyed and treasured. Sometimes we need to go on one kind of journey and sometimes we need to go on the other. It can be argued that social work, like many other activities, has concentrated too much on the first goal-oriented type of journey and ignored the importance of the journey of discovery. Yet it is the latter, for which only very limited 'planning' can be undertaken, that is the essence of empowerment-based social work, and that is necessary if we are to seek creative alternatives to the oppressive and dehumanising structures that affect workers and clients alike. This is the journey of dialogical praxis, which social workers and clients can take together. It is a harder, less predictable and more dangerous road to travel, but ultimately we have no alternative unless we want to remain trapped within the stultifying paradigm of rationalist modernist practice, which has significantly failed to meet the aims of social justice and human rights. And it is only by embarking on this kind of journey, alongside those with whom they work, that social workers can truly respect their clients' right to self-determination and the whole range of human rights that flow from it.

Management

Many social workers find themselves in management roles, and the question must therefore be asked whether it is possible to practise management in such a way as to respect and promote human rights. At one level this might be questioned – the very idea of management seems to symbolise control and domination, and it is not unlike 'supervision', as discussed earlier. Certainly the management discourse seems to locate the manager in a position of superiority and to imply an unequal power relationship with at least the potential for oppressive practice and the denial of human-rights. Indeed the discourse of managerialism has been criticised on precisely these grounds (Rees & Rodley 1995; Ife 1997b). The reality of social work, however, is that management positions will continue to exist, some social workers will fill them, and it is necessary to see whether management can be practised in such a way as to respect and further human rights.

Management, of course, is not a monolithic enterprise. There are many different approaches to it, and the idea of what constitutes 'good management' is contested (Jones & May 1992; Harlow & Lawler 2000). Instead of simply being negative and only criticising managerial discourse (though such a critique needs to be strongly made), it is important also to examine how social workers who find themselves in managerial positions might practise so as to enhance the cause of human rights. The key to such practice is to ensure that it is set up with genuinely participatory and dialogical structures and processes, so that it is not a case of the word of the manager being law, or of the manager exercising her/his power in such a way that it is oppressive or denies the other actors full participation. Management can be participatory and dialogical as long as the manager takes steps to create the space for the participation of the others involved and does not seek to use the potentially unequal power relationship to dominate or control. One way to achieve this is for the manager to be very clear that he/she is also able to learn and grow from the process, that wisdom lies with the people she/he is 'managing', and that the process will not be a one-way transfer of expertise. Thus dialogical relationships can begin to be established, though, as is the case with the worker–client relationship, it is necessary to take specific steps to redefine the power relationship that the worker may initially construct in the more conventional form of a power imbalance.

Of course there will be times when the manager feels it is 'necessary to exert one's authority', for example in the case of a deliberate breaking of agency policy, dereliction of duty, or unethical behaviour. This is analogous to a social worker deciding that he/she must 'act in the best interests of' another, implying that the worker knows best. Sometimes it is justified and necessary, but it should always be undertaken with caution and deep moral anguish on the part of the manager, because of the temptation to wield power for its own sake to meet the needs of the manager, and because of knowledge of so many occasions in the past where such power has been misused. The test here is the same as that for the social worker: is such a decision necessary to safeguard or promote human rights, and can the apparent denial of rights that is involved be justified on the grounds of preventing even more widespread and significant human rights denial or abuse? Such questions are never easy, and the role of the manager is in this sense as much an ongoing moral struggle as the role of the direct-service worker. The other important principle is, of course, that the decision is better shared, and taken dialogically in partnership with the person concerned.

Other management practices can also support or hinder human rights. The introduction and support of organisational practices that maximise worker and client participation in decision-making is one important initiative that needs to be undertaken by human rights-oriented managers. This can be achieved in different ways, depending on the organisational context, and cannot be described in any more detail here. The institution of good work practices, occupational health and safety measures, child care provision, access for people with disabilities, sympathetic and flexible provision for leave taking for personal and family reasons, maternity and paternity leave, recognition and support of trade unions, and the elimination of discriminatory policies and practices are all important ways in which managers can support human rights in the workplace.

The above discussion has focused on the manager's responsibility to respect the human rights of workers. But the social work manager also has a clear responsibility to institute policies and procedures that respect and further the human rights of clients. This involves, for example, making sure that all clients are treated with respect and dignity and that they have maximum opportunity to control and direct the services they receive and to provide feedback to the organisation so that services can be improved. It also involves ensuring that the programs of the agency are compatible with human rights standards as outlined in this book. For example, it may be important for a human rights-oriented manager to seek to renegotiate funding agreements so that the outcomes are not rigidly specified before a program commences, but rather to ensure that the participants will be able to have a genuine part in determining the outcomes, and to free both workers and clients to work dialogically.

Boundaries

The idea of professional boundaries has an important place in the construction of social work (Ragg 1977). The boundary between one's personal and professional life is seen as needing to be strongly drawn and maintained. This is justified on two grounds. First, the integrity of the profession, and of one's professional practice, is seen as requiring clear boundaries. If personal issues are allowed to cross into professional life, one's professional judgement is seen to be clouded and one will act as a result of one's own needs rather than the needs of the client. Professional and personal behaviour are seen as different; in a particular situation one may act very differently as a professional social worker than one would as an 'ordinary' human being. If the boundary is not clearly drawn and maintained, a social worker is likely to act 'unprofessionally' in the workplace, or annoy friends and family by 'acting the social worker' at home.

The other justification for professional boundaries is to maintain the worker's sanity, and as a defence against burnout from a stressful job. A clear boundary enables the worker to lead a balanced life. One is entitled to 'a life outside social work', and indeed one might even frame this in human rights terms; Article 24 of the Universal Declaration of Human Rights states: 'Everyone has the right to rest and leisure, including reasonable limitation of working hours ...'

Like much else in social work, however, the reality is not as clear-cut as this. Different workers will define their boundaries in different ways and at different points, depending on the nature of the job and on the particular worker. Thus some social workers would never agree to allowing a client to visit them at home, while for others this would be seen as quite natural and acceptable. Social workers may agree on the importance of boundaries, but they will not agree on where those boundaries should be drawn; and indeed most social workers would probably agree that in the real world of practice there cannot be hard-and-fast rules about such things. For some social work positions, the boundaries are necessarily drawn in very different places. For example, a social worker in an isolated rural community simply cannot avoid meeting her/his clients at the local store, at the weekend football, or anywhere else, however much she/he may want to avoid such contacts; that social worker is forced to draw the boundary rather differently from a worker in a large metropolis. For social workers in community development, the boundaries are inevitably more blurred, especially if the worker is living in the community as well as working in it. Some social work settings simply do not lend themselves to the drawing of rigid personal/professional boundaries, unless the worker wants to live the personal life of a hermit. But in other settings the establishment of clear boundaries is necessary in the interests of protecting the rights of both client and worker.

In some circumstances the drawing of clear boundaries might be seen as effectively distancing the worker from the people with whom he/she is working, and hence as disempowering. Some community development approaches, for example the Gandhian model as practised in India (Gaikwad 1981), require the worker to become completely involved in and absorbed by the community. Only in that way, it is claimed, can true identity with the people be achieved; a worker should simply not be allowed to 'escape' to a more comfortable lifestyle but should be required to live with the people she/he is trying to help.

Different cultural contexts will also play a part in the differing definition of boundaries. Indeed it might be claimed that the rigid separation of the professional and the personal is characteristically western and makes little sense in other cultural traditions that are more holistic in their world-view. Indigenous social workers, and some non-indigenous workers working with indigenous communities, are very likely to have a view of practice that questions the whole validity of rigid boundaries between the personal and the professional.

There is also evidence to suggest that social workers see their boundaries as permeable rather than rigid (Zubrzycki 1999). Workers will readily admit that they use insights from their personal experience (e.g. as parents, partners, siblings) to enrich their social work understanding and practice, and similarly they will acknowledge that their practice can enrich their private lives. It is not therefore a case of blocking each out from the other, but rather there is a level of controlled permeability: the worker needs to feel in control of what is allowed to cross the boundary in each direction, and what stays on the other side.

The idea of boundaries between the personal and the professional, then, is contestable and is worked out very differently in different social work locations. The question for present purposes is how a human rights perspective might inform such boundary issues. One concern is that by drawing clear boundaries between the personal and the professional the social worker is prevented from engaging in a truly dialogical relationship with the client. The client is allowed, indeed encouraged or required, to be her/himself in the relationship, but the social worker is required to put on a professional persona and define some parts of her/his human experience as 'out of bounds'. This can not only affect the development of genuine dialogue, it can also prevent the establishment of empathy in the relationship, and may in addition prevent the social worker from engaging in what, to the client, is culturally acceptable behaviour (e.g. regarding bodily contact, use of abbreviated names or nicknames, visiting in the home, or exchange of gifts). The client's right to the best standard of service may thus not be realised, and the capacity for furthering a human rights agenda may be seriously curtailed if the social worker feels unable to engage with it wholeheartedly.

More significantly, perhaps, the construction of professional boundaries by the social worker may be seen as defining the worker and the client as different types of people (with the implication of superiority on the part of the social worker), and the social work relationship itself as unequal. This, as we have already seen, would be counter to a human rights perspective, as it could lead to the client's rights in the relationship (e.g. the right to privacy) being significantly different from the worker's.

In other cases, however, the setting of clear boundaries can be an important part of human rights practice. The role confusion caused for a client by a social worker who fails to define the personal/political boundary clearly can infringe the client's rights to privacy and to self-determination. And social workers' rights can readily be abused by a practice framework that requires them to cross the personal/professional boundary too readily.

Thus boundaries themselves are neither good nor bad, and it is important for a social worker to understand that the professional/personal boundary is problematic. How the worker will choose to construct or not to construct this boundary has implications for human rights, and the issue of boundaries therefore needs to be critically analysed in any practice context.

Supervision

The use of the word 'supervision' has already been discussed in the section above on language. Here our concern is more with the way supervision is practised. As indicated in the earlier discussion, there are important benefits from supervision, however problematic the word itself may be: it is clearly important for social workers to be able to reflect critically on their practice together with more experienced colleagues. Good 'supervision', if it can get over the serious problems about the connotations of the word itself, can be dialogical for those involved, both the supervisor(s) and the supervisee(s). There are several approaches that might be tried in order to free supervision from its limiting and control/surveillance image and make it potentially dialogical and supportive of human rights.

One possibility is to move supervision away from its traditionally individual construction, which can tend to individualise problems and lead to 'blaming the victim' in exactly the same way as is often the case in individualised social casework. Group supervision (Hawkins & Shoher 1989) allows for more interactions, more views to be expressed, and more wisdom to be shared, though of course the potentially negative impact of group dynamics can cause additional problems. It may not always be an ideal solution, but it may at times be worth consideration. Another possibility is to give the social worker more choice in whom she/he wishes to have as a supervisor. Personal compatibility, ideological or theoretical common ground, outside interests and factors such as age or gender will all enter the supervisory relationship, and it is naïve to assume that any senior social worker can successfully supervise any more 'junior' social worker. Some combinations will work better than others, and if one were to respect the rights of the social worker concerned, the choice of allocating a supervisor should not be a decision for management alone but should involve both the worker concerned and the potential supervisor(s). Another possibility is to acknowledge that not all of a social worker's needs for supervision may be able to be met by a single supervisor, and to examine the possibility of using different supervisors for different purposes. A further possibility is to look at ways in which the benefits of supervision might be better met in other ways, for example through peer groups, email lists, a mentor system, or retreats. These all represent potential ways in which some of the human rights issues in supervision might be addressed. None will be universally applicable but they are matters for negotiation, with the relevant actors taking account of the particular context. The key element, of course, is to construct supervision so that the 'supervisee' is an active contributor to the process with at least equal control and the 'supervisor' sees it in terms of dialogue from which he/she too can learn and develop, thus addressing the human rights issues of control and surveillance.

The structures of social work

This section deals with the structures within which social workers work. Social workers not only deliver services but they also practise within organisations and as part of a profession. Part of the social work role is to ensure that these social work organisations and professional structures are based on human rights principles.

The role of clients

If social workers are to uphold the principle stated at the beginning of this chapter, namely that human rights are served by the maximisation of self-determination, then this needs to be applied to the processes of the social agency. Often clients are not adequately consulted about a range of decisions that affect them, and the notion of client empowerment is applied to the client's life choices but not to her/his role within the agency. Such empowerment can be achieved in different ways in different locations – what is appropriate or possible will vary with different agency contexts, but the following are some ideas that need to be considered.

The capacity of a person to choose her/his social worker is often limited or non-existent. A social worker is 'assigned' to a client, often without the client being consulted. This decision is often made on the basis of an assessment of what sort of social worker would be 'best' for this particular person, but how often is the person her/himself involved in that assessment? In many cases she/he will not know the particular social workers who might be available, but there is still the possibility for a person to express a preference for a social worker with certain characteristics – sex, age, ethnicity, and so on, or with particular experience or practice orientation. In some instances the person will actually know some of the workers in the agency and may wish to express a preference for or against a particular worker being involved in his/her case. The way in which client preference for choice of worker can be effected will vary from agency to agency, but it is important for such choice to be maximised as part of a human rights approach to practice.

The issue of supervision has already been discussed at some length in this chapter, but the question also needs to be raised about the role of the client in the supervision of the worker. We think of supervision only as an activity between professionals, but if we are really serious about a human rights perspective on social work and maximising the rights of clients, supervision of workers by clients is a natural consequence. Clients, after all, are in a better position than anyone else to know how effective the 'professional help' of social workers has been, to reflect with the social worker on that worker's practice, and to help the worker on the path of professional development. Many agencies seek 'client feedback' through questionnaires or surveys, but this is essentially passive feedback which the agency or worker can accept or ignore at their discretion. A more active role for clients in 'supervision', however, would involve them in the ongoing reflexive development of the social worker.

Such client involvement need not, and indeed should not, stop at super-vision. It is worth considering, in any agency setting, the role clients play in the employment of social workers, including the development of selection criteria, the recruitment process, and the actual interview and selection panels. While there are sometimes good reasons for limiting such involve-ment, depending on the nature of the client group and the agency man-date, from a human rights perspective the full and active involvement of clients in the selection process should be the norm, and the onus should be on agency management to show why such practices are not followed in any particular circumstance. And this principle should apply not only to the initial selection and recruitment of social workers but also to perfor-mance review, promotion, managerial appointments, and other processes regarding social work employment. Indeed the ideal would be for social workers actually to be employed by, and formally accountable to, clients, and hence the clients become the agency managers. This is a natural out-come of a human rights empowerment-based approach to social work, and it can achieve significant results (Liffman 1978; Benn 1981). Although such an ideal is far removed from the reality of practice in most social work agencies, it should not be dismissed as naïve and unrealistic, but rather thought of as a goal towards which social workers should be striving, even if at the present time it is only possible through small incremental changes or the occasional demonstration project.

Client involvement in the policies, procedures and overall direction of the agency is another key component of a human rights approach to practice. This has been an ongoing issue in many social agencies, and there are considerable problems associated with it; it is too easy for such involvement to become tokenistic, or for 'client representatives' to be co-opted into the existing power structure of the agency so that they have little impact. Genuine client involvement that really makes a difference is hard to achieve, largely because of the tacit acceptance (by managers, workers and clients) that existing power differentials are somehow nat-ural and unchangeable. Such assumptions need to be actively challenged in the workplace as part of an approach to practice that respects human rights and seeks to maximise self-determination.

Organisational structures and practices

The issues of organisational structures have largely been covered in earlier sections. At this stage, it is worth noting that attention to organi-sational structures is important, as it is often organisational constraints that impede human rights-based practice. The way in which social work-ers practise in organisations, and the way they may seek to change such organisations (whether their formal structures or informal practices), can help to validate and extend human rights. Often the ways in which social workers can most effectively achieve this are through informal rather than formal channels (Jones & May 1992). Despite the efforts of many managers to reduce worker discretion and to formalise and standardise all activities, there remains in social work organisations an inevitable uncertainty, discretion and room to manoeuvre; the messiness of social work and of the human dramas it deals with can never be fully encapsulated in sets of rules and operational procedures. And the standards of practice are as much established through the informal processes of 'office culture' as by formal regulation. It is through these less formal channels that social workers learn what rules have to be obeyed to the letter and what rules in practice allow more discretion. Rule-bending has been part of social work since its inception, and will remain so. Policies, regulations and rules represent the rationalist modernist solution in an increasingly postmodern, random and chaotic world, and hence will never really work without 'creative interpretation' by people such as social workers who have to carry them out. It is in that creative interpretation (Lipsky 1980), which is often undertaken collectively through the discourse of the 'office culture', that social workers have opportunity to move towards more or less empowering forms of practice that may enhance or restrict human rights.

At a more formal organisational level, the obsession with managerial solutions to perceived problems means that organisational restructuring is a way of life for many social workers. From a managerialist perspective, any problem in an organisation can be solved by organisational change, usually in the form of a restructure. As social work organisations will always have perceived problems, due to the problematic and contradictory nature of social work itself, there will inevitably be continual organisational change in a futile attempt to resolve contradictions that actually lie elsewhere. Organisational change is also a favoured way for state (and increasingly non-state) authorities to make it look as if they are doing something about a social problem. For example the problem of substance abuse is, as social workers well know, the result of structural forces to do with inequality, perceived lack of opportunity for many young people, the potential profits of the illicit drug trade, and so on. It is quite unrealistic to expect a social agency providing services for users to be able to do very much about such structural forces and to make much of a difference. However, governments, for electoral reasons, have to appear to be doing something, and organisational change is a good way to make it seem as if a 'new initiative' is being taken in the 'fight against drugs'.

Social workers have become used to living in a state of constant organisational change, and while this can be destabilising in terms of developing good practice, it also presents opportunities. If the organisational context of social work is constantly being redefined, then it is important for human rights-based social workers to become part of that redefinition and actively engaged in the processes of restructuring, so that structures more conducive to the realisation of human rights can be facilitated.

Professional structures and processes

Social work is very much defined by its professional associations. In most countries where social work is practised there are one or more professional social work bodies. The International Federation of Social Workers, social work's global body, is in reality a federation of national social work associations. These associations vary considerably, depending on the context and the nature of social work in the country concerned (Mayadas et al. 1997; Tan & Envall 2000). Some are more activist, seeing their role as representing the voice of social workers in social issues and policy matters; some are more concerned with maintaining professional standards, professional exclusivity, accreditation, ethics and boundaries; some concentrate on meeting the needs of social workers for continuing education and support; and some are concerned with providing industrial protection for social workers. Most social work associations would in fact see themselves as doing all of these to some extent, though in each country the emphasis is different. In some countries the role of accrediting social work courses is undertaken by a separate body, while in others the professional association takes this role. The following discussion should be taken as applying to both sorts of bodies.

From a human rights perspective, a professional association can play a very important role. Through structures of accreditation and continual professional education, a professional association can encourage the kind of human rights-based practice discussed in this chapter and in Chapter 10. The association's role in defining social work practice in its particular national context gives it a powerful voice in establishing human rights as a fundamental basis for social work. This can be emphasised by professional associations in the way they establish accreditation guidelines, in their eligibility for membership, in their codes of ethics, in their representations to governments, in their publicity, in their dealings with schools of social work, and so on.

It is also important that a professional association reflect human rights principles in its own structures and practices. This requires it to pay attention to issues of inclusivity and to guard against practices that exclude certain people from becoming social workers. For example, it could ensure that indigenous traditions of practice and intellectual activity are included in the definition of standards, allowing for, and encouraging, diversity within the social work profession. It could also take an inclusive position with regard to social workers qualified in other countries (while being mindful of the need for social work to be grounded in the local culture). In addition, the structure of the professional association itself needs to reflect human rights principles, in terms of maximising participatory democracy within the association, ensuring that some social workers are not marginalised because of their background or their unpopular views, and making sure that the processes followed are transparent and participatory.

A further way in which professional associations can play an important part in human rights-based social work is by instituting human rights awareness and training workshops for social workers and others working in the human service field. Such workshops can help social workers to focus on human rights issues, define human rights priorities from their own perspective, establish networks among human rights-based workers, and develop appropriate action strategies.

The professional association has an important role in making representations to its national government about human rights issues, especially those of particular concern to social workers. A national government's commitment or otherwise to human rights (understood in a broad sense) should be a major concern of a national social work association, and it is important for the association to find ways that its voice, representing the social workers of that country, can be heard in government circles and public debates. Human rights issues are regularly matters of public concern and media attention, and social work, through professional associations, has a responsibility to be making a vigorous contribution to these debates. This will also include drawing attention (if necessary public attention) to practices in government and non-government organisations that violate human rights through their structures and processes.

A final and most important role for a professional association is to support social workers who are themselves taking a stand on human rights issues and who may themselves be victims of human rights abuse (or in danger of being so) as a consequence of their social work practice. Social workers have been threatened, imprisoned, beaten, tortured and killed as a result of their work, and the professional association has a clear responsibility to be working on behalf of such social workers and also seeking to prevent such abuse from happening by providing activist workers with full support. The intimidation of social workers, even if not so extreme, can still be of serious concern. Many social workers have lost their jobs, been denied promotion, been ostracised in the workplace, been told they will never get employment again, and so on, simply because they have dared to speak out or to confront injustice. These too are human rights abuses suffered by social workers, as are cases of discrimination against social workers in the workplace (e.g. on the grounds of race, sex, age, sexuality), and they demand strong action by a professional association committed to supporting the human rights of its members.

The education of social workers

A human rights perspective obviously has implications for social work education. The most obvious implication is the inclusion of material on human rights, and on a human rights approach to practice, in the social work curriculum. This would require theoretical exploration of the kind described in earlier chapters of this book, encouragement for students to think about human rights and what they mean for social work, and concentration on the kind of practice discussed in this chapter and Chapter 10. In this chapter, dealing with the human rights implications of the structures and processes of social work practice, we are primarily concerned with the actual process of social work education and what it means for human rights.

Banking education or critical pedagogy

Freire's description of critical pedagogy (1996), in contrast to the more conventional banking concept of education, has been very influential within social work theory and practice. Briefly, the banking concept sees education as about students acquiring something called 'knowledge', which is 'deposited' in the student's brain in the same way as money in a bank. This is objective, commodified knowledge, which the teacher imparts to the student and which the student absorbs, without any significant degree of critical engagement or reflection, and the student is then able to be tested on how well he/she has understood, absorbed and memorised the content. The skill of the teacher is judged entirely in terms of how effectively she/he can impart the knowledge, and the skill of the student is assessed on how effectively he/she can 'learn' it. The knowledge itself is unchanged in the process, and passes from teacher to student in a neutral, objective way.

By contrast, critical pedagogy requires that the teacher and the student actively engage, together, with the subject. Knowledge is not neutral but is contextualised, and both teacher and student construct and reconstruct the knowledge, in dialogue with each other; it is comparable to the process of dialogical praxis described in Chapter 10. From this perspective, knowledge can only be effectively acquired through a process of critical reflection, where the student relates the knowledge to her/his own direct environment and experience and uses the knowledge to engage in further reflection and action. This knowledge is not value-neutral but is part of a dynamic process of liberation and transformation. The skill of the teacher is judged on her/his capacity to enter into a critical dialogue with the student, and the skill of the student is judged on his/her capacity to reflectively integrate the dialogical experience in such a way that it leads to action and liberation. This is, of course, an oversimplification of Freire's philosophy of education, and the reader requiring a fuller explanation is referred to his *Pedagogy of the Oppressed* (1996).

Given the parallels between Freire's critical pedagogy and the dialogical praxis approach to social work described earlier, it is clear that a critical pedagogy approach to social work education will reinforce a human rights approach to social work. If the link between means and ends is to be respected, then such a form of education is necessary for human rights-based social work. It is also the form of educational practice that most respects the human rights of students as active and autonomous participants in the learning process rather than as passive recipients of commodified knowledge. Further, one of the important aspects of education is modelling, and if a dialogical praxis approach is modelled in a school of social work it will considerably strengthen the human rights perspective for students. It is hard to see how one can teach dialogical praxis without at the same time attempting to model such an approach to the educational task.

It is not easy to implement critical pedagogy in social work education. The educational socialisation of both educators and students usually means that such an approach does not come easily and is therefore likely to be resisted. There is more risk-taking, for both teacher and student. In addition, the structures of the university in which the education program is located are unlikely to be conducive to such an approach. Universities are no longer – if indeed they ever were – the free academic environment in which teacher and student can together seek wisdom, but are firmly embedded in banking concepts of education, emphasising specified learning objectives, objective evaluation of students' work, and marks/grades assigned on a linear scale. There are of course exceptions, particularly at the level of postgraduate research, and in various pockets of resistance that have been maintained in what are otherwise oppressive structures. Perhaps the strongest institutional constraint is time. Critical pedagogy takes time, and the time required of the educator is greater than is the case for banking education. It may simply be impossible to follow such practices given the staffing constraints experienced in many schools of social work.

Such institutional constraints can militate strongly against a critical pedagogy approach to social work education in many settings. But there may still be some aspects of the dialogical approach that can be incorporated into social work education programs, and creative educators can frequently find ways to achieve this, though often only at a more modest scale. However, the institutional constraints also suggest that seeking changes to the institutional practices of universities is a human rights issue that social work educators need to take up. Students can readily be made aware of the institutional factors that constrain students and staff alike, and they may form a partnership with educators to work towards progressive change.

Student choice

A human rights-based approach to social work education would seek to respect students' rights by allowing them maximum choice over, for example, units to be studied, field placements, allocated field educator, form of assessment, research supervisor, and so on. This defines the student as an active participant able to take responsibility for her/his own learning, and so is more respectful of human rights than the view of the student as a passive recipient who does not know what is best for her/him.

Student choice, however, must be informed. To expect a student to make such choices about his/her education without relevant information denies rather than promotes human rights. The student needs to be aware of the consequences of decisions, for example the employment opportunities likely to be gained or lost as a result of choosing a particular field placement or option, or the particular contributions specific supervisors may be able to make. There are also practical reasons why student choice cannot always be granted; for example, all students may request the same field placement or the same research supervisor. The student's choice should not be expected to be made in a vacuum, but rather as part of an ongoing dialogue between student and educator about what is likely to be in the student's best interests. But it still needs to remain the student's effective choice where at all possible, rather than the educator using her/his power and experience to 'persuade' the student otherwise. The principle to be followed cannot be one of unlimited choice by the student in all circumstances, but rather one of maximum feasible, effective and informed choice.

Collaborative learning

The idea of collaborative learning implies collaboration both among students and between student and educator. Each can serve to promote human rights in education by valuing the contribution of all involved in the process, and also by reinforcing students' rights, individually and collectively, to self-determination within the educational process. Collaborative learning is an important component of critical pedagogy. It requires that learning goals be set through dialogue between educator and students, that both be seen as having significant things to contribute to the learning process, and that both be active participants. This does not privilege 'knowledge' in books, journals and professors' brains over 'knowledge' that is grounded in students' experiences of the world. Rather it accepts both as important and seeks to have each inform the other so that all those involved, both students and educators, will learn. Each person, therefore, has an obligation to contribute to the educational process, and this promotes human rights within the educational experience.

Collaborative learning among students, using groups where possible, can not only be a way of maximising scarce teaching resources but can also serve the important purpose of challenging the individualist assumptions underlying both education and social work practice. The empowerment that is potentially present in a group situation can itself be an important learning experience for students, as the group is often the format in which consciousness-raising social work can most effectively take place, and where individual blame-the-victim perspectives can be readily challenged.

Clients and workers

So far the educational experience has been described as an interaction between student and educator. But there are two other actors who have a critical role to play in the education of social workers. The involvement of clients should be of central importance in social work education. By not including the voice of the clients, the client is tacitly devalued and the education process is constructed so as to exclude the people who are supposed to be the ultimate beneficiaries of the education program. Clients can and should have a critical role if the human rights perspective is to be maintained and all voices are to be heard.

In the earlier discussion of professional supervision, it was suggested that clients should play a part in the supervision and evaluation of practising social workers. The same argument applies to students. By framing field education in such a way that it is only social workers who are seen as competent to provide supervision or to judge the effectiveness of a student's practice, social work education is effectively silencing the clients, who clearly have a major stake in the process and who can offer important and unique insights into the effectiveness or otherwise of a student's learning. To include them in the supervision and evaluation of students on fieldwork is a significant human rights challenge facing social work educators. Obviously it is not an easy task to implement such a strategy effectively, but that is no reason for it not to be taken up. It is, of course, not only in field education that clients have a central role to play in the educating of future social workers. Their input into classroom learning, and their active involvement in the process of collaborative learning described above, can add significant human rights elements to social work education.

Practising social workers also have a great deal of wisdom to bring to social work education, and most social work schools already make good use of social workers as sessional instructors. But their participation in a collaborative learning program is much more than simply 'coming in to give a class' and then departing; it involves a higher level of commitment and risk, but also a higher level of potential reward. Such participation by both workers and clients could have significant benefits for them, as well as for students and educators, since they too would become part of a collaborative learning process comparable to the dialogical praxis model outlined in Chapter 10. Here we can see the potential for the merging of social work education and social work practice in a more fundamental way than commonly occurs in the field education program, where workers, students, clients and educators are all significant actors in a mutual education-practice-research activity. Such educational practice would value the contributions of all four groups and would significantly enhance the human rights project, as well as modelling a progressive human rights-based social work for future practitioners.

Assessment

The assessment of students is one of the aspects of education which can be problematic in human rights terms, since it is where the power difference between educator and student is most keenly felt. Assessment is constructed as the educator passing judgement on the value of the student's work; there is not necessarily any requirement for self-assessment by the student to become part of the process. Further, the educator evaluates the student, but there is often no corresponding mechanism for the student to evaluate the educator. The process therefore devalues the voice of the student and privileges the voice of the educator, thereby constructing an unequal and potentially oppressive relationship. This can easily undermine attempts to practise critical pedagogy within the social work school. The reality of student assessment is probably the biggest single obstacle to an education based on human rights practice.

While the unequal relationship involved in student assessment is to some extent inevitable within a university, some steps can be taken to minimise its impact and work towards a more dialogical relationship that is more respectful of the rights of the student. One way is to involve students in the process of determining the most appropriate forms of assessment. Sometimes this can be done individually where students can choose their assessment, while at other times it can be done by students and educators talking together as a group. Sometimes, also, a student may be able to have a choice of which faculty member will assess her/his work. Students could also be involved in the assessment process itself, by being asked to reflect on their own work and discuss it with the educator. In this way the assessment can become itself part of the dialogical process.

Educators can also change the nature of the assessment process by providing ample qualitative feedback to students, which moves assessment away from the linear grading system that is often incompatible with assessments for social work practice. Significant qualitative feedback can serve to render the letter or number grade less important for at least some students. This can be further reinforced by the educator providing informal feedback through the ongoing educator–student relationship. This can take place not only through formal written comments on assignments but also informally through conversations after class, with student groups over coffee, and so on.

Another way in which the inequality of the assessment relationship can be addressed is by building in appropriate mechanisms for the student to assess the educator, in a way that has more significance than occasional feedback survey questionnaires. Thus assessment can become something of a mutual reflective evaluation which can have significant positive outcomes for both parties, though in reality it is unlikely that this would ever completely equalise the relationship, simply because of the power structures within which education is located. However, mutual assessment is one way in which this power inequity can be reduced, and this would be more consistent with a human rights approach to education and practice.

Not all these initiatives may be possible in any one educational setting. For example in programs offering distance education for social work students, it is more difficult (though not necessarily impossible) to develop dialogical relations with students or involve them in the assessment process. Other institutional constraints may prevent further initiatives. But the point at issue is that assessment should where possible involve the student as well as the educator, and in any school of social work it should be possible to develop some sort of dialogue between educators and students about the assessment process. That alone can make a significant difference towards validating the student's right to have some control over her/his education and evaluation.

Field education

Field education is a major component of social work education. In the fieldwork setting there are several opportunities to implement a human rights perspective. Some of these have already been discussed, for example allowing the student maximum informed choice in the selection of agency, supervisor, university liaison staff, and work to be undertaken. Such choice validates the student and his/her right to maximum control over the direction and content of learning.

Supervision of social workers has already been discussed at some length, and the same issues can be seen as applying to the supervision of the social work student on placement. Learning is likely to be maximised, and the rights of the student respected, if that supervision process can also be dialogical, with mutual learning and feedback, where the student is an active learner and contributor to the process and can take some responsibility for the direction of the supervisory relationship and the learning to be undertaken.

The involvement of clients in the education process and in the evaluation of social workers has also been discussed in earlier sections, and again a natural extension would apply this to the field supervision of students. Ways need to be found in which clients can have an active role in the supervision and evaluation of social work students, as this affirms the clients' rights to a voice in a process that will eventually have a significant impact on them through the practice of newly graduating social workers. In the earlier discussion of clients' role in classroom teaching it was suggested that this could lead to a merging of education, practice and research, involving students, educators, clients and social workers in a collaborative process. Such a collaboration can take place at least as easily in the fieldwork setting as in the classroom, and it may provide a different framework for field education from the traditional apprenticeship model, which largely reproduces the unequal educational relationship where the student can easily be defined as relatively powerless and the client does not even rate a mention.

Similarly, the above comments about assessment can be translated into the fieldwork setting. Assessment mechanisms that provide an active role for the student are probably more common in field education than in classroom learning, and there is ample opportunity for the further development of collaborative assessment in the field, as part of the dialogical approach to supervision mentioned above.

Finally, field education provides many opportunities for students to engage with human rights issues in a practical way, by using the whole range of social work skills. The social work field education program could, indeed, be framed around human rights issues, covering the three generations and the variety of social work methods, but specifically using human rights terms to define the social work role and task, and to examine issues such as ethics, values, needs, cultural diversity, and so on. Indeed the human rights perspective increases the potential range for field education placements beyond more traditional social work settings, including activist agencies, environmental agencies, and overseas aid and development agencies. Many such placements are already used by schools of social work, but they frequently have only marginal status and are often constructed as not 'real' social work; they are for students who have a particular interest, who may not see themselves working as 'social workers' after graduation, or are optional extras for the 'good' student who has already demonstrated competence in 'mainstream' social work. A human rights perspective can help to move beyond the marginalisation of such placements by seeing them as central to creative practice.

Curriculum design

The design of the social work curriculum is an important location for the discursive construction of social work. By deciding what does and does not go into the social work curriculum, how it will be integrated and how it will be taught, those who design the curriculum have a major role in determining how social work is understood and practised by future generations of social workers. Traditionally, these decisions are largely made by three groups: social work educators, employers, and the professional association or accrediting body. It is in the interplay between these groups – the framework established by accrediting bodies, the ideas of social work educators, and the demands of employers and the professional association – that the curriculum is designed. Curriculum design is a fluid and ever-changing process. Despite apparently fixed curriculum statements, the social work curriculum in any social work school will effectively change every year in response to different requirements from the field, changing views of educators, change in faculty, and student demand. Indeed the context of social work is changing so quickly that any social work school that does not make frequent changes to the curriculum (whether formally recognised or not) risks irrelevance.

How can curriculum design meet the requirements of a human rights approach to social work? Obviously the inclusion of material on human rights and the development of a human rights perspective on practice are essential. But in this chapter we are more concerned with the process than the content, and this requires an examination of who designs the curriculum and how. As indicated above, traditionally the curriculum is designed with input from educators, employers and the profession. Once again, there are two key groups that are largely excluded from the process, namely clients and students. If the process of curriculum design is to be true to human rights principles, it is important that these voices also be heard and that processes be established to ensure that they have not just a token input but are able to play a meaningful part in the design of the curriculum and in decisions about what is taught and how it should be taught. That way these two key groups are given the right of self-determination, and control over processes that directly affect them. Otherwise the process of curriculum design remains in the hands of the more powerful and privileged groups, and in itself reinforces the relationships of inequality and power that can be seen as impinging on the rights of the less powerful clients and students.

Of course it is easier to make such a statement than to implement it. Involvement of both clients and students in curriculum design processes is neither easy nor straightforward, and like other attempts at participation it can result in tokenism and co-option. But if the obstacles to such involvement can be overcome, the curriculum design process can itself become a dialogical collaborative effort, and the result will in all likelihood reflect better the needs of all those involved in the process. And simply by engaging clients and students in this way, the power imbalances in education can to some extent be addressed.

The same applies not only to curriculum review and design processes but also to ongoing structures. The two important structures are the board or advisory committee of the social work school and the accreditation panel of the professional association or accrediting body. Both bodies need to address the issues of client and student input, and membership, if they are to reflect the human rights perspective of social work.

Academic appointments and evaluation

If the human rights perspective is to be maintained in the operation of social work education, it is important that there be input of both students and clients in the processes of recruitment, appointment, evaluation and promotion of academic staff. The traditional methods for these processes involve other university staff but do not often involve either students or the recipients of the professional services those students will offer after graduation. Again, it is a case of these less powerful voices being marginalised by the more powerful, and a human rights perspective would require that some way be found for them to be heard. This might involve student and client representatives on recruitment and selection panels, tenure committees, promotion committees, and so on. But such formal bodies can easily intimidate those with less experience in university structures, and simple representation may only reinforce rather than address the marginalisation of the student and client voices. It may be that genuine and effective involvement is better achieved by using a less formal process, for example through group discussions and consultations, the results of which can then be fed into the formal processes.

Like the other instances discussed in this section, the issues of genuine participation by the less powerful need to be addressed, and it should be recognised that this is not a simple process. Social workers, however, have been dealing with the dilemmas and contradictions of participation for a long time and should be in a better position than most other professions to address these issues effectively. The important point is that a human rights perspective requires that the voices of the less powerful be effectively heard, and that this applies to the internal workings of social work agencies and university social work departments as well as to the world of the social work client. If social workers cannot observe human rights principles in their own practices, they cannot presume to impose a human rights regime on others.

Conclusion

Human rights principles apply as much to *how* social workers do their work as to *what* they do. They must therefore be concerned with the processes of social work practice and education, as well as with their outcomes. Social work practice or education that does not reflect human rights principles in its own structures and processes, even though it may ultimately seek human rights goals, is not only contradictory but is likely to be counter-productive, given the necessary connection between means and ends. This chapter has identified a number of issues that are raised by a human rights perspective when we consider the processes and structures of the social work profession, and has shown that often the conventional language, structures, processes and educational practices of social work are counter to human rights principles

It is therefore important that social workers who claim a commitment to human rights should be critically reflective of their own practices, as well as analysing their clients' problems from a human rights perspective. It is not enough to be a dedicated human rights activist; one also has to be able to apply the analysis to one's own day-to-day actions.

Some of the ideas in this chapter might be seen as arguably more radical than those of the remainder of the book. This is because, for social workers, to apply the critique to social work itself brings the analysis much 'closer to home' and defines social work as potentially part of the problem rather than only as the means to the solution. Applying a human rights perspective to client outcomes is one thing, but to apply it to social work itself is quite another. After all, it is easier, and more comfortable, to apply a radical critique to something else (such as oppressive structures or institutions) than to one's own practice. This suggests that as well as promoting action to change oppressive structures within society, a major task for those seeking to bring about radical change through social work is also to apply the analysis to social work itself.

CHAPTER 12

Conclusion: Prospects for Human Rights Practice

There are two views one can take of the notion of human rights. One is that it is an idea whose time has come. This view sees human rights as being a necessary counter to economic globalisation, and asserts that in the newly globalised world ideas of global citizenship, based on ideals of human rights, are important in the same way that ideas of national citizenship rights became important with the emergence of the nation state. It suggests that the apparently increasing interest in a human rights discourse is a source of hope for a future based on collective human values rather than individual greed and consumption. Human rights can be the basis for a future of humanity that until now has been an apparently impossible dream.

The other view of human rights is that it is an idea whose time has passed. This view sees human rights as a leftover remnant from the disappearing world of modernist certainty and western imperialism. In the newly emerging postmodern world of relativism, multiple voices, fragmented realities and the 'death of the meta-narrative', there is no room for, and no point in, a universal discourse such as human rights. The idea of human rights is so tied up with the modernist project, and so western in its construction, that to persist with it is both an irrelevance and a disservice to humanity rather than a positive contribution to the future.

We cannot fully reject or ignore the postmodernist critique of traditional constructions of human rights. But this book is written from a position that embraces the former rather than the latter of the above alternatives. The postmodernist critique requires us to reject the idea of universal human rights as a static, natural or somehow god-given reality, inherent in 'the nature of man'. The idea of human rights as discursively constructed, however, frees us from such a notion, and sees human rights as a discourse that is changing and evolving but still universal in that it is about how we construct universal values about what it means to be human, and about the implications of a perception of our common humanity for the way people should be treated. Such a discourse of common humanity will inevitably be contested, and the issue of whose voices are heard in the construction of human rights is therefore crucial.

The common discourses of social science are discourses of division. They divide people into two or more groups, on the basis of power, gender, class, race, ethnicity, sexuality, location or nationality. The analysis of oppression, on whatever dimension, divides humanity into an oppressing group and an oppressed group. Such analysis of course is essential – if we are to do something about overcoming oppression and its resultant inequality and inequity we need to understand its structural basis.

The danger of such discourses of division, however, is that they construct the world as consisting of people divided into two or more competing groups, thereby excluding or devaluing discourses of unity. Discourses of unity are about the things that unite the human race, rather than the things that divide it. In the final analysis, if two people are brought together who are different on any dimension(s) of inequality one might imagine – race, class, gender, ability, sexuality, age – the things that those two people still have in common, reflected in their common humanity, are far stronger and more significant. It is out of an understanding of our common humanity that we condemn racism, sexism, colonialism, or any other form of discrimination; this is a view that says that the basis of the discrimination is irrelevant when we consider the essential humanness of the person concerned. Thus in condemning discrimination, or any form of oppression, we are taking a human rights position, arguing that no person should be treated in that way because of our common human rights.

A human rights perspective represents such a discourse of unity, which needs to be put alongside (not to replace) the discourses of division. It is only by understanding the things that unite human beings as well as the things that divide them that we can develop an adequate basis for social and political practice. Conventional social science has provided social workers with sophisticated understandings of difference and division, and a human rights perspective can complement this by emphasising the important things that also bring people together. Social science, especially in its postmodern versions, helps us to validate and celebrate difference. Human rights, by contrast, help us to validate and celebrate our common humanity. Each is important, not only for social work practice, but for all people who care about the future of the human race.

A human rights perspective, however, does not negate an analysis or a celebration of difference. Thinking about human rights immediately poses the question of why some people are denied the human rights that others take for granted, and this inevitably leads into an analysis of inequality and structural oppression. And a human rights perspective does support the valuing of difference: the right to be different, to define one's life in different ways, to live a different lifestyle and to proclaim and celebrate difference can indeed be understood as a human right – we can unite in a celebration of difference as part of our common humanity.

Human rights also represent perhaps the strongest position from which to mount an opposition to the economic fundamentalism that is driving globalisation. In this sense a human rights perspective is more than just a nice idea. It provides a basis for a critique of and alternative to the global regime about which many people are becoming increasingly concerned because of its reinforcing of structures of oppression and disadvantage, and its blatantly undemocratic processes, which result in benefits for the few rather than for the many. Because of the impact of globalisation on social work, and especially on the people social workers claim to serve and to represent, it is important for social workers to be able to understand something about human rights and to think about the way human rights can serve as a basis for practice. A human rights discourse allows social workers to engage with universal themes of what is right and just, rather than to define morality only in terms of the fragmented personal politics described by Bauman (1999) and Beck (1997). Social workers are concerned with issues of social justice, fairness and equity, and hence a human rights perspective that focuses on these can be of considerable value.

Because of the discursive nature of human rights, and because of the need for human rights to be contextualised in different locations, a book like this cannot come up with 'definitive answers' or prescriptions about how to practise human rights-based social work. It can make some suggestions, identify some possible avenues for further exploration, and suggest the kind of things that should concern social work if it is to define itself as a human rights-based profession. How these are worked out in the varied, messy and changing world of social work practice, in different cultural and political contexts, is a matter both for each social worker individually and also for social workers working collectively, through formal or informal structures.

In the first decades of the new century the global–local dialectic is likely to be a major factor not only for social workers but throughout the newly emerging global society. How this plays out, how the local and global relate, how people relate to each, how (or if) they are consciously connected, and how each is understood in terms of the other will profoundly affect the lives of every person on the planet. It is in this context that a discourse of human rights becomes particularly important. Human rights represent a global discourse, given their concern with ideas of common humanity and global citizenship; the human rights dis-

course, by definition, applies universally. Yet statements of right are readily translated into local contexts, often, as we have seen, by their redefinition as statements of need. Human rights thus represent a discourse that
readily moves between the global and the local, and can provide a basis
for creative practice that links them in an empowering way. This makes it
of particular value for social workers struggling to practise in the new
environment of globalisation and the weakening of the state structures
within which social work has traditionally been located. The capacity of
social workers to link the local and the global in creative practice holds
the key to the future of the social work profession.

The realisation and the protection of human rights will not be
achieved without a struggle. Despite an apparent consensus on the importance of human rights (who would argue against them?), it is nevertheless
true that there are powerful forces with an interest in not following a
human rights agenda too closely, and indeed considerable profits are
being made because of the denial or violation of the human rights of large
numbers of people, particularly in poorer countries. It is not simply a case
of moral suasion. The history of human rights has been a struggle, often
against the odds, by people who have stood firmly and courageously on
the side of humanity and dared to resist the forces of oppression and domination. The struggle, inevitably, will continue. Human rights are not simply defined, they have to be struggled for and are hard won. Then once
won, there is a continuing struggle to protect them. The human rights
struggle is one that, in all probability, will never end. But defining social
work as a human rights profession locates social work practice firmly
within that ongoing struggle to assert the values of a common humanity.

A human rights discourse is, by nature, a discourse of hope. It concentrates not only on what is wrong (characteristic of so much social and
political analysis) but also articulates a vision of what is right, of where we
can be heading, of the human ideal. We may never get there, but that
should not diminish the strength of the vision. Such a discourse of hope
is significantly lacking in the social and political discourse at the dawn of
the twenty-first century, and is particularly lacking in the discourse of
social work. The only optimistic vision in the general public domain
seems to be the naïve and simplistic 'get rich quick' consumerist ideology of the free market, which has been shown to be both fundamentally
inequitable and fatally unsustainable. Whether a discourse of human
rights can provide a more tenable and sustainable hope remains to be
seen, but the promise is certainly there. Social work is, arguably, the core
human rights profession, given its value base and its encompassing of all
three generations of human rights within its practice. Social work practice, therefore, is in a unique and potentially powerful position to help
make the vision of human rights a reality.

APPENDIX I

The Universal Declaration of Human Rights

The Universal Declaration of Human Rights was passed by the UN General Assembly and assented to by the nations of the world in 1948. It represents a remarkable global consensus on human rights, and although some of its wording may now be open to re-evaluation, and certainly its articles are not by any means universally adopted in practice, it still remains the international human rights document with the greatest moral force. From the point of view of this book it is a key reference for all social workers.

Preamble

Whereas recognition of the inherent dignity and of the equal and inalienable rights of all members of the human family is the foundation of freedom, justice and peace in the world,

Whereas disregard and contempt for human rights have resulted in barbarous acts which have outraged the conscience of mankind, and the advent of a world in which human beings shall enjoy freedom of speech and belief and freedom from fear and want has been proclaimed as the highest aspiration of the common people,

Whereas it is essential, if man is not to be compelled to have recourse, as a last resort, to rebellion against tyranny and oppression, that human rights should be protected by the rule of law,

Whereas it is essential to promote the development of friendly relations between nations,

Whereas the peoples of the United Nations have in the Charter reaffirmed their faith in fundamental human rights, in the dignity and worth of the human person and in the equal rights of men and women and have determined to promote social progress and better standards of life in larger freedom,

Whereas Member States have pledged themselves to achieve, in co-operation with the United Nations, the promotion of universal respect for and observance of human rights and fundamental freedoms,

Whereas a common understanding of these rights and freedoms is of the greatest importance for the full realization of this pledge,

Now, therefore,

The General Assembly,

Proclaims this Universal Declaration of Human Rights as a common standard of achievement for all peoples and all nations, to the end that every individual and every organ of society, keeping this Declaration constantly in mind, shall strive by teaching and education to promote respect for these rights and freedoms and by progressive measures, national and international, to secure their universal and effective recognition and observance, both among the peoples of Member States themselves and among the peoples of territories under their jurisdiction.

Article 1

All human beings are born free and equal in dignity and rights. They are endowed with reason and conscience and should act towards one another in a spirit of brotherhood.

Article 2

Everyone is entitled to all the rights and freedoms set forth in this Declaration, without distinction of any kind, such as race, colour, sex, language, religion, political or other opinion, national or social origin, property, birth or other status.

Furthermore, no distinction shall be made on the basis of the political, jurisdictional or international status of the country or territory to which a person belongs, whether it be independent, trust, non-self-governing or under any other limitation of sovereignty.

Article 3

Everyone has the right to life, liberty and security of person.

Article 4

No one shall be held in slavery or servitude; slavery and the slave trade shall be prohibited in all their forms.

Article 5

No one shall be subjected to torture or to cruel, inhuman or degrading treatment or punishment.

Article 6

Everyone has the right to recognition everywhere as a person before the law.

Article 7

All are equal before the law and are entitled without any discrimination to equal protection of the law. All are entitled to equal protection against any discrimination in violation of this Declaration and against any incitement to such discrimination.

Article 8

Everyone has the right to an effective remedy by the competent national tribunals for acts violating the fundamental rights granted him by the constitution or by law.

Article 9

No one shall be subjected to arbitrary arrest, detention or exile.

Article 10

Everyone is entitled in full equality to a fair and public hearing by an independent and impartial tribunal, in the determination of his rights and obligations and of any criminal charge against him.

Article 11

1. Everyone charged with a penal offence has the right to be presumed innocent until proved guilty according to law in a public trial at which he has had all the guarantees necessary for his defence.
2. No one shall be held guilty of any penal offence on account of any act or omission which did not constitute a penal offence, under national or international law, at the time when it was committed. Nor shall a heavier penalty be imposed than the one that was applicable at the time the penal offence was committed.

Article 12

No one shall be subjected to arbitrary interference with his privacy, family, home or correspondence, nor to attacks upon his honour and reputation. Everyone has the right to the protection of the law against such interference or attacks.

Article 13

1. Everyone has the right to freedom of movement and residence within the borders of each State.
2. Everyone has the right to leave any country, including his own, and to return to his country.

Article 14

1. Everyone has the right to seek and to enjoy in other countries asylum from persecution.
2. This right may not be invoked in the case of prosecutions genuinely arising from non-political crimes or from acts contrary to the purposes and principles of the United Nations.

Article 15

1. Everyone has the right to a nationality.

2. No one shall be arbitrarily deprived of his nationality nor denied the right to change his nationality.

Article 16

1. Men and women of full age, without any limitation due to race, nationality or religion, have the right to marry and to found a family. They are entitled to equal rights as to marriage, during marriage and at its dissolution.
2. Marriage shall be entered into only with the free and full consent of the intending spouses.
3. The family is the natural and fundamental group unit of society and is entitled to protection by society and the State.

Article 17

1. Everyone has the right to own property alone as well as in association with others.
2. No one shall be arbitrarily deprived of his property.

Article 18

Everyone has the right to freedom of thought, conscience and religion; this right includes freedom to change his religion or belief, and freedom, either alone or in community with others and in public or private, to manifest his religion or belief in teaching, practice, worship and observance.

Article 19

Everyone has the right to freedom of opinion and expression; this right includes freedom to hold opinions without interference and to seek, receive and impart information and ideas through any media and regardless of frontiers.

Article 20

1. Everyone has the right to freedom of peaceful assembly and association.
2. No one may be compelled to belong to an association.

Article 21

1. Everyone has the right to take part in the government of his country, directly or through freely chosen representatives.
2. Everyone has the right to equal access to public service in his country.
3. The will of the people shall be the basis of the authority of government; this will shall be expressed in periodic and genuine elections which shall be by universal and equal suffrage and shall be held by secret vote or by equivalent free voting procedures.

Article 22

Everyone, as a member of society, has the right to social security and is entitled to realization, through national effort and international co-operation and in accordance with the organization and resources of each State, of the economic, social and cultural rights indispensable for his dignity and the free development of his personality.

Article 23

1. Everyone has the right to work, to free choice of employment, to just and favourable conditions of work and to protection against unemployment.
2. Everyone, without any discrimination, has the right to equal pay for equal work.
3. Everyone who works has the right to just and favourable remuneration ensuring for himself and his family an existence worthy of human dignity, and supplemented, if necessary, by other means of social protection.
4. Everyone has the right to form and to join trade unions for the protection of his interests.

Article 24

Everyone has the right to rest and leisure, including reasonable limitation of working hours and periodic holidays with pay.

Article 25

1. Everyone has the right to a standard of living adequate for the health and well-being of himself and of his family, including food, clothing, housing and medical care and necessary social services, and the right to security in the event of unemployment, sickness, disability, widowhood, old age or other lack of livelihood in circumstances beyond his control.
2. Motherhood and childhood are entitled to special care and assistance. All children, whether born in or out of wedlock, shall enjoy the same social protection.

Article 26

1. Everyone has the right to education. Education shall be free, at least in the elementary and fundamental stages. Elementary education shall be compulsory. Technical and professional education shall be made generally available and higher education shall be equally accessible to all on the basis of merit.
2. Education shall be directed to the full development of the human personality and to the strengthening of respect for human rights and fundamental freedoms. It shall promote understanding, tolerance and friendship among all nations, racial or religious groups, and shall further the activities of the United Nations for the maintenance of peace.
3. Parents have a prior right to choose the kind of education that shall be given to their children.

Article 27

1. Everyone has the right freely to participate in the cultural life of the community, to enjoy the arts and to share in scientific advancement and its benefits.

2. Everyone has the right to the protection of the moral and material interests resulting from any scientific, literary or artistic production of which he is the author.

Article 28

Everyone is entitled to a social and international order in which the rights and freedoms set forth in this Declaration can be fully realized.

Article 29

1. Everyone has duties to the community in which alone the free and full development of his personality is possible.
2. In the exercise of his rights and freedoms, everyone shall be subject only to such limitations as are determined by law solely for the purpose of securing due recognition and respect for the rights and freedoms of others and of meeting the just requirements of morality, public order and the general welfare in a democratic society.
3. These rights and freedoms may in no case be exercised contrary to the purposes and principles of the United Nations.

Article 30

Nothing in this Declaration may be interpreted as implying for any State, group or person any right to engage in any activity or to perform any act aimed at the destruction of any of the rights and freedoms set forth herein.

APPENDIX II

Other Human Rights Declarations, Treaties and Conventions

As well as the Universal Declaration of Human Rights, there are a number of other United Nations human rights declarations, treaties and conventions of potential relevance to social workers. The texts are not reproduced here, because of space limitations, but they are readily available from UN sources, from the Internet, or from various books in which they are reprinted (e.g. Ishay 1997).

This list does not include important regional human rights documents, such as the European Convention for the Protection of Human Rights, the American Convention on Human Rights, the African Charter on Human and People's Rights, and so on. These are important for social workers working in those regions but are not included here because the list is meant to be of use for social workers in any country. It also does not include national bills of rights or human rights declarations and legislation. Readers are encouraged to investigate the national and regional human rights documents, agreements, conventions and charters that apply to their own regional and national settings.

The full texts of the following documents, in different translations, can be found through the website of the United Nations High Commission for Human Rights (www.unhchr.ch).

- International Covenant on Economic, Social and Cultural Rights
- International Covenant on Civil and Political Rights
- Optional Protocol to the International Covenant on Civil and Political Rights allowing for an individual to appeal to the UN if their rights have been violated
- Second Optional Protocol to the International Covenant on Civil and Political Rights, aiming at the abolition of the death penalty
- Declaration on the Right and Responsibility of Individuals, Groups and Organs of Society to Promote and Protect Universally Recognized Human Rights and Fundamental Freedoms
- Proclamation of Teheran (a further declaration of human rights twenty years after the Universal Declaration)
- Declaration on the Granting of Independence to Colonial Countries and Peoples
- United Nations Declaration on the Elimination of All Forms of Racial Discrimination

- International Convention on the Elimination of All Forms of Racial Discrimination
- Discrimination (Employment and Occupation) Convention
- Convention against Discrimination in Education
- Equal Remuneration Convention
- Declaration on the Elimination of All Forms of Intolerance and of Discrimination Based on Religion or Belief
- Declaration on Fundamental Principles concerning the Contribution to the Mass Media to Strengthening Peace and International Understanding, to the Promotion of Human Rights and to Countering Racialism, Apartheid and Incitement to War
- Declaration on Race and Racial Prejudice
- Declaration on the Rights of Persons Belonging to National or Ethnic, Religious and Linguistic Minorities
- Declaration on the Elimination of All Forms of Discrimination against Women
- Convention on the Elimination of All Forms of Discrimination against Women
- Declaration on the Elimination of Violence against Women
- Convention on the Political Rights of Women
- Declaration on the Protection of Women and Children in Emergency and Armed Conflict
- Optional Protocol to the Convention on the Elimination of Discrimination against Women (allowing cases of discrimination against women to be appealed to the UN)
- Declaration on the Rights of the Child
- Convention on the Rights of the Child
- Optional Protocol to the Convention on the Rights of the Child on the involvement of children in armed conflicts
- Optional Protocol to the Convention on the Rights of the Child on the sale of children, child prostitution and child pornography
- Declaration on Social and Legal Principles relating to the Protection and Welfare of Children, with Special Reference to Foster Placement and Adoption Nationally and Internationally
- Slavery Convention
- Protocol amending the Slavery Convention
- Supplementary Convention on the Abolition of Slavery, the Slave Trade, and Institutions and Practices Similar to Slavery
- Forced Labour Convention
- Abolition of Forced Labour Convention
- Convention for the Suppression of the Traffic in Persons and of the Exploitation of the Prostitution of Others
- Standard Minimum Rules for the Treatment of Prisoners
- Basic Principles for the Treatment of Prisoners
- Body of Principles for the Protection of All Persons under Any Form of Detention or Imprisonment
- United Nations Rules for the Protection of Juveniles Deprived of Liberty
- Declaration on the Protection of All Persons from Being Subjected to Torture and Other Cruel, Inhuman or Degrading Treatment or Punishment
- Convention against Torture and Other Cruel, Inhuman or Degrading Treatment or Punishment

- Principles of Medical Ethics relevant to the Role of Health Personnel, particularly Physicians, in the Protection of Prisoners and Detainees against Torture and Other Cruel, Inhuman or Degrading Treatment or Punishment
- Safeguards guaranteeing protection of the rights of those facing the death penalty
- Code of Conduct for Law Enforcement Officials
- Basic Principles on the Use of Force and Firearms by Law Enforcement Officials
- Basic Principles on the Role of Lawyers
- Guidelines on the Role of Prosecutors
- United Nations Standard Minimum Rules for Non-custodial Measures (The Tokyo Rules)
- United Nations Guidelines for the Prevention of Juvenile Delinquency (The Riyadh Guidelines)
- United Nations Standard Minimum Rules for the Administration of Juvenile Justice (The Beijing Rules)
- Declaration of Basic Principles of Justice for Victims of Crime and Abuse of Power
- Declaration on the Protection of All Persons from Enforced Disappearances
- Principles on the Effective Prevention and Investigation of Extra-legal, Arbitrary and Summary Executions
- Freedom of Association and Protection of the Right to Organise Convention
- Right to Organise and Collective Bargaining Convention
- Workers' Representatives Convention
- Labour Relations (Public Service) Convention
- Employment Policy Convention
- Convention (No. 154) concerning the Promotion of Collective Bargaining
- Convention (No. 168) concerning Employment Promotion and Protection against Unemployment
- Convention (No. 169) concerning Indigenous and Tribal Peoples in Independent Countries
- Convention on Consent to Marriage, Minimum Age for Marriage and Registration of Marriages
- Recommendation on Consent to Marriage, Minimum Age for Marriage and Registration of Marriages
- Declaration on the Promotion among Youth of the Ideals of Peace, Mutual Respect and Understanding between Peoples
- Declaration on Social Progress and Development
- Declaration on the Rights of Mentally Retarded Persons
- Principles for the protection of persons with mental illness and the improvement of mental health care
- Universal Declaration on the Eradication of Hunger and Malnutrition
- Guidelines for the Regulation of Computerized Personal Data Files
- Declaration on the Rights of Disabled Persons
- Declaration on the Right of Peoples to Peace
- Declaration on the Right to Development
- International Convention on the Protection of the Rights of All Migrant Workers and Members of Their Families
- Declaration of the Principles of International Cultural Co-operation
- Recommendation concerning Education for International Understanding, Co-operation and Peace and Education relating to Human Rights and Fundamental Freedoms

- Convention on the Nationality of Married Women
- Convention on the Reduction of Statelessness
- Convention relating to the Status of Stateless Persons
- Convention relating to the Status of Refugees
- Protocol relating to the Status of Refugees
- Statute of the Office of the United Nations High Commissioner for Refugees
- Declaration on Territorial Asylum
- Declaration on the Human Rights of Individuals Who are not Nationals of the Country in which They Live

References

Aguilar, M. 1997, 'Mexico'. In Mayadas et al., *International Handbook on Social Work Theory and Practice*, pp. 60–75.

Alinsky, S. 1971, *Rules for Radicals: A Practical Primer for Realistic Radicals*, New York: Random House.

Alston, P. 1994, *The Best Interests of the Child: Reconciling Culture and Human Rights*, New York: Oxford University Press.

Attfield, R. 1983, *The Ethics of Environmental Concern*, Oxford: Basil Blackwell.

Aziz, N. 1999, 'The Human Rights Debate in an Era of Globalization'. In P. Van Ness (ed.), *Debating Human Rights: Critical Essays from the United States and Asia*, London: Routledge, pp. 32–55.

Baier, A. C. 1994, *Moral Prejudices: Essays on Ethics*, Cambridge, Mass.: Harvard University Press.

Barber, J. 1991, *Beyond Casework*, London: Macmillan.

Barnes, C. 1990, *Cabbage Syndrome: The Social Construction of Dependence*, Basingstoke: Falmer Press.

Bateman, N. 1995, *Advocacy Skills: A Handbook for Human Service Professionals*, Aldershot, UK: Ashgate.

Bauer, J., and D. Bell (eds) 1999, *The East Asian Challenge for Human Rights*, Cambridge University Press.

Bauman, Z. 1993, *Postmodern Ethics*, Oxford: Blackwell.

Bauman, Z. 1995, *Life in Fragments: Essays in Postmodern Morality*, Oxford: Blackwell.

Bauman, Z. 1998, *Globalization: The Human Consequences*, Cambridge: Polity Press.

Bauman, Z. 1999, *In Search of Politics*, Cambridge: Polity Press.

Beck, U. 1997, *The Reinvention of Politics: Rethinking Modernity in the Global Social Order*, Cambridge: Polity Press.

Beck, U. 2000, *What is Globalization?*, Cambridge: Polity Press.

Beetham, D. (ed.) 1995, *Politics and Human Rights*, Oxford: Blackwell.

Beetham, D. 1999, *Democracy and Human Rights*, Cambridge: Polity Press.

Benn, C. 1981, *Attacking Poverty Through Participation: A Community Approach*, Melbourne: PIT Publishing.

Benn, C. 1991, 'Social Justice, Social Policy and Social Work', *Australian Social Work* 44(4): 33–42.

Benn, S., and R. Peters 1959, *Social Principles and the Democratic State*, London, Allen & Unwin.

Bentham, J. 1983, 'Deontology: Theoretical'. In A. Goldworth (ed.), *The Collected Works of Jeremy Bentham: Deontology Together with a Table of Springs of Action and Article on Utilitarianism*, Oxford: Clarendon Press, pp. 117–247.

Berger, T. 1991, *A Long and Terrible Shadow: White Values, Native Rights in the Americas 1492–1992*, Vancouver: Douglas McIntyre.

Biggs, S., C. Phillipson and P. Kingston 1995, *Elder Abuse in Perspective*, Buckingham: Open University Press.

Blickle, R. 1993, 'Appetitus Liberatis, A Social Historical Approach to the Development of the Earliest Human Rights: The Example of Bavaria'. In Schmale, *Human Rights and Cultural Diversity*, pp. 143–62.

Bobbio, N. 1996, *The Age of Rights*, transl. A. Cameron, Cambridge: Polity Press.

Bookchin, M. 1990, *Remaking Society: Pathways to a Green Future*, Boston: South End Press.

Booth, K. 1999, 'Three Tyrannies'. In Dunne and Wheeler, *Human Rights in Global Politics*, pp. 31–70.

Braidotti, R., E. Charkiewicz, S. Hausler and S. Wieringa 1994, *Women, The Environment and Sustainable Development*, London: Zed Books.

Brecher, J., and T. Costello 1994, *Global Village or Global Pillage: Economic Reconstruction from the Bottom Up*, Boston: South End Press.

Bröhmer, J. 1997, *State Immunity and the Violation of Human Rights*, The Hague: Kluwer Law International.

Brown, C. 1998, 'Human rights'. In J. Baylis and S. Smith (eds), *The Globalization of World Politics: An Introduction to International Relations*, New York: Oxford University Press, pp. 469–82.

Brown, C. 1999, 'Universal human rights: a critique'. In Dunne and Wheeler, *Human Rights in Global Politics*, pp. 103–27.

Bryson, L. 1992, *Welfare and the State: Who Benefits?*, London: Macmillan.

Burrows, R., and B. Loader (eds) 1994, *Towards a Post-Fordist Welfare State?*, London: Routledge.

Carter, A. 1999, *A Radical Green Political Theory*, London: Routledge.

Carty, A. (ed.) 1990, *Post-Modern Law: Enlightenment Revolution and the Death of Man*, Edinburgh: Edinburgh University Press.

Cassese, A. 1990, *Human Rights in a Changing World*, Philadelphia: Temple University Press.

Castells, M. 1996, *The Information Age: Economy, Society and Culture*, vol. 1 *The Rise of the Network Society*, Malden, Mass.: Blackwell.

Castells, M. 1997, *The Information Age: Economy, Society and Culture*, vol. 2 *The Power of Identity*, Malden, Mass.: Blackwell.

Castells, M. 1998, *The Information Age: Economy, Society and Culture*, vol. 3 *The End of Millennium*, Malden, Mass.: Blackwell.

Centre for Human Rights 1994, *Human Rights and Social Work: A Manual for Schools of Social Work and the Social Work Profession*, Professional Training Series No. 1, Geneva: United Nations.

Chomsky, N. 1998, 'The United States and the Challenge of Relativity'. In T. Evans (ed.), *Human Rights Fifty Years On: A Reappraisal*, Manchester University Press, pp. 24–56.

Clapham, A. 1993, *Human Rights in the Private Sphere*, Oxford: Clarendon Press.

Clark, C. 2000, *Social Work Ethics: Politics, Principles and Practice*, London: Macmillan.

Clegg, S. 1989, *Frameworks of Power*, London: Sage.

Coleman, J. 1993, 'Medieval Discussions of Human Rights'. In Schmale, *Human Rights and Cultural Diversity*, pp. 103–20.

Compton, B., and B. Galaway 1999, *Social Work Processes*, 6th edn, Pacific Grove, Calif.: Brookes/Cole Publishing Co.

Cook, W., and R. Herzman 1983, *The Medieval World View: An Introduction*, New York: Oxford University Press.

Coote, A., and B. Campbell 1982, *Sweet Freedom: The Struggle for Women's Liberation*, Oxford: Blackwell.

Corey, G., M. Corey and P. Callanan 1998, *Issues and Ethics in the Helping Professions*, 5th edn, Pacific Grove, Calif.: Brooks/Cole Publishing Co.

Cornely, S., and D. Bruno 1997, 'Brazil'. In Mayadas et al., *International Handbook on Social Work Theory and Practice*, pp. 93–110.

Cox, K. R. (ed.) 1997, *Spaces of Globalization: Reasserting the Power of the Local*, New York: Guildford Press.

Craig, G., and M. Mayo (eds) 1995, *Community Empowerment: A Reader in Participation and Development*, London: Atlantic Highlands, NJ: Zed Books.

Crotty, M. 1998, *The Foundations of Social Research: Meaning and Perspective in the Research Process*, Sydney: Allen & Unwin

Czerny, M. 1993, 'Liberation theology and human rights'. In Mahoney and Mahoney, *Human Rights in the Twenty-First Century*, pp. 33–9.

Dauncey, G. 1988, *After the Crash: The Emergence of the Rainbow Economy*, Basingstoke: Green Print.

Davis, M. (ed.) 1995, *Human Rights and Chinese Values: Legal, Philosophical, and Political Perspectives*, New York: Oxford University Press.

Deacon, B. 1997, *Global Social Policy: International Organizations and the Future of Welfare*, London: Sage.

Deacon, B. 1999, 'Social Policy in a Global Context'. In A. Hurrell and N. Woods (eds), *Inequality, Globalization and World Politics*, Oxford: Oxford University Press, pp. 211–47.

De Bary, W., and T. Weiming (eds) 1998, *Confucianism and Human Rights*, New York: Columbia University Press.

De Schweinitz, K. 1943, *England's Road to Social Security*, New York: Barnes & Co.

Dobson, A. 1995, *Green Political Thought*, 2nd edn, London: Routledge.

Dominelli, L., and E. McLeod 1989, *Feminist Social Work*, London: Macmillan.

Doyal, L., and I. Gough 1991, *A Theory of Human Need*, London: Macmillan.

Dreidger, D. 1989, *The Last Civil Rights Movement: Disabled Peoples' International*, London: Hurst & Co.

Du Bois, E. 1998, *Woman Suffrage: Women's Rights*, New York University Press.

Dunne, T., and N. Wheeler (eds), *Human Rights in Global Politics*, Cambridge University Press.

Duparc, C. 1993, *The European Community and Human Rights*, Luxembourg: Office for Official Publications of the European Communities.

Dupont-Bouchat, S. 1993, 'Criminal Law and Human Rights in Western Europe (14th–18th Centuries). The Example of Torture and Punishment. Theory and Practice'. In Schmale, *Human Rights and Cultural Diversity*, pp. 183–97.

Eckersley, R. 1992, *Environmentalism and Political Theory*, New York: SUNY Press.

Ekins, P. 1992, *A New World Order: Grassroots Movements for Global Change*, London: Routledge.

Falk, R. 1993, 'The Making of Global Citizenship'. In J. Brecher, J. Childs and J. Cutler (eds), *Global Visions: Beyond the New World Order*, Boston: South End Press, pp. 39–50.

Falk, R. 2000a, *Human Rights Horizons: The Pursuit of Justice in a Globalizing World*, New York: Routledge.

Falk, R. 2000b, 'Global Society and the Democratic Prospect'. In Holden, *Global Democracy*, pp. 162–78.

Fatic, A. 1995, *Punishment and Restorative Crime-Handling: A Social Theory of Trust*, Aldershot, UK: Avebury.

Fattore, T., M. Galloway-Smith and N. Turnbull 2000, 'Managerialism Meets Human Rights: the Consequences for Children'. In Rees and Wright, *Human Rights and Corporate Responsibility*, pp. 210–32.

Fay, B. 1975, *Social Theory and Political Practice*, London: Allen & Unwin.

Fay, B. 1987, *Critical Social Science*, Cambridge: Polity Press.

Feinberg, J. 1973, *Social Philosophy*, Englewood Cliffs, NJ: Prentice-Hall.

Fisher, R., and H. Karger 1997, *Social Work and Community in a Private World: Getting Out in Public*, New York: Longman.

Fook, J. 1993, *Radical Social Work: A Theory of Practice*, Sydney: Allen & Unwin.

Fook, J. 1996, *The Reflective Researcher: Social Worker's Theories of Practice Research*, Sydney: Allen & Unwin.

Foucault, M. 1970, *The Order of Things: An Archaeology of the Human Sciences*, London: Tavistock Publications.

Foucault, M. 1972, *The Archaeology of Knowledge*, transl. S. Smith, London: Routledge.

Foucault, M. 1986, 'Truth and Power'. In P. Rabinow (ed.), *The Foucault Reader: An Introduction to Foucault's Thought*, Harmondsworth: Penguin Books.

Foucault, M. 1991, *Discipline and Punish: The Birth of the Prison*, Harmondsworth: Penguin Books.

Fox, J., and D. Brown (eds) 1998, *The Struggle for Accountability: The World Bank, NGOs and Grassroots Movements*, Cambridge, Mass.: MIT Press.

Fox, W. 1990, *Towards a Transpersonal Ecology: Developing New Foundations for Environmentalism*, Boston: Shambhala.

Franklin, B., and N. Parton (eds) 1991, *Social Work, the Media and Public Relations*, London: Routledge.

Freire, P. 1972, *Cultural Action for Freedom*, Harmondsworth: Penguin Books.

Freire, P. 1985, *The Politics of Education: Culture, Power, and Liberation*, transl. D. Macedo, Westport, Conn.: Bergin & Garvey.

Freire, P. 1996, *The Pedagogy of the Oppressed*, Harmondsworth: Penguin Books.

French, M. 1992, *The War Against Women*, Oxford: Blackwell.

Gaha, J. 1997, 'A Professional Code of Ethics – an Imperfect Regulator'. In A. Alexandria, M. Collingridge and S. Miller (eds), *Proceedings of the Annual Conference of the Association for Professional and Applied Ethics*, Wagga Wagga NSW: Keon Publications.

Gaikwad, V. 1981, 'Community Development in India'. In R. Dore and Z. Mars (eds), *Community Development: Comparative Studies in India, The Republic of Korea, Mexico and Tanzania*, Paris: UNESCO.

Galtung, J. 1994, *Human Rights in Another Key*, Cambridge: Polity Press.

Galtung, J. 2000, 'Alternative Models for Global Democracy'. In Holden, *Global Democracy*, pp. 143–61.

Gandhi, M. 1964, *Gandhi on Non-violence: Selected Texts from Mohandas K. Gandhi's 'Non-violence in Peace and War'*, ed. T. Merton, New York: New Directions Publishing.

Gangjian, D., and S. Gang 1995, 'Relating Human Rights to Chinese Culture: the Four Paths of the Confucian Analects and the Four Principles of a New

Theory of Benevolence'. In M. Davies (ed.), *Human Rights and Chinese Values: Legal, Philosophical and Political Perspectives*, New York: Oxford University Press, pp. 35–56.

Gastil, J. 1993, *Democracy in Small Groups: Participation, Decision Making and Communication*, Philadelphia: New Society Publishers.

George, V., and P. Wilding 1984, *The Impact of Social Policy*, London: Routledge.

George, V., and P. Wilding 1994, *Welfare and Ideology*, London: Harvester Wheatsheaf.

Germaine, C. 1991, *Human Behaviour in the Social Environment: An Ecological View*, New York: Columbia University Press.

Geuss, R. 1981, *The Idea of a Critical Theory: Habermas and the Frankfurt School*, Cambridge University Press.

Gil, D. 1998, *Confronting Injustice and Oppression: Concepts and Strategies for Social Workers*, New York: Columbia University Press.

Giroux. H. 1989, *Schooling for Democracy: Critical Pedagogy in the Modern Age*, London: Routledge.

Goddard, C., and R. Carew 1993, *Responding to Children: Child welfare Practice*, Melbourne: Longman Cheshire.

Goodin, R. 1992, *Green Political Theory*, Cambridge: Polity Press.

Goodin, R., H. Headey, R. Muffels and H. Dirven (eds) 1999, *The Real Worlds of Welfare Capitalism*, Cambridge University Press.

Griffin, J. 1996, *Value Judgement: Improving our Ethical Beliefs*, Oxford: Clarendon Press.

Habermas, J. 1984, *The Theory of Communicative Action*, vol. 1, *Reason and the Rationalisation of Society*, transl. T. McCarthy, Boston: Beacon Press.

Harcourt, W. (ed.) 1994, *Feminist Perspectives on Sustainable Development*, London: Zed Books.

Harlow, E., and J. Lawler (eds) 2000, *Management, Social Work and Change*, Aldershot, UK: Ashgate.

Harvey, D. 1989, *The Condition of Postmodernity: An Enquiry into the Origins of Cultural Change*, Oxford: Blackwell.

Havel, V. 1991, *Vaclav Havel: Open Letters*, London: Faber & Faber.

Havel, V. 1992, *Summer Meditations: on Politics, Morality and Civility in a Time of Transition*, London: Faber & Faber.

Hawkins, P., and R. Shoher 1989, *Supervision in the Helping Professions: An Individual, Group, and Organizational Approach*, Birmingham: Open University Press.

Hazlehurst, K. (ed.) 1995, *Popular Justice and Community Regeneration: Pathways of Indigenous Reform*, Westport, Conn.: Praeger.

Healy, K. 2000, *Social Work Practices: Contemporary Perspectives on Change*, London: Sage.

Healy, W., J. Rimmer and J. Ife 1986, 'Cultural Imperialism and Social Work Education in Australia'. In R. Berreen, D. Grace and T. Vinson (eds), *Advances in Social Work Education*, Sydney: University of NSW.

Held, D. 1987, *Models of Democracy*, Stanford University Press.

Held, D. 1999, 'The Transformation of Political Community: Rethinking Democracy in the Context of Globalization'. In I. Shapiro and C. Hacker-Cordon (eds), *Democracy's Edges*, Cambridge University Press.

Held, D. 2000, 'The Changing Contours of Political Community: Rethinking Democracy in the Context of Globalization'. In Holden, *Global Democracy*, pp. 17–31.

Held, D., A. McGrew, D. Goldblatt and J. Perraton 1999, *Global Transformations: Politics, Economics and Culture*, Cambridge: Polity Press.

Herman, E., and N. Chomsky 1988, *Manufacturing Consent: The Political Economy and the Mass Media*, New York: Pantheon.

Heron, J. 1990, *Helping the Client: A Creative Guide*, London: Sage.

Hershock, P. 2000, 'Dramatic Intervention: Human Rights from a Buddhist Perspective', *Philosophy East and West* 50(1): 9–33.

Hines, C. 2000, *Localization: A Global Manifesto*, London: Earthscan.

Hirst, P., and G. Thompson 1996, *Globalization in Question*, Cambridge: Polity Press.

Hirst, P., and G. Thompson 2000, 'Global Myths and National Policies'. In Holden, *Global Democracy*, pp. 47–59.

Holden, B. (ed.) 2000, *Global Democracy: Key Debates*, London: Routledge.

Holmes, S., and C. Sunstein 1999, *The Cost of Rights: Why Liberty Depends on Taxes*, New York: Norton.

hooks, b 1981, *Ain't I A Woman? Black Women and Feminism*, London: Pluto Press.

Howard, R. 1995, *Human Rights and the Search for Community*, Boulder, Col.: Westview Press.

Howe, D. 1994, 'Modernity, Postmodernity and Social Work', *British Journal of Social Work* 24(1): 513–32.

Human Rights and Equal Opportunity Commission (HREOC) 1996, *Annual Report 1995–96*, Canberra: Australian Government Publishing Service.

Human Rights and Equal Opportunity Commission (HREOC) 1997, *Bringing Them Home: National Inquiry into the Separation of Aboriginal and Torres Strait Islander Children from their Families*, Sydney: Commonwealth of Australia.

Humphreys, M. 1994, *Empty Cradles*, London: Doubleday.

Ife, J. 1980, 'The Determination of Social Needs: A Model of Need Statements in Social Administration', *Australian Journal of Social Issues* 15(2): 92–107.

Ife, J. 1995, *Community Development: Creating Community Alternatives – Vision, Analysis and Practice*, Melbourne: Longman.

Ife, J. 1997a, 'Australia'. In Mayadas et al., *International Handbook on Social Work Theory and Practice*, pp. 383–407.

Ife, J. 1997b, *Rethinking Social Work: Towards Critical Practice*, Melbourne: Longman.

Ife, J. 1999, 'Postmodernism, Critical Theory and Social Work'. In R. Pease and J. Fook (eds), *Transforming Social Work Practice: Postmodern and Critical Perspectives*, Sydney: Allen & Unwin, pp. 211–23.

Ife, J. 2000, 'Localized Needs in a Globalized Economy: Bridging the Gap with Social Work Practice,' *Canadian Social Work* 2(1)/*Canadian Social Work Review* 17 (Joint issue): 50–64.

Illich, I., I. Zola, J. McKnight, J. Caplin and S. Shaiken 1977, *Disabling Professions*, London: Marion Boyars.

Ishay, M. R. (ed.) 1997, *The Human Rights Reader*, New York: Routledge.

Jacobsen. J. 1994, *The Economics of Gender*, Cambridge, Mass.: Blackwell.

Jamrozik, A., and L. Nocella 1998, *The Sociology of Social Problems: Theoretical Perspectives and Methods of Intervention*, Cambridge University Press

Janke, T. 2000, 'Our Culture/Our Future: Indigenous Cultural and Intellectual Rights'. In Rees and Wright, *Human Rights and Corporate Responsibility*, pp. 69–88.

Jenkins, K. 1999, *Why History? Ethics and Postmodernity*, London: Routledge.

Jenks, C. 1993, *Culture*, London: Routledge.

Jessop, B. 1994, 'The Transition to Post-Fordism and the Schumpeterian Workforce State'. In Burrows and Loader, *Towards a Post-Fordist Welfare State?*, pp. 13–37.

Jones, A., and J. May 1992, *Working in Human Service Organisations*, Melbourne: Longman.

Jones, P. 1994, *Rights: Issues in Political Theory*, London: Macmillan.

Kadushin, A., and G. Kadushin 1997, *The Social Work Interview: A Guide for Human Service Professionals*, 4th edn, New York: Columbia University Press.

Keat, R. 1981, *The Politics of Social Theory: Habermas, Freud and the Critique of Positivism*, Oxford: Blackwell

Keck, M., and K. Sikkink 1998, *Activists Beyond Borders: Advocacy Networks in International Politics*, Ithaca, NY: Cornell University Press.

Kellert, S. 1993, *In the Wake of Chaos*, Chicago University Press.

Kenny, S. 1999, *Developing Communities for the Future: Community Development in Australia*, Melbourne: Nelson.

Kirby, S., and K. McKenna 1989, *Experience, Research, Social Change: Methods from the Margins*, Toronto: Garamond Press.

Knudtson, P., and D. Suzuki 1992, *Wisdom of the Elders*, Sydney: Allen & Unwin.

Kumar, K. 1995, *From Post-Industrial to Post-Modern Society: New Theories of the Contemporary World*, Oxford: Blackwell.

Lawler, J. 2000, 'The Rise of Managerialism in Social Work'. In Harlow and Lawler, *Management, Social Work and Change*, pp. 33–55.

Lawson, H. 2000, 'Globalization, Knowledgescapes and the Social Work Imagination'. Paper presented at Joint Conference of International Federation of Social Workers and International Association of Schools of Social Work, Montreal.

Lee, E. 1996, 'Marxism and Feminist Theory'. In S. Wolton (ed.), *Mysticism, Marxism and Modern Theory*, London: Macmillan.

Lee, J. 1994, *The Empowerment Approach to Social Work Practice*, New York: Columbia University Press.

Leighninger, L., and J. Midgley 1997, 'United States of America'. In Mayadas et al., *International Handbook on Social Work Theory and Practice*, pp. 9–28.

Leonard, P. 1997, *Postmodern Welfare: Restructuring an Emancipatory Project*, London: Sage.

Li, X. 1999, 'Why the Republic was Refused in Australia?', *Beijing Review* 42(47): 9.

Liffman, M. 1978, *Power for the Poor: The Family Centre Project, an Experiment in Self-Help*, Sydney: Allen & Unwin.

Lipsky, M. 1980, *Street-Level Bureaucracy: Dilemmas of the Individual in Public Services*, New York: Russell Sage Foundation.

Little, D. 1999, 'A Different Kind of Justice: Dealing with Human Rights Violations in Transitional Societies', *Ethics and International Affairs* 13: 65–80.

Lloyd, M., and A. Thacker (eds) 1997, *The Impact of Michel Foucault on the Social Sciences and Humanities*, New York: St Martin's Press.

Loescher, G. 1999, 'Refugees: a Global Human Rights and Security Crisis'. In Dunne and Wheeler, *Human Rights in Global Politics*, pp. 233–58.

Loewenberg, F., R. Dolgoff and D. Harrington 2000, *Ethical Decisions for Social Work Practice*, 6th edn, Itasca, Ill.: Peacock.

Machan, T. 1989, *Individuals and Their Rights*, La Salle, Ill.: Open Court Publishing.

Mahoney, K., and P. Mahoney (eds) 1993, *Human Rights in the Twenty-First Century: A Global Challenge*, Dordrecht: Martinus Nijhoff.

Mandela, N. 1994, *Long Walk to Freedom: the Autobiography of Nelson Mandela*, Boston: Little Brown.

Marshall, P., 1992, *Demanding the Impossible: A History of Anarchism*, London: HarperCollins.

Martin, S., and H. Schumann 1997, *The Global Trap: Globalization and the Assault on Democracy and Prosperity*, transl. P. Camiller, Sydney: Pluto Press.

Maslow, A. 1970, *Motivation and Personality*, 2nd edn, New York: Harper & Row.

Mayadas, N., T. Watts and D. Elliott (eds) 1997, *International Handbook on Social Work Theory and Practice*, Westport, Conn.: Greenwood Press.

McDonald, C. 1999, 'Human Service Professionals in the Community Service Industry', *Australian Social Work* 52(1): 17–25.

McIntyre, J. 1995, *Achieving Social Rights and Responsibility: Towards a Critical Humanist Approach to Community Development*, Melbourne: Community Quarterly.

McKillip, J. 1987, *Need Analysis: Tools for the Human Services and Education*, Newbury Park, Calif.: Sage Publications.

McLaren, P., and C. Lankshear (eds) 1994, *Politics of Liberation: Paths from Freire*, London: Routledge.

McLaren, P., and P. Leonard (eds) 1993, *Paulo Freire: A Critical Encounter*, London: Routledge.

Meyer, B., and P. Geschiere (eds.) 1999, *Globalization and Identity: Dialectics of Flow and Closure*, Oxford: Blackwell.

Mills, C. W. 1970, *The Sociological Imagination*, Harmondsworth: Penguin.

Mishra, R. 1984, *The Welfare State in Crisis: Social Thought and Social Change*, Brighton: Wheatsheaf.

Mishra, R. 1999, *Globalization and the Welfare State*, Cheltenham: Edward Elgar.

Mittelman, J. 2000, *The Globalization Syndrome: Transformation and Resistance*, Princeton University Press.

Mitterauer, M., and R. Seider 1982, *The European Family: Patriarchy to Partnership from the Middle Ages to the Present*, transl. K. Oosterveen and M. Hörzinger, Oxford: Blackwell.

Mullaly, R. 1997, *Structural Social Work: Ideology, Theory and Practice*, 2nd edn, Toronto: Oxford University Press.

Narayan, L. 2000, 'Freire and Gandhi: Their Relevance for Social Work Education', *International Social Work* 43(2): 193–204.

Neuwahl, N., and A. Rosas (eds) 1995, *The European Union and Human Rights*, The Hague: Kluwer Law International.

Neysmith, S. (ed.) 1999, *Critical Issues for Future Social Work Practice with Aging Persons*, New York: Columbia University Press.

Nozick, M. 1992, *No Place Like Home: Building Sustainable Communities*, Ottawa: Canadian Council on Social Development.

Offe, C. 1984, *Contradictions of the Welfare State*, London: Hutchinson.

Office of Seniors' Interests 1999, *Final Report 1998/99* Government of Western Australia, www.osi.wa.gov.au/pubs/seniors99.pdf.

Parekh, B. 1999, 'Non-ethnocentric Universalism'. In Dunne and Wheeler, *Human Rights in Global Politics*, pp. 128–59.

Parker, S., B. Pease and J. Fook 1999, 'Empowerment: The Modernist Social Work Concept *par excellence*'. In Pease and Fook, *Transforming Social Work Practice*, Sydney: Allen & Unwin.

Parton, N., and P. O'Byrne 2000, *Constructive Social Work: Towards a New Practice*, London: Macmillan.

Pease, R., and J. Fook (eds) 1999, *Transforming Social Work Practice: Postmodern and Critical Perspectives*, Sydney: Allen & Unwin.

Pereira, W. 1997, *Inhuman Rights: The Western System and Global Human Rights Abuse*, Penang: The Other India Press, The Apex Press and Third World Network.

Pettman, J. 1996, *Worlding Women: A Feminist International Politics*, London, Routledge.

Pincus, A., and A. Minahan 1976, *Social Work Practice: Model and Method*, Itasca, Ill.: Peacock.

Plumwood, V. 1993, *Feminism and the Mastery of Nature*, London: Routledge.

Queiro, I. 1997, 'Latin America'. In Mayadas et al., *International Handbook on Social Work Theory and Practice*, pp. 51–9.

Ragg, N. 1977, *People Not Cases: A Philosophical Approach to Social Work*, London: Routledge & Kegan Paul.

Ratner, S., and J. Abrams 1997, *Accountability for Human Rights Atrocities in International Law: Beyond the Nuremberg Legacy*, New York: Oxford University Press.

Ray, L. 1993, *Rethinking Critical Theory: Emancipation in the Age of Global Social Movements*, London: Sage.

Rayner, M. 1998, *Rooting Democracy: Growing the Society We Want*, Sydney: Allen & Unwin.

Rees, S. 1991, *Achieving Power: Practice and Policy in Social Welfare*, Sydney: Allen & Unwin.

Rees, S., and G. Rodley (eds) 1995, *The Human Costs of Managerialism: Advocating the Recovery of Humanity*, Sydney: Pluto Press.

Rees, S., and S. Wright (eds) 2000, *Human Rights and Corporate Responsibility*, Sydney: Pluto Press.

Rees, S., G. Rodley and F. Stilwell (eds) 1993, *Beyond the Market: Alternatives to Economic Rationalism*, Sydney: Pluto Press

Riches, G. (ed.) 1997, *First World Hunger: Food Security and Welfare Politics*, New York: St Martin's Press.

Roberts, J., and L. Stalans 1997, *Public Opinion, Crime, and Criminal Justice*, Boulder, Col.: Westview Press.

Robinson, D., and C. Sidoti 2000, 'The Status of Human Rights in Australia'. In Rees and Wright, *Human Rights and Corporate Responsibility*, pp. 24–40.

Rodger, J. 2000, *From a Welfare State to a Welfare Society: The Changing Context of Social Policy in a Postmodern Era*, London: Macmillan.

Roemer, J. 1999, 'Does Democracy Engender Justice?' In I. Shapiro and C. Hacker-Cordon (eds), *Democracy's Value*, Cambridge University Press.

Rooney, R. 1992, *Strategies for Work With Involuntary Clients*, New York: Columbia University Press.

Rorty, R. 1998, *Truth and Progress: Philosophical Papers*, Cambridge University Press.

Rosenau, P. 1992, *Post-Modernism and the Social Sciences: Insights, Inroads and Intrusions*, Princeton University Press.

Said, E. 1993, *Culture and Imperialism*, New York: Random House.

Said, E. 1995, *Orientalism*, Harmondsworth: Penguin.

Saunders, P. 1994, *Welfare and Inequality: National and International Perspectives on the Australian Welfare State*, Cambridge University Press.

Saward, M. 1998, *The Terms of Democracy*, Cambridge: Polity Press.

Schmale, W. (ed.) 1993, *Human Rights and Cultural Diversity*, Goldbach, Germany: Keip.

Seidman, S. (ed.) 1994, *The Postmodern Turn: New Perspectives on Social Theory*, Cambridge University Press.

Setälä, M. 1999, *Referendums and Democratic Government: Normative Theory and the Analysis of Institutions*, London: Macmillan.

Shields, K. 1991, *In the Tiger's Mouth: An Empowerment Guide for Social Action*, Sydney: Millennium Books.

Simmons. A. 1992, *The Lockean Theory of Rights*, Princeton University Press.

Sinclair, R. 1988, *Democracy and Participation in Athens*, Cambridge University Press.

Smith, S., D. Williams and A. Johnson 1997, *Nurtured By Knowledge: Learning to Do Participatory Action Research*, New York: Apex Press.

Solas, J. 2000, 'Can a Radical Social Worker Believe in Human Rights?,' *Australian Social Work* 53(1): 65–70.

Stapleton, J. 1995, *Group Rights: Perspectives Since 1900*, Bristol: Thoemmes Press.

Strauss, A., and J. Corbin 1990, *Basics of Qualitative Research: Grounded Theory, Procedures and Techniques*, Newbury Park, Calif.: Sage.

Tan, N., and E. Envall 2000, *Social Work Around the World*, Schwarztorstrasse, Switzerland: IFSW Press.

Timms, N., and R. Timms 1977, *Perspectives in Social Work*, London: Routledge & Kegan Paul.

Tong, R. 1989, *Feminist Thought: A Comprehensive Introduction*, London: Routledge.

Torgerson, D. 1999, *The Promise of Green Politics: Environmentalism and the Public Sphere*, London: Duke University Press.

Touraine, A. 1995, *Critique of Modernity*, Cambridge, Mass.: Blackwell.

Towle, C. 1965, *Common Human Needs*, New York: National Association of Social Workers.

Tutu, D. 1999, *No Future Without Forgiveness*, London: Random House.

Twine, F. 1994, *Citizenship and Social Rights: The Interdependence of Self and Society*, London: Sage.

Uhr, J. 1998, *Deliberative Democracy in Australia: the Changing Place of Parliament*, Cambridge University Press.

Uhr, J. 2000, 'Testing Deliberative Democracy: The 1999 Australian Republic Referendum', *Government and Opposition* 35(2): 189–211.

Umbreit, M. 1999, 'Victim-offender Mediation in Canada: The Impact of an Emerging Social Work', *International Social Work* 42(2): 197–210.

UNDP (United Nations Development Programme) 2000, *Human Development Report 2000*, New York: Oxford University Press.

Van Den Bergh, N., and L. Cooper (eds) 1986, *Feminist Visions of Social Work*, Silver Spring, Md.: National Association of Social Workers.

Van Ness, P. (ed.) 1999, *Debating Human Rights: Critical Essays from the United States and Asia*, London: Routledge.

Von Senger, H. 1993, 'From the Limited to the Universal Concept of Human Rights: Two Periods of Human Rights'. In Schmale, *Human Rights and Cultural Diversity*, pp. 47–100.

Walby, S. 1990, *Theorizing Patriarchy*, Oxford: Blackwell.

Wendell, S. 1996, *The Rejected Body: Feminist Philosophical Reflections on Disability*, New York: Routledge.

Wheeler, M. 1997, *Politics and the Mass Media*, Oxford: Blackwell.

Wilhelmsson, T., and S. Hurri (eds) 1999, *From Dissonance to Sense: Welfare State Expectations, Privatisation and Private Law*, Aldershot, UK: Ashgate.

Wilkes, R. 1981, *Social Work With Undervalued Groups*, New York: Tavistock.

Woodiwiss, A. 1998, *Globalisation, Human Rights and Labour Law in Pacific Asia*, Cambridge University Press.

Woodroofe, K. 1962, *From Charity to Social Work in England and the United States*, University of Toronto Press.

Wronka, J. 1992, *Human Rights and Social Policy in the 21st Century: A history of the idea of human rights and comparison of the United Nations Universal Declaration of Human Rights with United States federal and state constitutions*, Lanham, Md.: University Press of America.

Yeatman, A. (ed.) 1998, *Activism and the Policy Process*, Sydney: Allen & Unwin.

Younghusband, E. 1964, *Social Work and Social Change*, London: Allen & Unwin.

Zubrzycki, J. 1999, 'The Influence of the Personal on the Professional: A Preliminary Investigation of Work and Family Issues for Social Workers', *Australian Social Work* 52(4): 11–16.

Index